An Anthology of I Ching

by the same authors

The Astrology of I Ching

An Anthology of I Ching

W. A. Sherrill, M.A.
Fellow of the China Academy

and

W. K. Chu, Ph.D.
*Director, East-West Essence Society,
Santa Ana, California*

Routledge & Kegan Paul

London, Henley and Boston

First published in 1977
by Routledge & Kegan Paul Ltd
39 Store Street
London WC1E 7DD,
Broadway House
Newtown Road
Henley-on-Thames
Oxon RG9 1EN and
9 Park Street
Boston, Mass. 02108, USA
Set in 11/12 pt Walbaum
and printed in Great Britain by
Western Printing Services Ltd, Bristol

British Library Cataloguing in Publication Data

An anthology of I Ching

1. Philosophy, Chinese
I. Chu, Wen Kuan   II. Sherrill, Wallace Andrew
181'.11   B126

ISBN 0 7100 8590 7

First published as a paperback 1983
ISBN 0 7100 9520 1

Contents

Contents

Figures

Tables

Tables

Preface

Westerners are not as familiar with the *I Ching* and its many and varied usages as the Chinese. There are numerous books and manuscripts in Chinese dealing with the *I Ching*. Regrettably most of them cover only part of a discipline or subject and few of them are objective; to a large extent, they are the product of single individuals' minds and must be evaluated on that basis, along with ascertaining the probable reason for which they were written. Therefore, in researching material on the *I Ching* much chaff has to be separated from the grain. This is no easy task. And there are few English-language sources for the researcher, for books in English, so far, have confined themselves mainly to discussion of the *I Ching* itself.

The reader will note that no bibliography has been included. This is not an oversight but a deliberate decision. The basic material is centuries old, reprints having either been pirated or published in a manner that involves no infringement of copyright. Since different publishing houses have reproduced the same material, it would be unfair to credit one version in preference to another. Furthermore, with the few exceptions noted in the text, none of the material we have used has been taken from English-language sources.

We have both worked with and used the *I Ching* extensively and thus are aware of the additional applications to which the basic text has been put in China. These extensions of its use are of great interest to all lovers of the *I Ching* in the Orient and we believe that they will also interest Western savants, scholars and readers.

It would be no mean task for those who neither read nor speak Chinese to gather together and apply all the appropriate material.

It would not be easy even for the average Chinaman, for the original sources are all in classical Chinese, which only a small percentage of the population can read and understand. Fortunately Dr Chu has this ability as well as a broad understanding of the *I Ching*. After a little pressure I was able to convince him that we ought to produce a book that would open up to Westerners at least some of the more unusual aspects of the *I Ching* that are available to the Chinese.

This anthology is the result of our efforts. It is only a beginning, but we hope that Westerners will benefit from what is presented here. Apart from the background material in Chapter 1, which is included to make the subsequent text more clear (and some of this, too, is new), the reader will find much that is unusual, enlightening, exceptional in this text, as well as gaining access to several new systems which he can subsequently employ as tools to make his life more meaningful.

It is our hope that readers will derive as much pleasure and benefit from perusing and studying this work as we had in preparing it for them.

W. A. SHERRILL

W. K. CHU

1 | Basic Information

Introduction and background history

For the Chinese, the *I Ching* is the equivalent of the Bible. No other book pervades the lives of the people in the same way. It encompasses an ontological concept of a divine creator and a unified universe. It is considered as embracing all that is manifested in the universe through the sixty-four hexagrams, or Gwa (Kua). The result is that the Chinese have made the principles of Yin and Yang, and the evolution of these into hexagrams, into an integral part of their lives, as well as of the various disciplines covered in this anthology. A remarkable point to note is that these same principles underlie Chinese philosophy, astrology, divination, geomancy, meditation, and other related subjects. This book outlines these disciplines for the reader and brings together the basic material in a single volume for the first time. All the disciplines have their origin or background in the *I Ching*.

Researching Chinese material is somewhat difficult. Many Chinese scholars take Confucius's statement too literally, that is, 'If I give a student one-fourth of what he should know I expect him to get the other three-fourths himself, otherwise I do not want him as a student.' As any Sinologue can tell you, no book in China is complete in itself. Some key essence or ingredient is always left out. As a result one has to refer to several texts in order to get the complete story. This has been our basic task: to collect and collate the information from its various sources and convert it into a series of brief essays.

It is impossible, of course, for a comprehensive anthology of this nature to cover in full any of the subjects discussed. We do, however, expect to give the reader sufficient material on each subject to provide him with a good foundation from which to begin further research, if that is what he wants to do, or to enable him to use the material presented to a greater or lesser extent, according to his degree of personal absorption and interest in the subject.

As has already been said, this is the first time that this material has been brought together in a single volume. Nowhere in England, America, China, Hong Kong, or anywhere else, does a book as comprehensive in scope exist. Although much further work still needs to be done, our presentation covers all the available sources and takes account of all the known research results.

In attempting a task of this magnitude many difficulties can be encountered; not least of these is the paucity of material available. Since this book is only a beginning, the following estimates will give the reader some idea of what he can expect to gain from this volume.

Some new thoughts are included in the basic material. So far as divination is concerned, the Chinese material is about 85 per cent clear; the remaining 15 per cent requires hard study, additional research and practice. Anyone interested in divination will find much of value in the advanced divination section, as well as, perhaps, obtaining further clarification of the basic material. The number of uses to which advanced divination can be put is almost limitless.

With respect to the astrologies, this book covers those with a time concept which are related to the *I Ching*. Thus, Tzu Pin, Tzu Wei, Nine Star (House) astrology and the astrology of the *I Ching* will all be discussed. Both Japanese and Chinese books are about 95 per cent clear with respect to Tzu Pin astrology, about 80 per cent are clear regarding Tzu Wei, and both are fairly comprehensive regarding Nine Star (House) astrology. The astrology of the *I Ching per se*, is not generally known in Japan and is now for the first time being introduced to the Western world. It is only about 50 per cent clear in any single Chinese book and many works have to be consulted. Our own recent volume, *The Astrology of I Ching*, published by Routledge & Kegan Paul (London, 1976) is complete in itself but contains only about 70 per cent of all the material on the subject.

Only a smattering of knowledge and material exists regarding the remaining topics in this anthology. Geomancy and directionology are little known anywhere. The Chinese material makes it only about 15 per cent clear. For meditation we estimate about 10 per cent. In our discussions of the *I Ching* and its history we also present brief comments on the Tai-I method, a counterpart to Western mundane[1] astrology. It differs in that it covers thousands of years as well as current matters. What the reader can get out of all that is presented will depend on his own state of development. Everyone, however, can learn something which could potentially improve his or her life.

Obviously, in the light of the foregoing percentages, none of the subjects discussed here can be covered in minute detail. The reader will find, however, that he can become sufficiently well versed in each area to do elementary work in that subject, as well as being provided with a base which will enable him to undertake further research if he so wishes. Instruction from so-called 'Chinese Masters' will not clear up the remaining questions because these 'Masters' are not academically oriented. The further material has to be sought in books and manuscripts. We ourselves are still carrying out further research, but felt it vital to present what we had learned thus far, so that others, too, could carry out additional research.

THE *I Ching*

To best understand this anthology it is desirable to begin with the history of the *I Ching* and its application.

Scholars generally agree that Fu Hsi originated the trigrams and the hexagrams some time before 3000 BC. According to the Chinese, Fu Hsi is the Father of our present civilization. He taught men the use of fire, and how to build homes, live in communities and engage in agriculture. For those who could understand it he taught a system of ontology and a code of ethics which was passed down in the form of the *I Ching*.

For many centuries this was transmitted orally to a select few by means of easily memorized verses and consisted of the statements one finds at the beginning of each hexagram and at the beginning of each line in any book of the *I Ching*. The holders of

---

[1] Mundane, as used in this book, refers to that branch of Western astrology which deals with nations and other entities, their life, growth, character, personality, events, situations, etc., as if they were individuals.

this wisdom were free to make their own interpretations. According to some scholars these verses were primarily used for divination for kings and rulers. The oracles, in many cases, were supposedly recorded on shell and bones, that is, tortoiseshell and human or animal bones. This was done by means of carvings. The hexagrams of the *I Ching* were supposedly represented by dots, whereas the oracles themselves were in early Chinese characters. In our examination of a number of records, pictures and shells and bones themselves, we did not find any evidence of dots. This does not mean that they might not be found elsewhere. It does indicate that the *I Ching* was limited to relatively few persons.

Another method of divination used at that same general period was the heating of tortoiseshells until they cracked, predictions being made from the patterns formed by the cracks.

Certainly oracles were recorded on shell and bones, but which of them used the *I Ching* as a source and which were based to the cracking of tortoiseshell is difficult to determine. If you look in your copy of the *I Ching* you will find tortoises mentioned in line 5 of Hexagram 41 and line 2 of Hexagram 42. 'Someone does indeed increase him. Ten pairs of tortoises cannot oppose it. (Supreme) good fortune.' This, in essence, indicates that the good auspices of these lines cannot be opposed by any number of predictions made by using tortoiseshell divination.

Around 1700 BC is thought to be the first time that the *I Ching* was recorded on other than shell or bones and this was by burning characters on bamboo strips. Most of these strips would hold only one line each. This is believed to be the origin of Chinese writing in an organized form, for the writing on shell or bones was in groups relating to a particular concept only and not developed on a continuing basis, as was now done on the bamboo strips. The Chinese method of writing from top to bottom of a page is also thought to originate from these bamboo strips, and the way the strips were bound and rolled may account for the fact that the Chinese read and open books from right to left. As for the characters themselves, the fact that the hexagrams were composed of lines made by strokes makes many people attribute the origin of Chinese characters to Fu Hsi, since Chinese characters, too, are formed by using lines and strokes. Archaeologists have evidence that the characters originated in the north-west section of China, so it is quite probable that this may be true. Of course, one must not forget the Chinese tendency to attribute everything written to a great sage or a well-known person, just to have it accepted. (Many other people do the same.)

Two ancient books have influenced the thought and character of China. One is the *I Ching*; the other is the *Shu Ching*. The *I Ching* came from the north-west, which in the early days was the normal route around the Himalayan mountains to the rest of Asia. A scholarly book of philosophy, ontology, and practical advice, it originated with Fu Hsi and was re-emphasized by Huang Ti, the Yellow Emperor around 2400 BC. The *Shu Ching* came from the eastern part of China and was a chronicle of the reigns of kings and emperors. It was used as a guide by subsequent rulers. However, each could and often did have the records altered to suit his purposes, so that the interpretations would be favourable for what he was trying to impose. As a result, the true historical value of the *Shu Ching* is questionable. The *Shu Ching* makes no mention of the *I Ching*. This seems further to substantiate that the *I Ching* came from the north-west.

The next major step in the genesis of the *I Ching* was, as previously mentioned, the verses being inscribed on bamboo strips around the eighteenth century BC. At that time the *I Ching* still consisted simply of terse, basic verses.

King Wên and the Duke of Chou made a tremendous contribution by amplifying the meanings of the short verses. King Wên, during the time he was imprisoned by the last emperor of the Shang or Yin dynasty in 1152–51 BC, wrote explanations to the Judgments and Images of the *I Ching*. Later, his son, the Duke of Chou, wrote explanations for the moving lines. Both of these efforts were masterpieces of correlation of the total action and interaction of the sixty-four hexagrams. To do this and develop a usable work without contradictions or conflicts was definitely sage-like. What these men set forth is still in use today. It was a magnificent piece of scholarly workmanship and we owe them much.

Around the sixth century BC Confucius wrote commentaries on the *I Ching* and Lao Tze wrote the *Tao Te Ching*. Both of these had their foundation in the work done by King Wên and the Duke of Chou. Confucius was greatly impressed with the value of the *I Ching*. In his analects he is quoted as saying, 'If I

5

had more years to my life I would devote them to the *I Ching*', and 'Give me a few more years to study the *I Ching*, then I should have a good philosophy of the mutation of human events'. Confucius's commentaries are quoted in part in Book II of the English version of Richard Wilhelm's translation of the *I Ching*. A number of scholars have used the commentaries to interpret the *I Ching* as a guide to good government, good government having been one of the chief aims and purposes of Confucius during the early and middle part of his life.

The comparison of the *Tao Te Ching* and the *I Ching* can be the basis of lengthy research, with material enough for one or more books. In some people's opinion the *Tao Te Ching* extracts and reformulates the religious aspects of the *I Ching*, so that Taoism as a religion can be said to stem from the *I Ching*. Whether or not the *I Ching* has such a religious basis does not concern us here. Suffice to say that *I Ching* was the foundation from which the *Tao Te Ching* developed. The *Tao Te Ching* was written at about the same time as Confucius's commentaries, around 500 BC. Further mention will be made of the *Tao Te Ching* in the discussion on the *I Ching* and meditation.

The period between roughly 500 BC and 229 BC was known as the era of the Warring States and the 100 Philosophy Schools. These Schools produced a wide range of works (both favourable and hostile), interpreting the *I Ching*, and commenting on the *Tao Te Ching*, on Lao Tze's and Chuang Tze's thoughts on Taoism, on Confucius's and Mencius's concepts, and on many other writings of lesser import. Even communism was proposed in some of Mo Tze's writings. It was a period during which most people were confused as to just what to believe. Their dilemma could be compared to what ours might be today if we had to decide which protestant sect was the right one. Then, as now, a man could only make his choice on the basis of which suited him best. As far as we are concerned, since each man's choice answers his own individual needs at a given time, each philosophic concept or religion serves a purpose and 'all roads eventually lead to Rome', as the saying goes. All lead to higher evolvement.

The choices came to an end during the Chin Dynasty, in 229–207 BC. After Emperor Chin unified China in 221 BC he continued to have great difficulty with the many factions who still wanted to be independent. In addition to the military means he employed, he decided that changing the people's thinking would further help unify China, so in 213 BC he ordered the burning of all books which did not conform with state-approved doctrine. Many philosophies were thus done away with. The basic *I Ching* was not burned (just as today the basic *I Ching* has not been destroyed or done away with in Communist China), but all of Confucius's works, including his commentaries on the *I Ching*, were ordered to be burned. Wandering gypsies who had the same disregard for laws then as they have today, kept the books in their possession, and many were passed on to scholars of the Han dynasty after it took over in 206 BC. So it is to the gypsies that we have to be grateful for the preservation of these valuable works; our debt is to people, who, on the face of it, would seem the least likely to want to help preserve culture. Many philosophies and isms did not survive, but Confucius's works did. Tung Chung Shu, an adviser and a power in the government in 138 BC, had the Emperor establish a 'recommendation' system for appointment to government positions from provincial and state areas, based on filial piety, morality and wisdom. In the Sui dynasty (*c.* AD 600) the 'recommendation' system was modified to a civil service examination system for which the six[1] Confucian classics were the principal basis.[2] The

---

[1] The six Confucius classics are:

a *The Book of Odes* (*Shih Ching*). This consists of 305 poems and sacred odes, together with 6 others set to music, edited by Confucius.

b *The Book of History* (*Shu Ching*). A collection of early historic documents, chiefly kings' proclamations; they are the earliest Chinese documents known.

c *The Book of Music*. A compilation of early music written to produce harmony and stir emotions.

d *I Ching*. A restatement of King Wên's and the Duke of Chou's versions of the *I Ching*, with an explanation of the book's origin, and a guide to its use and practical interpretation.

e *Spring and Autumn Annals* (*Chun Ch'iu*). A chronicle of some events in Chinese history during the years 722–481 BC.

f *The Book of Rites* (*Li Chi*). Allegedly a record of the governmental systems of the early Chou dynasty relating to the correct conduct of affairs in government, and setting out the required customs of the time and the form and practice of the many ceremonial rites and diplomatic procedures.

[2] Examinations were held at the local level, with the winner advancing to a city examination, the city winner to county examination, the county winner to state examination, the state winner to federal examination, with applicants being selected to fill positions at each level. Many stories have been written about the methods employed by those anxious to win, and some of the hardships and difficulties involved. These make interesting reading.

I Ching was one of these and the primary requirement was to interpret it for the guidance and proper conduct of good government.

Chinese scholars have shown interest in the *I Ching* in every period of their country's history, some of them being more active than others. Ching Fang, for example, put forward his system of Advanced Divination related to the *I Ching* during the Han dynasty (206 BC–AD 220), and it was he who invented the 'self' and 'other' aspects of hexagrams and gave special interpretations for each line (see the section on Advanced Divination on p. 57). Among the astrologies related to the *I Ching*, Tzu Pin astrology was developed during the Tang dynasty (AD 618–907) and Tzu Wei astrology during the Northern Sung dynasty (AD 960–1126). Chou Tung Yi (AD 1017–1075), among others, revitalized and provoked added interest in Confucianism and the *I Ching* through his writings and advanced philosophic concepts regarding them.

Coming to more modern times, Chiao Hsun is perhaps the most noteworthy scholar of the Ch'ing dynasty (AD 1644–1912) as regards the *I Ching*. He studied the text for over twenty years, writing fourteen volumes, known as *I T'ung Shih*, in which he reveals how Fu Hsi used the *I Ching* to teach and guide people as well as to impart ethical precepts. This was over and beyond the basic divination to which most persons give consideration. In a sense then, he made it serve a universal purpose.

In this century many people have studied and used the *I Ching*, including Chiang Kai-shek, who extolled it as the basis for the Eight Virtues of Chinese culture (Pa Te), the Four Supporting Pillars (Sze Wei) and the Three Ultimate Virtues (San Ta Te). The Eight Virtues correspond to the eight houses of the *I Ching*; the Four Supporting Pillars are symbolic of the greater and lesser Yang and the greater and lesser Yin, while the Three Ultimate Virtues symbolize the mental, physical and spiritual triumvirate of man, earth and heaven as equal partners.

The development of the trigrams

The philosophic fundamentals and method of development of the *I Ching* are deep and far-reaching. In them one finds a complete and orderly concept of the origin of the universe and everything in it, a concept which relates equally to the physical, mental and spiritual planes; or, to use the words of the *I Ching*, to earth, man and heaven. Thus their magnitude of application is limitless.

The trigrams, with their multitudinous meanings and interactions, form the foundation for an understanding of the *I Ching*. Three laws are basic to their formulation and development, and form the foundation for the philosophic as well as the practical aspects of the *I Ching*, which, in turn, makes them the basis of Chinese thinking and behaviour. The *I Ching*, the oldest Chinese book in continuing use today, would not have survived its many trials and tests across the ages had its intrinsic value not been great and the truths it incorporates self-evident. Man only continues to accept that which he instinctively and intuitively knows to be right. The three laws are the Law of Evolution, the Law of Change and the Law of Enantiodromia (Reversal *in extremis*).

THE LAW OF EVOLUTION

A Supreme Ultimate, Tao, a Divine Creator or Divine Creative Principle is posited in the formation and development of the *I Ching*. At our present state of human development it defies exact definition. As *Tao Te Ching* expresses it, the Tao is nameless yet exists everywhere. It is beyond the power of human words to describe it or human thoughts to encompass its limitless power and aspects. Each person does, however, in his own mind, have a concept of it, whether he calls it God, Allah, Mazda, Atman, or by any other seemingly appropriate appellation.

Whatever the name you choose to call it by, we are here positing that, resulting from its actions as accomplishments, the Supreme Ultimate possesses THOUGHT (Logos, the Word), FORCE (Vibrations, Direction) and MATTER, or SUBSTANCE (a store of undifferentiated atoms—atoms without positive or negative consciousness as yet imparted—and differentiated atoms—those with consciousness). This last implies immediately that there is an orderly development of atoms from a quiescent state to the vast variety that exist today. Atoms are at various levels and states of development, as is easily understood when one considers those forming the brain of man as compared with those in plants and minerals. An oak tree, for example, attracts mostly atoms related

9

to or compatible with itself, whereas the fir tree adjacent to it attracts only those which suit it. Similarly, individual persons attract only those atoms which are appropriate to their own state of development or evolvement.

To arrive at a state of being useful for specific purposes all atoms must be given consciousness and experience. They must start at the lowest level and work their way ever higher, just as man does. Further, as is well known, man sheds atoms constantly and replaces them continuously through the absorption of food, water, air, sunlight, the cosmic forces, etc. Everyone gives his or her atoms experiences which are necessary for those atoms at their particular state of development at that given time. After a reasonable period of experience they are shed off to make room for other atoms to gain experience. Thus, each individual, no matter who or where he is, nor what his physical condition may be, is serving the evolution of mankind.

The development of Yin and Yang into trigrams and hexagrams exemplifies the foregoing principles through the application of the Law of Evolution. The stages by which this happens are shown in Figure 1.

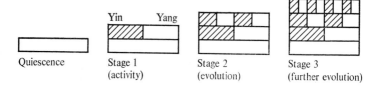

Figure 1. The development of Yin and Yang

If we analyse Figure 1 we see that for atoms to have a consciousness there must be activity, and that the basic activity is that of producing Yang and Yin, or the positive and negative aspects within the atoms. Scientific evidence verifies that all atoms have positive and negative characteristics. This consciousness is brought into being at the first stage of activity from quiescence. The second stage of development is of a more complex nature, and the third stage even more so.

Yin and Yang are considered to be equal yet complementary in value. There has to be a positive creative force and at the same time a negative or receptive one. One major reason for this is the fact that after things have served their purpose they must be destroyed in order to make room for the new. Also, the creative develops the thought or concept while the receptive brings things into being or fruition. This gives rise to the idea that all things have their archetype in the higher realm before they are manifested on earth. This was a favourite concept of Plato's many centuries after the initiation of the concepts in the *I Ching*. This same dichotomy exists in man; i.e., those things which are in the psychic body later become manifest in our physical bodies. It is man's thoughts, which have been deposited and accepted in his psychic body, that later become manifested in or through his physical body. As will be reflected later in this book, man who is an equal partner with heaven and earth, thereby determines his own fate and existence. It is man's thoughts which later form the experiences he undergoes. Man's health, happiness, success, financial status, security, etc., all are determined by his thinking. This naturally imposes a grave responsibility on man and one which many people would rather not have, namely that of controlling their lives and having no one to blame but themselves for what they are and what happens to them. This is one aspect of man's Yin and Yang in action. It is axiomatic, too, that everything must correspond and adhere to the same laws. Therefore, it follows that all type of actions must conform to the Divine Dictum that there shall be progress. There are many people who wonder whether things are not in fact declining, and who believe that they would rather have the 'good old days' back; but one has only to look at the overall history of this planet to recognize that there *has* been progress. Naturally, there are some reversals when the old is cast out and replaced by the new. But these instances of apparent retrogression are relative, for basically everything is a part of progress and therefore part of the evolutionary process. It follows then that everything is in a constant state of change.

THE LAW OF CHANGE

The Law of Change states that everything is progressing or retrogressing, standstills being but appearances. This can be illustrated by considering a rolling wheel. The point which touches the ground is stationary for a moment only. It will then rise and fall as the cycle repeats itself. A rolling wheel, of course, produces a sine curve. In the realities of life many things, such as the ebb and flow of the tides, day and night, winter and summer, and so on, are sine curves; but many, for instance, the way in which blood circulates through the body, travelling to all its parts by way of arteries and returning along the veins, are not. This, too, is cyclic, but the time taken for the blood to travel from the heart to some parts of the body is far less than is needed to reach others. Actions of this general nature are considered as special cyclic conditions.

Earlier, we stated that Thought, Force and Matter (atoms) formulate the universe and all there is in it. Force is vibratory and uses thought as the creative principle. By the application of Force (or Vibrations) to Matter, all forms are produced. The Force, of course, is brought about by the interaction of the Yin and Yang, just as force is brought about by the positive and negative poles in electricity or magnetism. Each form is thus the result of the interaction of the positive Yang and the negative Yin, just as it would be if these were poles of a circuit of electricity. Each form vibrating according to its own rate is the basis of selectivity of atoms between all forms, whatever the proximity of the atoms or the forms may be. Hence, plants, animals and minerals all take on atoms supporting their appropriate form's rate at a given time. The slowing down of the vibratory rates results in the form's dissolution since it is no longer vibrating at a rate sufficient to retain its original form. It follows, therefore, that the higher the rate of vibration the more evolved the form will be. Additionally, the fact that atoms have consciousness and vibratory rates provides a possible basis for ESP and psychokinesis. When an atom has consciousness and a vibratory rate it can be influenced by higher consciousnesses and higher vibratory rates. These raise the level of the lower consciousnesses or vibratory rates in keeping with the Divine Will for progress, as exemplified by the Law of Evolution. The Law of Change, therefore, supports and co-operates with the Law of Evolution.

It is not our intention in this work to go into a detailed treatise on these Laws, but rather to state them and briefly show their applicability to the *I Ching*, especially as regards the formation and development of the trigrams and the hexagrams.

THE LAW OF ENANTIODROMIA (Reversal *in extremis*)
This has quite different qualities from those ascribed to the Law
of Change and the Law of Evolution, but is of paramount importance in the development of hexagrams and trigrams and may be
considered as complementing both these Laws.

Briefly stated, the word Enantiodromia is a Greek word meaning that whatever goes to its ultimate extremity will revert to its
opposite. This Law plays two very strong roles in the *I Ching*.
The first is in the development of the trigrams and is manifested
at every stage of their development (see Figure 1). What it means
is simply this. Whenever the Yang reaches its extreme expression
it changes to the Yin, and whenever the Yin reaches *its* extreme
expression it converts itself into Yang. It can be posited that when
the Supreme Ultimate became active again after a 'night' of rest,
it produced the Creative first. When the Creative, the Yang,
reaches its extreme it converts itself into the opposite, the Receptive or Yin. This, in a broad sense, would parallel the Biblical
story that woman was created from the rib of man. The meaning,
as far as the activation and evolution of the trigrams is concerned,
is that at each stage of development a Yang converts itself into a
Yin, and a Yang and a Yin likewise converts itself into a Yang and
a Yin. Referring to Figure 1, we see that from Stage 1 (bottom to
top) the Yang produced a Yang and a Yin, and the Yin produced
a Yin and a Yang. Similarly, the two Yang and the two Yin of
Stage 2 produced four Yang and four Yin in Stage 3, as shown in
Figure 1a.

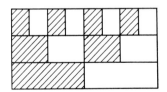

Figure 1a.   Stage 3 evolution (detail from Figure 1)

Starting at the top right-hand corner of Figure 1a, and moving
from top to bottom and from right to left, we discern the eight
trigrams, as follows (Yang lines being represented by solid lines
[——], Yin lines by broken ones [— —]):

Three Yang = ☰ This is called Ch'ien, or Father

Two Yang and one Yin = ☱ This is called Tui, Youngest Daughter

Yang–Yin–Yang = ☲ This is called Li, Middle Daughter

Yang and two Yin = ☳ This is called Chên, Eldest Son

Yin and two Yang = ☴ This is called Sun, Eldest Daughter

Yin–Yang–Yin = ☵ This is called K'an, Middle Son

Two Yin and a Yang = ☶ This is called Ken, Youngest Son

Three Yin = ☷ This is called K'un, or Mother

The progeny are determined and designated by the concepts that 'one rules many' and that 'changes enter from the bottom'. The sons, therefore, are those trigrams with one Yang and two Yin, the one with the solid line at the bottom being the Eldest Son, while the one with the single Yang line in the middle is the Middle Son, and the trigram with the single Yang line at the top is the Youngest Son. Similarly, ☴ Sun is the Eldest daughter, Li ☲ the Middle Daughter and Tui ☱ the Youngest Daughter.

It should be noted, too, that the Tai Ch'i symbol (Figure 2),

Figure 2.   Tai Ch'i

which is the first stage of evolution from quiescence, shows a bit of the Yang in the Yin and a bit of the Yin in the Yang. This is considered to be the seed by which and through which the Law of Enantiodromia operates.

The development of the trigrams can also be demonstrated in a circular manner, as in Figure 3.

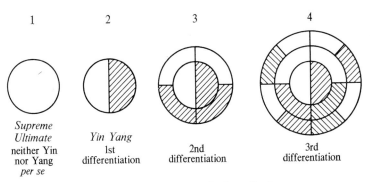

| 1 | 2 | 3 | 4 |

Supreme Ultimate neither Yin nor Yang *per se*

Yin Yang 1st differentiation

2nd differentiation

3rd differentiation

Figure 3. The circular evolution of trigrams

In three more stages of evolution the sixty-four hexagrams or Kua are produced. The Chinese call them Kua, since strictly speaking they are not hexagrams. For our purposes, however, these two terms will mean the same and may be used interchangeably.

The formation of the trigrams and the Kua can be substantiated by the use of algebra:

Let A = a Yang line
    B = a Yin line
then
$$(A + B)^3 = A^3 + 3A^2B + 3AB^2 + B^3$$

Converting this formula we get:

a trigram of three Yang lines

three trigrams of two Yang and a Yin

three trigrams of two Yin and a Yang

and a trigram composed of three Yin

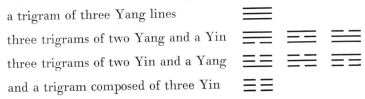

For the hexagrams the following formula can be used:

$$(A + B)^6 = A^6 + 6A^5B + 15A^4B^2 + 20A^3B^3 + 15A^2B^4 + 6AB^5 + B^6$$

By a conversion similar to that shown above for the trigrams, the sixty-four hexagrams can be verified as in Figure 4.

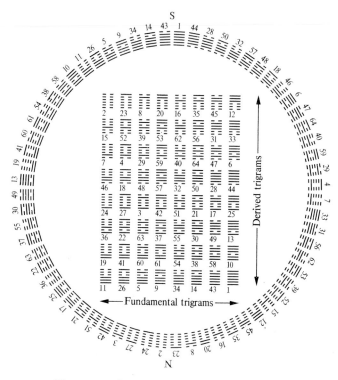

Figure 4. Circular diagram of hexagrams

Now that we have determined what the trigrams are and who they represent, the next thing to know is what their attributes and associations are (see Appendix A). In order to arrive at this, though, we must take into consideration several intermediate facts, the first of these being the Earlier Heaven sequence of trigrams (shown in Figure 5).

As mentioned earlier, the archetype for everything that exists was developed in heaven before being brought into fruition here on earth. This began when the Supreme Ultimate decided that the period of quiescence should end. The 'New Day' began by the activation of the first undifferentiated atom with Yin and Yang; i.e., a consciousness of positive and negative vibrations. Then, through the Word—the ideas of heaven, the Logos—vibrations were sent into being and forms were produced. Stars, planets, suns, moons and earths and everything on them came into being, the prototype in every case originating in heaven. From this concept the Earlier Heaven sequence of trigrams was developed, as shown in Figure 5.

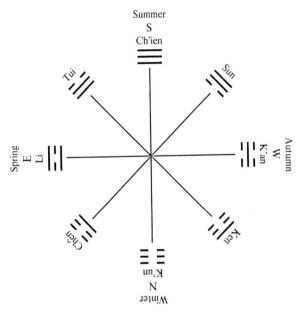

Figure 5. Earlier Heaven sequence

The conversion of the Word, or Logos, into ideas was done through what is now called the Later Heaven sequence. The patterns were prescribed and laid down in heaven and the products produced here on earth through the machinery and mechanisms applicable to earth and its needs. It is obvious that since heaven and earth are different they should have and use different mechanisms. Therefore, the sequence of trigrams for earth's applications varies somewhat from the heavenly one. Further, since heaven already had its sequence, earth's sequence of trigrams was called the Later Heaven sequence, since it had originated there for use on earth. See Figure 6.

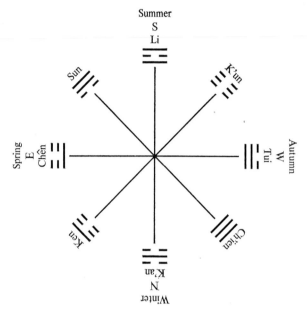

Figure 6. Later Heaven sequence

The Later Heaven sequence is very important, for together with the Lo Map (Figure 8), it forms the basis of most of those Chinese studies associated with the *I Ching*, such as medicine, astrology, geomancy, meditation, philosophy, and the proper conduct of one's life. The underlying concept combines numerology with the philosophy of the *I Ching*. The fundamental idea is that everything in the world is ordered, predetermined in heaven and in accordance with the Laws of Heaven and the Laws of Earth, and therefore predictable and understandable here on earth at any given time unless modified by the thoughts and actions of man. Since the Laws of Heaven and the Laws of Earth are constant, the results of their application can be foreknown. This constancy and orderliness comes from a combination of the Later

Heaven sequence as superimposed by a so-called Magic Square of Three, wherein the word 'magic' relates to the fact that the numbers in any column, horizontal, vertical or diagonal, add up to fifteen (see Figure 7). Note that this square is also directional.

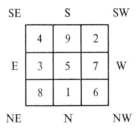

Figure 7. The Magic Square of Three

When the Magic Square is superimposed upon the Later Heaven sequence, we find that the trigrams, their direction and numerical values are as follows:

Ch'ien	NW	6	Father, Creative, Heaven
K'an	N	1	Middle Son, Water (River), Danger
Ken	NE	8	Youngest Son, Mountain, Keeping Still
Chen	E	3	Eldest Son, Arousing, Thunder
Sun	SE	4	Eldest Daughter, Penetration, Wind
Li	S	9	Middle Daughter, Fire, Clarity
K'un	SW	2	Mother, Receptive, Earth
Tui	W	7	Youngest Daughter, Lake, Joyousness

Note that the odd numbers form the cardinal directional points while the even numbers relate to the inter-cardinal points.

According to Chinese legend, the Lo River in the north-west of China is supposed to have brought forth the diagram shown in Figure 8, which is now known simply as the Lo Map. Basically it is the Magic Square of Three presented in such a manner as to readily distinguish the Yin and the Yang.

From this there developed a concept that if things work together and complement one another, the positive and negative sequences shown in the Lo Map should likewise work in pairs. This brought about what is sometimes known as the Ho Map, and at others simply as the River Map (see Figure 9). Beginning at the north and working clockwise, they brought the NW 6 to N, making it the fulfiller of the 1 in the north. By the same token and for the same reason the NE 8 (−) was co-joined with E 3 (+); SE 4 (−) with S 9 (+); and SW 2 (−) with W 7 (+).

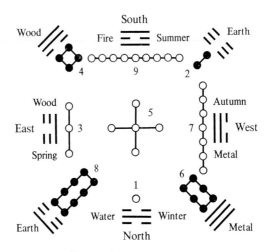

Figure 8. The Lo Map

Subsequently the problem arose of adapting the Five Celestial elements to this diagram for a graphic and numerological sequence of these celestial forces. The celestial elements of metal, water, wood, fire and earth, were already an integral part of Chinese experience. By observing the action of these in nature they determined their interaction. This also provided a basis for the concept that all begins with earth and subsequently returns to earth, since earth is the completer, that which brings all alse into fruition. Therefore, some commentators consider 5 as the number of the earth and the total of the elements as well, since they all are operative on the earth and brought to completion again through the number 10, which encompasses all the numbers before it. Consequently, 10 represents a complete cycle. Others say the elements are purely celestial and only named after things common on earth as a matter of convenience and for understanding. In any event, the sequence they established and which is still in common usage today is as shown in Table 1.

Table 1   *Generation of elements*

Earth generates (gives birth to) metal (W)

Metal generates (gives birth to) water (N)

Water generates (gives birth to) wood (E)

Wood generates (gives birth to) fire (S)

Fire generates (gives birth to) earth (Centre)

The Chinese sages took into account that while the foregoing was the way in which the elements worked with each other, there was also the matter of these elements (forces) opposing each other. The table of opposition, as they ascribed it, is as shown in Table 2.

Table 2   *Conquering of elements*

Earth conquers water (Absorption)

Water conquers fire (Quenching)

Fire conquers metal (Melting)

Metal conquers wood (Cutting)

Wood conquers earth (Extracting)

These sequences, and the trigrams representing them, together with the position and direction indicated by the trigrams, form the basis of Chinese astrology, divination, geomancy, medical science, meditation and philosophy. The sequences given in Tables 1 and 2 should be memorized to facilitate the understanding of much that subsequently occurs in this anthology.

The Ho Map (see Figure 9) forms the basis for the elemental aspects and numerology of the twelve Horary Branches; i.e., the twelve two-hour periods of each day. Note that there are two significant differences between the Lo and Ho Maps, the first being that the 5 Yang of earth in the Lo Map are balanced in the Ho Map by 5's counterpart, 10 Yin; the second being that the combination of 2 and 7 are now in the south representing fire, and 4 and 9 are in the west depicting metal. This change is brought about by the Horary Branch concept that the opposites 1/2 and 3/4 should be literal opposites. The same applies to the elements; i.e., that opposites should be those which oppose each other, as water does fire and metal does wood. From this we get the values for the Horary Branches set out as Table 3.

The values for the Celestial Stems will be given later in the text, at a point where they will be more appropriate. Different scholars and sages originated different philosophies, astrologies,

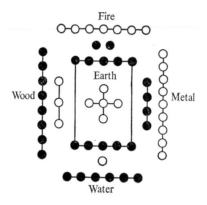

Figure 9.   The Ho Map

geomancies, meditations, etc., each having his own idea as to what was right and best. To set forth the relevant tables here would only lead to confusion, so they will be presented when and as applicable.

Table 3   *Numerological symbolism of the Horary Branches associated with the Ho Map*

Water	*Earth*	*Wood*	*Earth*	*Fire*
a+	b−	c+ & d−	e+	f− & g+
1 & 6	5 & 10	3 & 8	5 & 10	2 & 7

Earth	*Metal*	*Earth*	*Water*	
h−	i+ & j−	k+	l−	
5 & 10	4 & 9	5 & 10	1 & 6	

Figures 1–9 and Tables 1–3 are very important, since all subsequent sections of this anthology are either built upon them or related to them. For greater ease of understanding of the material,

and to avoid having to refer back at each mention, it would be wise to try and memorize them. One further table is also of general application: that tabulating the attributes and associations of the trigrams. For ease of reference, this is given at the end of the text, as Appendix A.

Basic divination

The most popular use of the *I Ching* is for divination, and perhaps always has been. From the earliest of times, following its inception, it has been the basis for oracles and predictions for kings and rulers. Beyond doubt, others used it for such purposes, too. Even Confucius did (as the footnote on p. 91 of the Wilhelm/Baynes translation of the *I Ching* shows), while at the same time emphasizing its additional aspects and usages in his commentaries on the text. For those who are experienced with it, understand it and are ready to accept that the *I Ching* knows much more about any given situation than humans do, it can be of great value as a guide. Basically, it is the aura of the questioner which determines the way the yarrow stalks are divided or the coins are cast. The aura reflects man's inner self and the inner self is in contact with the Divine storehouse of infinite wisdom and knowledge. Hence the use of the *I Ching* is a means of telling man what he inwardly knows but hasn't been able to discern for himself at the beta level of consciousness. It is probable that some readers will not agree with the foregoing statements. This is relatively immaterial, since all the guidance given by *I Ching* is of an ethical nature. Consequently there never is any danger of following advice which conflicts with a person's own beliefs regarding the validity of the oracles and whether chance or otherwise controls the fall of the coins or yarrow stalks. Experience will gradually show that the *I Ching* is a valid guide and that it does reflect greater consideration than mortals give to any situation. In other words, it cannot of itself be of harm to anyone. It only helps. That is why it has withstood criticisms and tests for over 5,000 years. Regrettably, those who interpret the hexagrams often do not know as much as they should about a given situation, so that even though thoroughly sincere and honest at the time, they may give erroneous predictions.

Furthermore, it is only with hindsight that one truly knows

what the *I Ching* meant. For example: two acquaintances of ours once asked the *I Ching* whether they would take a trip to Mexico the following week. All their plans had been laid and many preparations had been made. There was nothing to indicate that they wouldn't make their journey. The answer the *I Ching* gave was 'No'. As it turned out, on the day they were to have left the uncle of one of them was taken to hospital, the doctor advising them that the illness was terminal. Family affairs dictated that the trip should be postponed, which it was. This situation could not have been foreseen at the time the question was asked. Innumerable other cases could be cited. In our own case, experience has proved that our intuitive evaluation of the *I Ching*'s response to any question we have put to it has been between 70 per cent and 90 per cent accurate (according to our level of evaluation). We never cease to be amazed at its profound insight.

As stated above, the throwing of the coins or the separation of the yarrow stalks is a matter of the individual's own aura impinging upon and controlling the results. Each one of us is connected with Universal Intelligence at all times. A man whose development was at a sufficiently high stage and who was adequately spiritual, would have no need for a 'go between' such as the *I Ching* to give him guidance. He would either intuitively know what to do or else ascertain it from higher sources, since all is already known in what the *I Ching* calls 'heaven'. (Others speak of higher planes, etc.) Through the unconscious powers within man, one's inner self makes contact with the storehouse of Universal Knowledge and the response is given to us in a manner which comes up heads or tails when the coins are tossed, in such a way that the hexagram indicated will be the one best understood by the individual's intuition. There is no outside force controlling the manner in which the coins are tossed. Neither is it chance. It all stems from within one's own self. That is why it is so important to make the questions clear when formulating them, to concentrate on them while tossing the coins, and to meditate on the responses before implementing them.

In more detail, the method of obtaining a prediction is as follows. When one wishes to obtain an oracle the first step is to formulate one's question clearly, concisely and in the present tense. Although mention is made of Universal Time elsewhere in this book—i.e., things happening in accordance with Divine time rather than man's concept of time—it is man's time we are considering here. In fact, time as man knows it does not exist in the heavenly dimension. But since the answers from the *I Ching* relate to things here on earth, and since these do involve man's concept of time, any question relating to time should be clearly and specifically spelled out so as to avoid any ambiguity. Questions phrased positively also seem to get clearer responses than those with a negative aspect, so that it is best to avoid 'no' and 'not' or any implication of these. Indefinite words, such as 'will' and 'shall' should never be used alone, since they could mean any (man's concept of) time between now and eternity. Thus words must be finitely circumscribed and limited; for example, Will I go to the mountains *this weekend?* . . . *this year?*, etc. Should I become a writer of books *this summer?*, etc. The phrasing should be terse yet using active verbs. Any ambiguity generally results in a weak response or one easily open to misinterpretation. Furthermore, one of the keys of Logos is Love, hence the mind responds to emotional words with greater strength and intuition than it does to passive or technical words. Therefore, if an emotional word can be used without changing the meaning of a question, use it. As a suggestion, until real experience has been gained in using the *I Ching*, it is desirable to write out all questions to see that the best possible wording has been used and that it accurately reflects what the questioner wants to know, before tossing the coins.

The method of tossing the coins will be mentioned shortly. As for oracles through the selection of yarrow stalks, very few people know the procedure nor care to learn it, so it will not be described here. Those who are interested in knowing about it should refer to Richard Wilhelm's book *The I Ching or Book of Changes*. Its Appendix, 'The Yarrow Stalk Oracle', on pp. 721–3 of the one-volume edition of Cary F. Baynes's English translation (Routledge & Kegan Paul, 1968), adequately describes the procedure.

The coins used for consulting the *I Ching*, whether old Chinese coins or modern Western or Oriental ones, should be preserved and used for that purpose only. Having decided on the coins you will be using, wash them thoroughly to clean off other people's vibrations, and then hold them in your hands, preferably for about half an hour, to allow them to adequately absorb your vibrations. When not in use they should be kept in such a place and manner that they do not absorb someone else's vibrations. Remove them from storage and bring them out only when you want to use them for oracular purposes.

With the question well formulated and with your coins in your hands, ask the question mentally before each of the six times you toss the coins to obtain a hexagram. When you have finished using them, restore the coins to their private location.

The values assigned to the coins are as follows: heads have a value of 3, tails a value of 2. The results can only be a choice of the following:

(a) Three tails $3 \times 2 = 6$
(b) Two tails and one head $(2 \times 2) + 3 = 7$
(c) Two heads and one tail $(2 \times 3) + 2 = 8$
(d) Three heads $3 \times 3 = 9$

A 6 represents a moving Yin line and is written   —x—
A 7 represents an unmoving Yang line and is written   ———
An 8 represents an unmoving Yin line and is written   — —
A 9 represents a moving Yang line and is written   —ө—

The construction of a trigram or a hexagram is from the bottom upwards. Therefore, the results of the first toss of the coins will represent the bottom line, the second the second line from the bottom, the third toss the third line from the bottom, etc., for all six tosses. Suppose the results in sequence of tossing, were 6–7–8–9–8–6. The hexagram would be:

—x—
— —
—ө—
— —
———
—x—

A Yang moving line—i.e., 9 or —ө——represents the present or past situation with regard to the question asked, while a 6 or —x— represents the future, as it relates to the meanings given for a particular line. When the action indicated by the moving lines has been taken, the result is the formation of a new hexagram; this is what the situation or circumstance will become in the future, after action has been taken. A moving Yang converts into a Yin and this is considered retrogression, whereas a moving Yin converts itself into a Yang and is considered progression. In the foregoing example the conversion action would be:

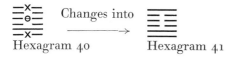

Hexagram 40   Hexagram 41

As a result of having moving and fixed lines every hexagram, as is obvious, can change into every other hexagram. Thus a situation or circumstance depicted by any hexagram can, through appropriate action, be changed into any other. This can be used to advantage in personal matters, in that if one does not like the present situation or circumstance one can select a hexagram representing what one would like the situation to be and then look up the action that needs to be taken to attain the new situation. Suppose, for example, that the present situation is one of conflict and one would like to have peace instead. Conflict is Hexagram 6 and Peace is Hexagram 11. What then is needed to change Hexagram 6 into Hexagram 11?

Hexagram 6   Hexagram 11

A glance at the hexagrams shows that the lines which need to change into their opposites are 1, 3, 4, 5 and 6. Therefore, these need to be moving lines, as represented thus:

One would then read Hexagram 6 and the action required for the moving lines in order to determine the course to pursue for the situation to become one of peace. This same method can be applied to any circumstance. For instance, one can ask the question, 'What is the present situation regarding ——?' and then use the hexagram thus derived as the basis for making the change into what one would like the situation to be.

To return to the matter of the interpretation of the hexagrams derived from tossing the coins, the following commentaries will be found useful and beneficial in arriving at the meaning of any oracle thus obtained. They are somewhat similar to those set forth in the Chinese book *The Hidden Meaning of I*:

(a) Read the Judgment and Image of the hexagram as a whole to get a good feel for the overall meaning of the hexagram.

If there are no moving lines, use the Judgment and Image statements for your evaluation.

(b) One Moving Line: Make the judgment and final evaluation on the text of the one moving line.

(c) Two Moving Lines: Consider the text of both moving lines and give the upper line more weight in the evaluation than the lower.

(d) Three Moving Lines: Consider the text of all the moving lines and give the greatest weight to the text of the middle moving line, and to the text of both the present and future hexagram.

(e) Four Moving Lines: Read all the lines and give greatest weight to the meaning of the two unmoving lines as they are described in the future hexagram. Emphasize the meaning of the lower non-moving line as it is found in the future hexagram.

(f) Five Moving Lines: Read all the lines and give greatest weight to the meaning of the single non-moving line as it is described in the future hexagram along with the final outcome depicted in the future hexagram.

(g) Six Moving Lines: Read everything but make the evaluation on the basis of the final outcome (future) hexagram.

Altogether, there are ten important considerations we should remember in connection with every interpretation of a hexagram. These are the points which King Wên and the Duke of Chou emphasized in their amplification of the *I Ching* and are among the important elements in the Confucian commentaries. All the 'Judgments' made by King Wên, and both the Big and Little 'Images' put forward by the Duke of Chou (see p. 5) are based on the interplay and interrelationship of the lines of the trigrams. In combination with the natural symbolism involved, the direction of movement predicted by the heavenly sequences (i.e. Later Heaven and Earlier Heaven), and the agreement or disagreement between the strong and the weak lines, the upper and lower trigrams, and the inner and outer trigrams, we find a full, and in one sense, scientific, basis for every explanatory statement made.

For a comprehensive evaluation of any line, trigram or hexagram, the ten important considerations are as follows:

(1) The first question to answer is, Which hexagram is under consideration and what is the nature of the trigrams involved? Identifying a hexagram is simple and done in the normal manner. As for the trigrams, there are two: the upper trigram, composed of the upper three lines and spoken of as being on top of the lower one; and the lower trigram, consisting of the lower three lines. Let us use the following hexagram to illustrate all the ten points we are about to discuss:

On identification we find that this is Hexagram 40, Deliverance, with moving lines. The moving line in the first place is designated 6–1; the moving line in the third place is designated as 6–3; the moving line in the fourth place is designated 9–4.

Breaking down Hexagram 40 we find that our two trigrams are:

Upper trigram: Thunder, movement, Chên ☳

Lower trigram: Water, rain, danger, K'an ☵

Chên, movement, tends to rise, while rain falls and water flows downhill. So we have movement away from danger, hence deliverance. Also, after a thunderstorm and rain the air has been cleared and is refreshed and the earlier tension in the atmosphere has been released. These then are the factors which give the hexagram its name of 'Deliverance'.

(2) Our second point relates to the body of the hexagram; that is, the inner and the outer trigrams, sometimes also referred to as the upper and the lower trigrams. In our example, we have shown what they are and how they interact. However, by way of amplification we are told that the inner trigram generally relates to self or the particular question or situation under consideration, whereas the outer one relates to external conditions and external effects. On some occasions, one may want to look at them as having possibly heavenly and earthly considerations.

(3) The position of the lines likewise is important:

From the point of view of trigram construction
    6 = heaven

    5 = man
    4 = earth
    3 = heaven
    2 = man
    1 = earth

From the point of view of hexagram construction

    6 Outside the situation
    5 King or ruler, husband
    4 Minister
    3 Transitional state
    2 Wife or follower
    1 Seeds of the change to the situation

    6 Symbolic of heaven's considerations
    5 Symbolic of heaven's considerations
    4 Symbolic of man's considerations
    3 Symbolic of man's considerations
    2 Symbolic of earth's considerations
    1 Symbolic of earth's considerations

In our example, we have:

6⎱ — — Two Yin, so heaven's consideration is to be re-
5⎰ — — ceptive (to guidance).

4⎱ ——— Here a Yang is leading a Yin, the positive is
3⎰ — — leading the negative, in keeping with natural law.

2⎱ ——— Same interpretation as for 4/3 above. Here the
1⎰ — — positive in nature (earth) is leading the negative,
        which is also in keeping with natural law.

As for the natural balanced position of the lines of a hexagram, they are said to be in their rightful position when they are

    6 — —
    5 ———
    4 — —
    3 ———
    2 — —
    1 ———

In other words the odd number positions are Yang, positive, strong, whereas the even numbers are Yin, negative, gentle.

Several factors have to be taken into consideration when deciding whether lines are favourable or not, but for the purpose of moving lines—i.e., a moving Yang line or a moving Yin line—the following algebraic table applies:

$(-) \times (+) = (-)$ lines disagree
$(-) \times (-) = (+)$ lines agree
$(+) \times (+) = (+)$ lines agree
$(+) \times (-) = (-)$ lines disagree

(4) This step involves the assignment and use of appropriate symbolism for the determination and correct evaluation of the Big and Little Images (the Big Image refers to the Image as shown in the *I Ching* for each hexagram; the Little Image is the interpretation set forth for each line).

Under (1) above, we discussed the symbolism of movement and danger, illustrating how in this instance there was movement away from danger, and hence 'deliverance'. The symbolism for all the trigrams is shown in Appendix A and need not be repeated here. From these it is possible to see (from the way in which they tend to interact with one another as a result of either being over or under another trigram) how each hexagram received its name. These names for hexagrams are not in any respect arbitrary but are based on the processes of nature and its laws. They are all founded on natural principles and natural phenomena.

(5) In this step we determine the position of the governing ruler of the hexagram (not to be confused with the term ruler or king in connection with line 5, as mentioned under (3) above).

Basically, if a trigram or hexagram has a single Yin or Yang line, then that single line determines the nature and position of the governing ruler of the trigram or hexagram. If you refer back to page 14 you will see that a single Yang line in a trigram determined that it was a son and the position of the Yang line determined whether it was the eldest, middle or youngest son. Similarly, a single Yin and its position determined the eldest, middle and youngest daughters.

The normal position for the ruler is line 5. However, if there is only one Yang line or one Yin line in a hexagram it usually is the ruler (as in trigrams). The principle is that one and only one can rule many. In some cases a trigram having a minority of Yang or Yin lines is used to determine the ruler and in such cases the minority Yang or Yin line is assigned as the ruler. In cases where the upper and lower trigrams are equal, as in Hexagram 51 ䷲, the ruler is the single line in the upper trigram (in this case the Yang line in the fourth place). It is to be noted that there is only one case in all the sixty-four hexagrams where a line in the third position is assigned as the ruler, and that is Hexagram 15, Modesty ䷎. The third position is generally considered as unstable, transient, wavering, and hence unfavourable. It is the third line which when moving in a rising and declining cycle, is about to enter the upper trigram and as such the first consideration given is that it is a source of trouble until it proves itself to be favourable, as in Hexagram 15, where it exemplifies modesty.

(6) Here we determine whether the lines of the inner and outer trigrams agree or disagree, correspond or fail to correspond. This is done by matching lines 1 to 4, 2 to 5 and 3 to 6, the upper trigram being considered as leading the lower. In our example ䷲ lines 1 and 4 agree since a Yang is leading a Yin, the positive leading the negative. Lines 2 and 5 are opposites, so they can get along but not as favourably as when the Yang leads the Yin. Lines 3 and 6 are both alike, so difficulties between them as non-moving lines are apt to arise.

(7) A person cannot make a final judgment regarding a question or situation without knowing the background events which gave rise to them. We should know the hexagram which represented the preceding condition. Just as, in travelling, one can get to New York by several routes or modes of travel, so one can get into a particular situation or difficulty in one of several ways. We must know the point from which a situation has developed in order to make a proper and correct judgment. There are, of course, several ways in which one hexagram changes into another. As has already been said, the action of moving lines can change any one hexagram into any other. Changes entering from the bottom move up through a hexagram to the top. Then there is the natural circular diagram sequence described on p. 16, which Sau Yung changed into one of his own when evaluating

the history of China according to the *I Ching*. Another method is through the action of the Law of Enantiodromia (see p. 13). Recognizing that the background for a hexagram can be quite variable makes one believe that fortune-tellers using the *I Ching* are only guessing (if lucky, they can guess right) since they do not know and cannot determine the origin of those matters for which they are making predictions. It is true that they can use the *I Ching* as we have described here. But they do not know the underlying facts and related circumstances. Hence they should not be relied upon even though using such a valuable work as the *I Ching*. Only the questioner has adequate background information, and even this may not be complete.

As for our example, if we accept the statement (in accordance with the sequences developed by Yu Yen during the South Sung Dynasty, which can be found in most Chinese books on the *I Ching*) that the hexagram was derived from Hexagram 46, Pushing Upward, we can explain another statement made in the Judgment of the hexagram. For Hexagram 40 to be derived from Hexagram 46 means that the Yang line in the third place in Hexagram 46 has to move up into the outer trigram K'un to become the Yang line in the fourth place of Hexagram 40. K'un means a lot of people or the general public. Its position in the Later Heaven sequence is in the south-west. Therefore, the Judgment of the hexagram says there is good fortune in going to the south (line 3 in Hexagram 46 moving into the K'un trigram) and that this is beneficial to the public. It can be interpreted as meaning either that by going to the south there will be good fortune, or that when the majority or public need help there will be good fortune in going to their aid.

(8) We must remember that ancient symbolism was used and still exists in the basic text of the *I Ching*. This next step and our example illustrate this quite clearly. We now come to the inner hexagram, that is, the hexagram within the hexagram under consideration. The inner hexagram is that hexagram made up of the two nuclear trigrams (lines 2, 3 and 4; and lines 3, 4 and 5). In our example this gives us ☲☵, where lines 3, 4 and 5 = ☲ Li and are symbolized by fire and sun, and lines 2, 3 and 4 form trigram ☵ K'an, symbolizing water, danger and field. The inner hexagram plays a part in the overall view of a given

situation. Here we have 'three foxes in a field', the three lines of the Li trigram being the foxes who, mixing with lines 3, 4 and 5 show them to be in the field formed by the latter trigram. We read the following for 9–2: 'Nine in the second place means: One kills three foxes in the field and receives a yellow arrow. Perseverance brings good fortune.' So if line 2 is a moving line, then when such movement takes place the Li trigram is destroyed. This course is meritorious, eradicating the three foxes, so a reward of a yellow arrow is ascribed. In other words, one receives an appropriate reward for eliminating troublesome conditions. The foxes were a source of trouble in ancient times and a yellow arrow was a highly prized award. Today one would assign other symbols for the troublesome conditions along with a more up-to-date and appropriate reward. The main point of the foregoing is that everything that is said in a hexagram has a rational basis.

(9) The ninth consideration relates to individual lines and what type of line they are resting on. Except for the bottom line of each hexagram all lines are 'resting' on another line which is either Yin or Yang. Since Yang lines are strong, active and creative, they are difficult to ride on, whereas Yin lines are gentle and receptive. Yang lines also have a tendency to rise, which makes them additionally difficult. So depending on their own strength, a line has more or less difficulty in its position by virtue of the strength and type of line under it.

(10) Our last consideration is, in a sense, the reverse of (9), yet different. Here the line has comfort or difficulty depending on whether a gentle Yin line or a strong Yang line is on top of it.

Thus we see that there are nine conditions which have to be taken into account when considering each line, namely:

(a) Is it in its right place?
(b) Does it agree with the corresponding line of the other trigram?
(c) Is it favourable or unfavourable as a part of heaven (lines 5 and 6), man (lines 3 and 4) or earth (lines 1 and 2)?
(d) What type of line is it riding on?
(e) What type of line is on top of it?
(f) Is it a Yang or Yin line?
(g) Is it a fixed or moving line?

(h) What is its favourable or unfavourable action as a moving line?

(i) Which line is the ruler of the trigram or hexagram?

Similarly, in considerating the trigrams one must ask:

(a) What is the symbolism of the trigram?
(b) What is the sex of the trigram?
(c) What is the nature of the trigram?
(d) What is its relation to the other trigram of the hexagram?
(e) Is it a male trigram leading a female trigram, or vice-versa?
(f) What is its direction of movement?
(g) What is the position of any moving line(s) in the trigram?
(h) What trigram does it change into, or does it remain the same?
(i) What is its position in the Later Heaven sequence?

When one comes to hexagrams themselves, the points to be considered are:

(a) All the considerations that were applied to the trigrams.
(b) The interaction of the symbolism of the trigrams.
(c) The interaction of the directional position of each trigram.
(d) The same considerations (a), (b) and (c) above for the nuclear trigrams within the inner hexagram (lines 2, 3 and 4; plus lines 3, 4 and 5).
(e) What effect does the inner hexagram have on the external hexagram?
(f) What other points of view regarding the situation or question, apply? In particular, what is said by
  (i) the opposite hexagram (change every line to its opposite)?
  (ii) the reverse hexagram (turn the hexagram upside-down)?
  (iii) the inner hexagram?
  (iv) the reverse inner hexagram?
(g) What are the courses of action which augur good fortune and success?
(h) What actions or courses should be avoided?
(i) What is the proper timing?
(j) Is the proposed action in keeping with the Supreme Will?

While the foregoing rules and suggestions may seem lengthy, it will not be long, if one consults the *I Ching* regularly, before one applies them automatically to evaluate and consider the oracles one receives.

Like everything else, the more experience one gains, the closer to perfection one comes. One must remember, however, that, irrespective of who makes a prediction and how good it may be, it is only with hindsight that the full and true import of the oracle can be seen. The *I Ching* will grow on you, and the more you use it, the more its value to you will increase, and the more benefit you will be able to derive from it. Like any other gem, its value increases with age.

2 | *Advanced Divination*

The expression Advanced Divination applies to methods of making predictions other than only those obtained by coins or dividing yarrow stalks and then evaluating the Judgments and Images developed by King Wên and the Duke of Chou. Our research and experimentations have brought to light (a) a method for making yearly predictions from the *I Ching*, (b) some methods for making predictions without the use of coins or yarrow stalks, (c) a method for obtaining predictions for almost anything, (d) a method for obtaining *yes* or *no* responses. Of course, if predictions beyond those normally attainable are to be made there must be added information on which to make or base such predictions.

Basically, the methods of prediction we are about to discuss go back to the scholars of the Han dynasty (206 BC to AD 220), among whom we have already mentioned Ching Fang. Subsequently, great impetus was given to these concepts by Sau Yung (*c*. AD 1000) and his contemporaries. Broadly speaking the predictions are made partly on a time concept and partly on the symbolic representations, interactions and direction of application of the *I Ching* trigrams. By synthesizing what the trigrams represent (whatever the subject or object one has in mind), which trigrams generate one another or which are conquered by others (see Tables 1 and 2), as well as the timing according to the Horary Branches and the direction of applicability from the Lo Map, skilful predictions can be made. Naturally, the better one understands all the factors involved the more likely it is that the prediction will be valid and fulfilled. Most of these aspects have been mentioned earlier. The Chinese concept of time, however, may be new to the Westerner.

It is more appropriate to discuss the Chinese concept of time in full in the chapter on astrologies associated with the *I Ching*, so it will not be presented in detail here. In broad terms, it posits that for any given instant of time, the moment in question is a synthesis of all the Cosmic forces acting together and can be represented by a symbol rather than trying to work out each force independently and correlating and collating all the factors concerned. Man, too, is an element of time and can be represented by a symbol.

The first system of interest to the dedicated user of the *I Ching* is that for making yearly predictions.

A   Yearly predictions

The most popular of the yearly prediction methods in China to-day is the one which combines the Five Elements, the Celestial Stems, the Horary Branches and certain other salient considerations.

For these yearly predictions the individual should toss the coins and obtain a hexagram in the usual manner; from this, by following the rules, guidelines and procedures given below, his prospects for the year can be known. The year, in this case, goes from winter solstice to winter solstice. Therefore, the prediction is only applicable up to the next winter solstice, regardless of when it is made during the year involved. The steps are given in the sequence considered most practical.

Step 1:   Toss the coins and develop a hexagram in the usual manner, keeping the question in mind before and during each cast of the coins.

Step 2:   Determine the hexagram number from the result of tossing the coins.

Step 3:   Using Figure 10, determine the applicable 'House', and the position within the 'House' of the hexagram.

Step 4:   Using Figure 11, determine which line represents the 'self' and which represents the 'other' (the word 'position' on Figure 11 being the position of the hexagram in its House, as ascertained from Figure 10).

For example, the House of Ch'ien gives the 'self' and 'other' lines shown as Table 4.

House	Position							
	1	2	3	4	5	6	7	8
Ch'ien — Metal	1	44	33	12	20	23	35	14
K'an — Water	29	60	3	63	49	55	36	7
Ken — Earth	52	22	26	41	38	10	61	53
Chên — Wood	51	16	40	32	46	48	28	17
Sun — Wood	57	9	37	42	25	21	27	18
Li — Fire	30	56	50	64	4	59	6	13
K'un — Earth	2	24	19	11	34	43	5	8
Tui — Water	58	47	45	31	39	15	62	54

Figure 10.   House positions

	Position							
	1	2	3	4	5	6	7	8
Line for Self	6	1	2	3	4	5	4	3
Line for Other	3	4	5	6	1	2	1	6

Figure 11.   'Self' and 'Other' lines

Table 4   *'Self' and 'Other' lines in the House of Ch'ien*

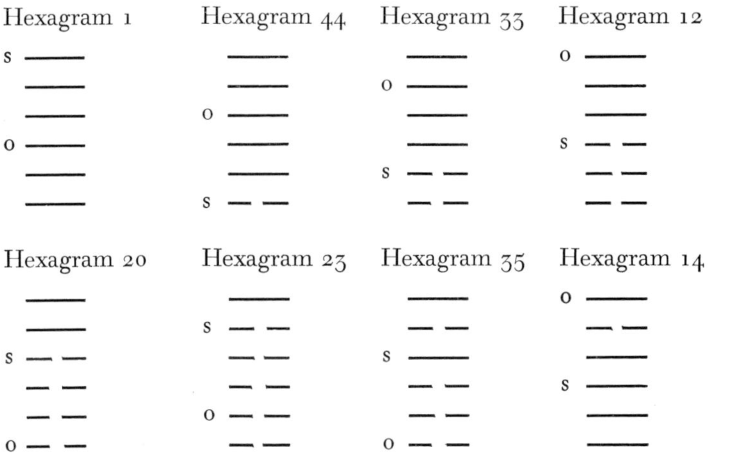

Step 5: (a) Having established the 'self' and 'other' lines in your hexagram, now identify its upper and lower trigrams; then, using Table 5, match each trigram to its appropriate position and note its letter sequence.

Table 5   *Horary Branch symbols related to trigrams*

——— k	— — k	— — a	——— c
——— i	— — i	——— k	— — a
——— g	——— g	— — i	— — k
——— e	— — e	— — g	——— i
——— c	— — c	——— e	— — g
——— a	——— a	— — — c	— — e
— — j	——— d	——— f	— — h
— — l	——— f	— — h	——— j
— — b	— — h	——— j	——— l
— — d	——— j	——— l	— — b
— — f	——— l	— — b	——— d
— — h	— — b	——— d	——— f

Note: The letter symbols are applicable to each trigram of any hexagram, the top three lines forming the upper trigram and the bottom three designating the lower. Notice that the male trigrams and hexagrams use the positive symbols in ascending sequence whereas the female ones use the negative in a descending sequence.

Step 6: (b) Select from Table 6 the element representations for the letter symbols you have obtained.

Table 6   *Horary Branch sequences and meanings*

f—	g+	h—	i+
e+			j—
d—			k+
c+	b—	a+	l—

a = water	g = fire
b = earth	h = earth
c = wood	i = metal
d = wood	j = metal
e = earth	k = earth
f = fire	l = water

EXAMPLE

Suppose you tossed the coins and came up with the following hexagram:

This is Hexagram 44. Its upper trigram is Ch'ien , Father, and the lower trigram is Sun ☴, Eldest Daughter.

Checking Table 5 we find that Ch'ien as the upper trigram

—— k

has the symbol —— i and Sun as the lower trigram has the

—— g

—— j

symbol —— l

— — b

Putting the two trigrams back together in the form of a hexagram, we have:

—— k
—— i
—— g
—— j
—— l
— — b

We then assign the elemental representations for the symbols from Table 6. Using our same example, we find that these are:

—— k (earth)
—— i (metal)
—— g (fire)
—— j (metal)
—— l (water)
— — b (earth)

Step 7: Entering Figure 10, we find that Hexagram 44 is in position 2.

From Figure 11 we find that the line for the 'self' for position 2 is line 1 and that line 4 designates the 'other'. Designate the appropriate lines of your hexagram with an 's' and 'o'.

```
——— earth
——— metal
o ——— fire
——— metal
——— water
s — — earth
```

Step 8: For convenience's sake, the information given in Tables 1 and 2 is repeated here:

Earth generates (gives birth to) metal
Metal generates (gives birth to) water
Water generates (gives birth to) wood
Wood generates (gives birth to) fire
Fire generates (gives birth to) earth

Earth conquers water (absorption)
Water conquers fire (quenching)
Fire conquers metal (melting)
Metal conquers wood (cutting)
Wood conquers earth (extracting)

The foregoing interactions are used to develop the predictions by correlating them with the 'House' to which the hexagram belongs. Check Figure 10 to determine to which 'House' the

Table 7   *Relatives and relationships*

1	Those lines which give birth to the 'House' are parents and ancestors.
2	Those lines which are the same as the 'House' are brothers, sisters and peers.
3	Those lines which conquer the 'House' are bosses, officials, troublemakers, one's office, one's position, etc.
4	Those lines which are generated by the 'House' are the descendants.
5	Those lines which are conquered by the 'House' are wives, sweethearts, money, business, professions, etc.

Note: When a woman tosses the coins and gets a hexagram for this purpose, lines 3 and 5 are interchanged as far as 'husband' or 'wife' are concerned; i.e., the lines which conquer the 'House' also represent the husband.

hexagram belongs. The analysis develops favourable or unfavourable relationships with relatives and associates and can also be used to determine the response to specific questions, such as those referring to financial activity, if the questions are phrased properly. The correlation is as set out in Table 7.

Figure 10 tells us that our example, Hexagram 44, is in the house of Ch'ien, metal. From Tables 1 and 2 we find that

Earth gives birth to metal
Metal gives birth to water
Fire conquers metal
Metal conquers wood.

Our example is:

——— earth
——— metal
——— fire
——— metal
——— water
— — earth

ANALYSIS

Line 1 is earth. Earth gives birth to metal (the House). Therefore, line 1 represents 'parents'.

Line 2 is water. Metal gives birth to water. Therefore, line 2 represents 'descendants'.

Line 3 is metal. This is the same as the 'House'. Therefore, line 3 represents brothers, sisters, peers, etc.

Line 4 is fire. Fire conquers metal. Therefore, line 4 represents one's office or one's position.

Line 5 is metal. This is the same as the 'House'. Therefore since it is the same as line 3 it must be evaluated with line 3 for the predictions relating to brothers, sisters and peers.

Line 6 is earth. Earth gives birth to metal. This line is the same as line 1 and therefore must be considered with line 1 in evaluating the prediction for 'parents'.

Enter your copy of the *I Ching* and make your evaluation on the basis of what is said for each line and relate it to the proper individuals or relationships.

For more detailed analysis or predictions, use the method

described in Section B below, in which the influence of the month and day are additionally considered.

B   Specific questions

The foregoing system gives a broad and general overview of the situation or circumstance for the questioner and obviously does not cover all the aspects he or she may wish to know. If more information is desired additional hexagrams should be developed in the usual manner, with one for each specific question. When this is done the Cosmic Forces as synthesized by time have to be considered for the month and day involved. The value for the month includes the general forces for the year, while those for the day pinpoint those especially applicable at that moment. The values are determined from the figures given in Tables 8 and 9.

Table 8   *Yearly cycle and daily cycle additive values*

Year	Yearly cycle	Daily cycle
1975	52	44
1976	53	49
1977	54	55
1978	55	60
1979	56	5
1980	57	10
1981	58	16
1982	59	21
1983	60	26
1984	1	31
1985	2	37
1986	3	42
1987	4	47
1988	5	52
1989	6	58
etc.	etc.	etc.

Note: For a more detailed table, see our volume *The Astrology of I Ching* (Routledge & Kegan Paul, 1976).

Table 9   *Sexagenary cycle*

1 Aa+	11 Ak+	21 Ai+	31 Ag+	41 Ae+	51 Ac+
2 Bb−	12 Bl−	22 Bj−	32 Bh−	42 Bf−	52 Bd−
3 Cc+	13 Ca+	23 Ck+	33 Ci+	43 Cg+	53 Ce+
4 Dd−	14 Db−	24 Dl−	34 Dj−	44 Dh−	54 Df−
5 Ee+	15 Ec+	25 Ea+	35 Ek+	45 Ei+	55 Eg+
6 Ff−	16 Fd−	26 Fb−	36 Fl−	46 Fj−	56 Fh−
7 Gg+	17 Ge+	27 Gc+	37 Ga+	47 Gk+	57 Gi+
8 Hh−	18 Hf−	28 Hd−	38 Hb−	48 Hl−	58 Hj−
9 Ii+	19 Ig+	29 Ie+	39 Ic+	49 Ia+	59 Ik+
10 Jj−	20 Jh−	30 Jf−	40 Jd−	50 Jb−	60 Jl−

PROCEDURE

Step 1: Determine the yearly cycle number from Table 8 and then enter Table 9 and pick out the capital letter (Celestial Stem) for the yearly number involved.

EXAMPLE:

The yearly cycle number of 1975 is 52 (Table 8).
The capital letter relating to 52 is B.
The Celestial Stem is therefore B.

Table 10   *Celestial Stem representations*

A+ and B−	= Wood
C+ and D−	= Fire
E+ and F−	= Earth
G+ and H−	= Metal
I+ and J−	= Water

Step 2: Enter Table 11 with the Celestial Stem for the year from Step 1 and pick out the symbol for the date of asking the question from the appropriate column under the Celestial Stem symbol for the year.

EXAMPLE:

Taking 10 July 1975 as the date for which the question is propounded, we see that:

45

1975 is a 52 Yearly Cycle year (Table 8).

The Celestial Stem for 52 is B (Table 9).

Under column B of Table 11, we find that

July 10 is Jh

h is therefore the Horary Branch symbol for the month involved.

Table 6 shows that h represents earth.

Table 11 *Monthly Celestial Stems and Horary Branches applicable to yearly Celestial Stems*

| Month | Applicable years | | | | |
	A & F	B & G	C & H	D & I	E & J
Winter solstice to 5 Jan.	Aa	Ca	Ea	Ga	Ia
6 Jan. to 3 Feb.	Bb	Db	Fb	Hb	Jb
4 Feb. to 5 Mar.	Cc	Ec	Gc	Ic	Ac
6 Mar. to 4 Apr.	Dd	Fd	Hd	Jd	Bd
5 Apr. to 5 May	Ee	Ge	Ie	Ae	Ce
6 May to 5 June	Ff	Hf	Jf	Bf	Df
6 June to 7 July	Gg	Ig	Ag	Cg	Eg
8 July to 7 Aug.	Hh	Jh	Bh	Dh	Fh
8 Aug. to 7 Sept.	Ii	Ai	Ci	Ei	Gi
8 Sept. to 8 Oct.	Jj	Bj	Dj	Fj	Hj
9 Oct. to 7 Nov.	Ak	Ck	Ek	Gk	Ik
8 Nov. to 7 Dec.	Bl	Dl	Fl	Hl	Jl
8 Dec. to winter solstice	Ca	Ea	Ga	Ia	Aa

Note: This table begins with the winter solstice, so that dates are *approximate*. Is is therefore suggested that when an important question is asked and this method is used for determining the prediction, the questioner should use a date other than one near the beginning or end of each monthly cycle. In this way more useful results can be obtained.

Step 3: Pick out the appropriate daily cycle value from Table 12 and add it to the daily cycle value for the appropriate year from Table 8. If the sum is less than 60 use it directly. If the sum is over 60, subtract 60 and use the remainder.

Table 12 *Daily cycle values*

Day	1	2	3	4	5	6	7	8	9	10	11	12	13	14	15
Month															
Jan.	0	1	2	3	4	5	6	7	8	9	10	11	12	13	14
Feb.	31	32	33	34	35	36	37	38	39	40	41	42	43	44	45
*Mar.	59	60	1	2	3	4	5	6	7	8	9	10	11	12	13
*Apr.	30	31	32	33	34	35	36	37	38	39	40	41	42	43	44
*May	60	1	2	3	4	5	6	7	8	9	10	11	12	13	14
*June	31	32	33	34	35	36	37	38	39	40	41	42	43	44	45
*July	1	2	3	4	5	6	7	8	9	10	11	12	13	14	15
*Aug.	32	33	34	35	36	37	38	39	40	41	42	43	44	45	46
*Sept.	3	4	5	6	7	8	9	10	11	12	13	14	15	16	17
*Oct.	33	34	35	36	37	38	39	40	41	42	43	44	45	46	47
*Nov.	4	5	6	7	8	9	10	11	12	13	14	15	16	17	18
*Dec.	34	35	36	37	38	39	40	41	42	43	44	45	46	47	48

Day	16	17	18	19	20	21	22	23	24	25	26	27	28	29	30	31
Month																
Jan.	15	16	17	18	19	20	21	22	23	24	25	26	27	28	29	30
Feb.	46	47	48	49	50	51	52	53	54	55	56	57	58			
*Mar.	14	15	16	17	18	19	20	21	22	23	24	25	26	27	28	29
*Apr.	45	46	47	48	49	50	51	52	53	54	55	56	57	58	59	
*May	15	16	17	18	19	20	21	22	23	24	25	26	27	28	29	30
*June	46	47	48	49	50	51	52	53	54	55	56	57	58	59	60	
*July	16	17	18	19	20	21	22	23	24	25	26	27	28	29	30	31
*Aug.	47	48	49	50	51	52	53	54	55	56	57	58	59	60	1	2
*Sept.	18	19	20	21	22	23	24	25	26	27	28	29	30	31	32	
*Oct.	48	49	50	51	52	53	54	55	56	57	58	59	60	1	2	3
*Nov.	19	20	21	22	23	24	25	26	27	28	29	30	31	32	33	
*Dec.	49	50	51	52	53	54	55	56	57	58	59	60	1	2	3	4

Note: Add one day during leap years for the months bearing an asterisk.

EXAMPLE:

28 July 1975

The daily cycle value for 28 July from Table 12 is 28.

1975 daily cycle value is 44 (Table 8)

Total = 44 + 28 = 72

Since the total is over 60, subtract 60 from 72:

72 − 60 = 12

12 is the corrected value for the day.

Step 4: Re-enter Table 9 and select the Horary Branch symbol for the corrected value for the day.

EXAMPLE:

For 12 the symbol is Bl

l therefore is the Horary Branch symbol for the day.

Step 5: Assign the element values to the Horary Branch symbols for the month and the day, using Table 6.

EXAMPLE:

From Step 2 the symbol for the month is h.

From Step 4 the symbol for the day is l.

From Table 6: h = earth, l = water

Step 6: One is now ready to ask one's question and should concentrate on it while tossing the coins and developing the hexagram in the usual manner.

Let us suppose that the question is, 'Will I have financial success during the balance of this year?', and that from tossing the coins we get Hexagram 25 with a moving line in the second place:

Step 7: From Figure 10 we see that Hexagram 25 is in the fifth position in the House of Sun—wood.

From Figure 11 we find that line 4 represents self.

Step 8: Table 5 shows that the Horary Branch symbols for Hexagram 25 are:

```
k ——
i ——
g —— (self)
e — —
c — —
a —— (other)
```

Line 3 = e = earth (Table 6) and is the money line (Table 7).
Line 4 = g = fire (Table 6) and is the self line (Figure 11).

Therefore, fire represents self; and earth represents money.

Step 9: Initial analysis: We have the fire of self intermingling with the force of h—earth and l—water. From Table 1 we see that water conquers fire and fire generates earth.

Step 10: Further analysis: Determine the following:

(a) What does the hexagram as a whole represent? Read the Judgment and Images of the hexagram. This symbolizes the present situation. Also note any moving lines, for any action indicated by them later changes the lines into their opposite.

(b) What will the hexagram change into; i.e., what will be the future hexagram after all moving lines have changed?

(c) What is the general picture of the new situation?

(d) How do I fit into the present situation; i.e., read the text for the 'self' line as well as finding out its element designation. In our present example, it is fire. Also read the text for the money line, which will indicate the general tendency at the present time.

(e) What is the action of the monthly element on self? On the money line?

(f) What is the action of the daily element on self? On the money line?

SIMPLIFIED ANSWERS TO ANALYSIS

The following is a simplified version of the answers to the above analysis, as they relate to our question and the response from the *I Ching* in the form of Hexagram 25 with line 2 being a moving line, line 3 the money line and line 4 the self line:

(a) This hexagram represents the birth of all things in primal innocence.

(b) The changed hexagram (future hexagram) is Hexagram 10.

(c) Hexagram 10 represents correct conduct and actions.

(d) Line 2, the moving line, indicates that one should take action for action's sake only. We should not 'count on the harvest while plowing'.

(e) Line 3, the money line, says that adversities due to our fate, or karma, often befall the best of persons. Remain firm.

(f) Line 4, the self line, says that man's innocence is being tested; in other words to be wary of possible temptations.

(g) The monthly element is earth and the self element is fire. If the monthly element supports the self element the interaction is favourable. Here, however, the self is generating the monthly element, so this is a case of taking something away from self, hence unfavourable.

(h) The monthly element is earth and the money element is earth. There is neither favourable nor unfavourable interaction.

(i) The daily action is water and the self action is fire. The interaction is that water conquers fire. This is inauspicious.

(j) The daily element is water and the money element is earth. Earth conquers water. This indicates some disharmony or loss but not as much as in (i) above.

CONCLUSION

Money will continue to be generated at the present rate if the current course of action is pursued. In that the hexagram as a whole relates to innocence, there is a probability of receiving a small amount from an unexpected source. We should not work for the sake of money but just let it come to us and not even be concerned as to how much it will be. During this period we will tend to spend more than we take in, which will be due to our karma, or fate. This is due to both the monthly and the daily interactions. All this happens to test our integrity in the process of spiritual development, to see how we handle the situation confronting us and whether we are making progress by the way in which we cope with minor troubles and difficulties. If we are capable of learning our lesson adequately we do not need to face this same karmic problem again. (We tested this particular method of prediction for ourselves when initially writing the foregoing, using the hexagram we obtained as an example. Several months later, we can now state that the analysis proved correct.)

Further possible examples of advanced divination

(Consult Tables 1–12 and Figures 10 and 11, obtaining your hexagram in the usual way.)

EXAMPLE 1

A man wants to take a trip for personal purposes on 'e' day of 'i' month and wishes to know if the trip will be successful. He obtained Hexagram 2, K'un.

(self) — — j
         — — l
         — — b

(other) — — d
         — — f
         — — h

Line 6 represents self, or the man in this case. Line 6 is metal and is generated by the daily element 'e', earth. Line 5, the other party, is wood. Metal conquers wood so the man will conquer the trip; i.e., the trip will go smoothly and he will achieve his purpose.

EXAMPLE 2

A man's child is seriously ill on 'g' day of 'c' month, and he obtained Hexagram 52, Keeping Still. The designations for this hexagram are as follows:

officer   ——— c
money   — — a
brother — — k
child   ——— i
parents —x— g
brother — — e

The child line, 'i', is repelled by the month, 'c',[1] conquered by 'g' day and also conquered by the moving line (the second line —g); therefore the child is in danger of dying.

EXAMPLE 3
What is my financial situation for the year (until the next winter solstice)?

This question was asked on 'b' day of 'g' month.
The hexagram:

```
'o'   brother ——— d
      child    ——— f
      money  —x— h (changed to 'g')
's'   money  — — e
      brother — — c
      parents ——— a
```

In this example there are two money lines, of which one, the third, is also the 'self' line. H, earth, is generated by the month g, fire, and also by the changed line g.

Since both money lines are earth and earth is generated by fire it is predicted that the questioner will make a fortune this year.

Note that line 4 reads 'h (changed to g)'. This is common usage when a moving line is involved in this type of divination.

EXAMPLE 4
Suppose a man is involved in a lawsuit and wishes to know the outcome. The question is asked in an 'f' month and a 'b' day. He casts Hexagram 22, with the following representations:

```
officer        —o— c wood
               — — a water
(other)        — — k earth
               —o— l water
               — — b earth
(self) officer ——— d wood
```

---

[1] For the further amplification of Celestial Stems and Horary Branches and their interactions see Tzu Pin astrology (pp. 121–4).

In any lawsuit it is important that the 'self' (my party) should be stronger than the 'other' (other party) and the officer (authority) line be unfavourable to the 'other'.

There are a number of things to be considered when analysing the hexagram. Here we find that the self line is also the lower officer line. The top line is also an officer line. Both officer lines conquer the 'other', which means that authority is unfavourable to the other party. Since the 'self' line also conquers the 'other' it means my party is going to win. The third line, water, is another moving line. Water generates wood. This is favourable to my party. The two lines between 'self' and 'other' are usually considered as the middlemen between the two parties. They are taken into consideration only if they are moving lines. In this case the third line is moving, so the middlemen could be witnesses, the judge or any person involved but not the object of the suit. Since the third line, water, is favourable to 'self', wood, it indicates that my party will get some advantage from the middlemen.

From this analysis we conclude my party must win. Next, since we would like to know something about the timing we must also consider the cosmic force (time) affecting this case:

(a) The month is 'f'; the Horary Branch for 'f' is fire. Fire generates earth, so during the 'f' month the 'other' gets the benefit of fire. Also, wood generates fire, so the 'self' line is being exhausted by generating fire. The 'f' month is not propitious for finalizing the lawsuit.

(b) It is a 'b' day and the Horary Branch for 'b' is earth. Wood conquers earth, so 'self' is not in harmony with the daily force either.

Since the above analysis indicates that the time is not favourable at present, we must analyse each succeeding month to find one in which the action is favourable, for we already know from the hexagram that my party will win. This is in keeping with reality, since normally it takes several months for a lawsuit to be concluded.

The next month after 'f' is a 'g' (fire) month. This is still favourable to the 'other', but since the other will not win this is not the month in which the case will be settled.

In the next month after 'g'—'h' month, earth—the 'other' no

longer gets help from the monthly force, but this alone is not of sufficient strength for the case to be settled.

The two following months are 'i' and 'j'. Both of these are metal, and metal conquers 'self' (wood), so one still can't expect to win in either of these months.

The next month after 'j' is 'k', an earth month. But, as in the case of the 'h' month, this is still not of sufficient strength for the case to be settled.

The following two months are 'l' and 'a'. Both are water, which generates 'self' (wood). Therefore the case will be won in either of these months and probably on an 'l' or an 'a' day, when both the day and the month are favourable to 'self'.

C   Divination without the use of coins or yarrow stalks

Sau Yung (*c.* AD 1020–1070), a famous sage in China, developed a number of usages for the *I Ching* in addition to its basic application for making predictions, of which his systems for advanced divination, astrology and the interpretation of history are the most widely known. Here we will discuss his rules and procedures relating to divination without the use of coins or yarrow stalks. They follow many of the principles set forth in earlier sections of this work and will be referenced or restated as may be appropriate.

An understanding of what is meant by Sau Yung's advanced divination can best be gained, perhaps, by presenting his well-known and famous story of divination, *Plum Blossoms I Number*. (It is necessary to note, however, that to many Chinese *Plum Blossoms I Number* has come to mean divination by mental evaluation in general and is not limited to the system exemplified in the story.)

In the year of Ch'en (Horary Branch number 5) in the twelfth month on the seventeenth day at the Shen hour (3–5 p.m., or daily Horary Branch number 9), while Sau Yung was viewing some plum blossoms, he observed two sparrows fighting on a branch and a moment or so later saw them fall to the ground. Sau Yung pondered on this and then observed:

When things are (apparently) motionless and in a quiescent state one cannot divine nor make predictions. It is only when there is activity that one has a basis for Divination. It is truly strange that both sparrows should fall to the ground over a normal quarrel. There must be some special reason behind this.

So he set about discerning a meaning. By using the year, month and day and adding them together—i.e., 5 (year) + 12 (month) + 17 (day)—he obtained the sum of 34. Since there are 8 trigrams, he divided 34 by 8 and the result was 4, with a remainder of 2. He decided to use the 'remainder' to determine the trigram (see section 2 below (p. 57) for the numbers applicable to trigrams). He next added the hour to the foregoing sum and again divided by 8; i.e., 34 + 9 = 43. 43 ÷ 8 = 5 and a remainder of 3. The trigram for 2 is ☱ Tui, which he used as the upper trigram, and the trigram for 3 is ☲ Li, which became the lower trigram of the hexagram. Dividing 43 by 6 (6 being the number of lines in a hexagram) he got 7 and a remainder of 1. Therefore, he considered 1 as the moving line; i.e., a moving line in the first or bottom place. Putting the two trigrams together he obtained the information set out as Table 13.

Table 13   *Hexagram obtained by the Sau Yung* Plum Blossoms I Number *System*

Present hexagram	Future hexagram (*after lines have changed*)
metal { ▬ ▬ / ▬▬▬ / ▬▬▬	▬ ▬ / ▬▬▬ } metal
fire { ▬▬▬ / ▬ ▬ / ▬⊖▬	▬▬▬ / ▬ ▬ } earth
Hexagram 49, Change	Hexagram 31, Influence

The nuclear trigrams (lines 2, 3 and 4, and 3, 4 and 5) of Hexagram 49 are ☴, wood, and ☰, metal.

Sau Yung reasoned that the action party must be represented by the upper trigram and time by the lower. Tui ☱ is the Youngest Daughter trigram, so the party was a girl. The trigram Li follows Tui in the sequence of trigrams, therefore the time would have to be tomorrow. The object of the action would be the nuclear upper trigram or Ch'ien, ☰ which, among other things, represents fruit trees. So a girl would come next day to pick plum blossoms (since they were in bloom) without the permission of the owner. The gardener would see her and frighten her by coming towards her. She would fall and injure her leg. This is because the girl ☱ trigram also represents metal, which is conquered by the lower trigram, Li, or fire. Wood, the lower nuclear trigram, generates fire—which implies even more fire. This indicates the likelihood of metal being conquered. The lower nuclear trigram ☴ also represents legs and the element wood.

The trigrams ☰ and ☱ both represent metal and metal conquers wood. So he divined that the girl would injure her leg.

Fortunately, in the changed or final outcome, Hexagram ䷏,

the lower trigram is earth which gives birth to metal. Since metal is the upper trigram the injury would not be serious.

It all turned out as Sau Yung had predicted and this type of divination, in general, became known as Plum Blossoms I Number Divination, based on the incident just related.

From this and other allied methods of mental divination, a few of which will be presented below, Sau Yung formulated a series of rules. Some of these duplicate or parallel rules have been presented previously, but they are reproduced here so that this section will be complete in itself. They can be used by the reader to make his own predictions.

THE RULES OF PLUM BLOSSOMS I NUMBER DIVINATION

1 Trigram and element designations

☰ and ☱ are metal.

☷ and ☶ are earth.

☳ and ☴ are wood.

☵ is water.

☲ is fire.

2 Trigram numbers

1 ☰ 2 ☱ 3 ☲

4 ☳ 5 ☴ 6 ☵

7 ☶ 8 ☷

3 Sequence of five elements

Wood generates fire, fire generates earth, earth generates metal, metal generates water and water generates wood.

Wood conquers earth, earth conquers water, water conquers fire, fire conquers metal and metal conquers wood.

4 Horary Branch hours

a (Tzu) hour	11 p.m.–1 a.m.	Yang hours	1
b (Ch'ou) hour	1 a.m.–3 a.m.	Yang hours	2
c (Yin) hour	3 a.m.–5 a.m.	Yang hours	3
d (Mao) hour	5 a.m.–7 a.m.	Yang hours	4
e (Ch'en) hour	7 a.m.–9 a.m.	Yang hours	5
f (Szu) hour	9 a.m.–11 a.m.	Yang hours	6
g (Wu) hour	11 a.m.–1 p.m.	Yin hours	7
h (Wei) hour	1 p.m.–3 p.m.	Yin hours	8
i (Shen) hour	3 p.m.–5 p.m.	Yin hours	9
j (Yu) hour	5 p.m.–7 p.m.	Yin hours	10
k (Hsü) hour	7 p.m.–9 p.m.	Yin hours	11
l (Hai) hour	9 p.m.–11 p.m.	Yin hours	12

5 Directions

In Plum Blossoms I Number Divination the Later Heaven sequence of directions is used, as set out in Figure 6 (see p. 18).

When using directions, man is considered as being in the centre of the diagram (Figure 6) and the object is either stationary in one direction, or moving towards him, or moving away from him in a specific direction. The object itself is the upper trigram, occupying that position in the hexagram, while the lower trigram is the directional aspect as determined from Figure 6.

6   The use of numbers in divination

In some cases it is desirable to use numbers to obtain an oracle. In such a case the part of the question to which the numbers would apply is extracted from the question and the letters of which that part is composed are counted. The total is divided by 8 and the remainder, 0–7, applies to the trigrams listed in Rule 2 above, with 0 being the same as 8, the number in such a case being exactly divisible. For example:

> 'Is *An Anthology of "I Ching"* a good title for this book?'
> Take the words '*An Anthology of "I Ching"* ' and count the words. Their number is five. The first two form the upper trigram and the last three the lower trigram. There are 11 letters in the first two words and 8 in the last three.
> $11 \div 8 = 1$ and a remainder of 3.
> $8 \div 8 = 1$ and no remainder (use 8).
>
>   Checking Rule 2, the trigram for 3 is Li ☲ and for 8 is K'un ☷.
>
>   The hexagram then is 35 ䷢ Progress, which is one of the

most favourable and auspicious Kuas in the *I Ching*.

7   Moving lines by numerology

To determine a moving line, add the numerical value for each trigram to the numerical value for the Horary hour for the time the question is asked and divide by 6. The 'remainder' after division will determine which is the moving line. A 'remainder' of 1 represents the bottom line; a 2 the second line from the bottom, and so on, and a zero refers to line 6 or the top line. For example, if one asks the same question as in Rule 6 during the sixth hour, one gets:

Upper trigram   Li ☲ = 3
Lower trigram   Li ☲ = 3
Szu hour (9 a.m.–11 a.m.) = 6

Adding together the numbers one has obtained, we get the total 12.

   $12 \div 6 = 2$, with zero remainder. So the moving line is line 6.

This too, gives a favourable aspect to the question, since line 6 in Hexagram 30, Li, is 'The height of clarity and no errors occur.'

8 Divination by date

In this method of divination the year, the month and the day of the month are added together to obtain the upper trigram. This total is divided by 8. Any remainder after division determines the upper trigram (from Rule 2), just as was done in Rule 6 above.

For the lower trigram, add the Horary Branch number for the hour to the previous total and divide this new total by 8. Any remainder after dividing determines the applicable trigram from Rule 2 above.

Remember that there are several systems of dating, including the sexagenary system, the lunar system, the Nine House system, the Gregorian calendar, and so on. Be careful not to 'mix oil and water', that is, to match a non-applicable part of one system with another.

EXAMPLE (using the lunar calendar):

8 January 1975   08.30 a.m.
January 1975 is part of lunar year 1974
1974 = year 51 (Table 8) = Ac (c = 3)
8 January 1975 is also the 26th day of the eleventh month by the Lunar calendar (see Appendix B)
3 + 11 + 26 = 40
40 ÷ 8 = 5, with no remainder
Therefore the upper trigram from Rule 2 is ☷
08.30 is the fifth Horary Branch so add 5 to 40
40 + 5 = 45
45 ÷ 8 = 5, with a remainder of 5
Therefore the lower trigram from Rule 2 is ☴

The hexagram is Hexagram 46 ䷭ Pushing Upward

For the determination of the moving line, the total number of the year, month, day and hour is used instead of Rule 7. Continuing the example above, we get:

$45 \div 6 = 7$ and a remainder of 3

Therefore line 3 is the moving line.

9   Use of the nuclear trigrams

In some instances it is desirable to use the nuclear trigrams just as Sau Yung did when he made his famous Plum Blossoms I Number prediction.

The rule for their prediction is simple: consider the trigrams only (lines 2, 3 and 4 as one trigram, and lines 3, 4 and 5 as the other) and evaluate their interactions according to Figures 9 and 10, or Rule 3. For example:

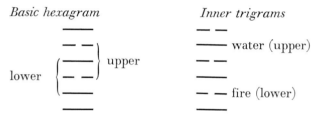

Basic hexagram   *Inner trigrams*

The resulting interaction between fire and water is opposition.

10   Divination by words and characters

(*a*) *Divination by Chinese words* (*presented for informative purposes*): If divination by words alone seems intuitively to be correct and appropriate for whatever one has in mind, then divide the number of words involved in half and use each half to get the upper and lower trigrams. If the number is odd the part with one word less will form the upper trigram and the one with the one word more, the lower. Apply the results to Rule 2. If more than eight words are involved in each half, divide the total by 8 and use the 'remainder' to determine the trigrams. Attributing the extra word to the lower trigram symbolizes that the heaven is clear while the earth is turbulent and clouded.

(*b*) *Divination by a single Chinese character* (*one word*): When the number is only one word (character) the number of strokes made to the left in forming the character are used to determine the upper trigram, while the number which go to the right determine the lower trigram, referring to Rule 2 for ascertaining the correct trigrams. Divide the total number of strokes by 6 and use the remainder to establish which is the moving line. For example:

2 strokes   8 strokes

The hexagram is ☰⊖☷ (shown)

2 + 8 = 10

10 ÷ 6 = 1 and a remainder of 4

Therefore, line 4 is the moving line.

(*c*) *Divination by two Chinese words:* When two words (characters) are involved use the first to determine the upper trigram and the second for the lower. Divide the total number of strokes by 6 and use the remainder obtained to establish the moving line. For example:

8 strokes   8 strokes

The hexagram is ☰×☷ (shown)

8 + 8 = 16; 16 ÷ 6 = 2, with a remainder of 4

Therefore, line 4 is the moving line.

(*d*) *Three words:* When three words are involved, use the first for determining the upper trigram and the other two to obtain the lower trigram. The moving line is determined as in (c) above.

(*e*) *Four words:* When four words are involved use the tones[1]

---

[1] There are four different ways to pronounce Chinese characters. The way they are spoken, i.e., the tones used, gives the listener the intended meaning. For example, the words 'buy' and 'sell' are both spoken as *mai* (*my*) in Chinese. When a rising intonation is used it means 'buy' and, conversely, if a descending tone is used it means 'sell'.

of the first two to determine the upper trigram and the tones of the last two for the lower. In all cases of four or more words use the intonation (phonetic) tones to decide the number for the word:

the first tone is 1
the second tone is 2
the third tone is 3
the fourth tone is 4

The moving line is determined in the usual manner.

(*f*) *Five words:* When five words are involved use the first two to get the upper trigram and the last three for the lower. Determine the moving line in the usual manner.

(*g*) *Six to ten words:* When the number of words divide evenly use the tones of the first half to determine the upper trigram and those of the last half for the lower. If the number is odd (7 or 9) include the odd word with the last half and again use phonetics to determine the trigrams. The moving line is found in the usual manner.

(*h*) *Eleven or more words:* Add up the number of words and divide by two. Give any odd word to the second half. The first half determines the upper trigram and the second half the lower. Divide the totals of the number of words in each half by 8 in each case and use the remainder to ascertain the trigrams. The moving line is found in the usual manner.

EXAMPLE:

Total 31 words
$31 \div 2 = 15$ and 1 remainder. Therefore, use 15 to get the upper trigram and 16 to get the lower.
$15 \div 8 = 1$ and 7 remainder
$16 \div 8 = 2$ and zero remainder
From Rule 2, Trigram 7 = ☷
                Trigram 8 = ☷

This gives Hexagram 23 ䷖, with the moving line in the first place ($31 \div 6 = 5$ and 1 remainder).

11   Divination by sound (such as someone rapping on a door)

Count the number of sounds to get the upper trigram and use the total of the number of sounds and the number of the Horary hour during which the sound was made to get the lower trigram (see Rule 4 for hours and numerical value). Divide the total in the usual manner to get the moving line.

12   Divination by number of objects

Count the number of objects (if over 8 divide the total by 8 and use the remainder) to get the upper trigram. Use the Horary hour number (Rule 4) of the time the objects were counted to get the lower trigram. Divide the total by 6 to get the moving line.

EXAMPLE:

22 objects counted at 8.30 p.m.

22 ÷ 8 = 2 and r 6   Trigram 6 is ⚏

8.30 p.m. is the 11th hour

11 ÷ 8 = 1 and r 3   Trigram 3 is ⚏

22 + 11 = 33   33 ÷ 6 = 5 and remainder 3.

The oracle is ䷒

13   Divination by length

Use the number of metres to get the upper trigram and the nearest number of centimetres remaining in the total length to get the lower trigram. If the total is less than a metre use centimetres and millimetres. Add the numerical values of the length to the numerical value for the Horary hour. Divide the total by 6 to get the moving line.

14   Divination by conversation and people

If the conversation is just one sentence divide it into two equal parts, if possible. Use the first part for the upper trigram and the second for the lower. If an odd word is involved assign it to the second part. Use the total to determine the moving line in the usual manner.

If the conversation is two sentences in length count the number of words in the first sentence for the upper trigram and the number of words in the second for the lower trigram. Get the moving line in the usual way.

If the speaker talks volubly, use only the first or the last sentence.

When observing people use appearance and age as the basis for the upper trigram (see attributes of trigrams, Appendix A) and the action of the object involved for the lower:

Shaking the head is	Ch'ien	☰
Shaking the feet is	Chên	☳
Moving the eyes a lot is	Li	☲
Using the hands a lot is	Ken	☶
Fidgeting is	K'un	☷
Talking volubly is	Tui	☱
Taciturnity is	Kan	☵
Profundity is	Sun	☴

15   Time for prediction to materialize

Only generalized guidance can be given here since this largely depends upon individual situations and the diviner's intuition. Broadly speaking, when an oracle is made about something which is moving the timing for materialization will be 'fast'. Conversely, if it is in regard to a person, animal or object which is sitting or lying down the 'time' will be slow. As a general guide 'fast' is about twice as rapid as 'slow'. Additional guidance can be found in some of the examples given below.

EXAMPLES USING THE RULES OF PLUM BLOSSOMS I NUMBER DIVINATION

(Note: The examples are from the Chinese book *Plum Blossoms I Number*, relating to Sau Yung, and dates refer to the Chinese lunar calendar. Regrettably, this will make it very difficult for the enthusiastic student to check the times and dates in order to verify the principles stated. However, setting out the principles involved side by side with the application of the rules, will enable him to experiment and verify his results on a current basis.)

EXAMPLE 1   Object and direction

One day, about noon, Sau Yung heard an ox bleating mournfully to the north of him. He decided to divine the circumstances involving the ox. Sau Yung knew that an ox is represented by ☷, Trigram 8. By Rule 5 this becomes the upper trigram. The direction was north, ☵, Trigram 6, which became the lower trigram. The time was noon, of the seventh Horary hour (Rule 4). To get the moving line he mentally computed $8 + 6 + 7 = 21$. $21 \div 6 = 3$, with the remainder 3 (Rule 7).

Therefore, the hexagram representing the situation was:

in which the moving line in the third place has been interpreted as meaning, 'Perchance the army carries corpses in the wagon. Misfortune.' This is a bad omen for the depicted situation.[1]

The nuclear trigrams (Rule 9) are ☴ wood and ☷ earth. Wood conquers earth (Rule 3) so this makes the situation additionally inauspicious.

Sau Yung judged that the ox would be killed within twenty-one days (21 being the numerical total). As it happened, the ox was sold twenty days later and slaughtered.

EXAMPLE 2   Sounds

One winter evening at the hour of Yu (5 p.m.–7 p.m.) a neighbour knocked on Sau Yung's door. The neighbour rapped once and then rapped another five times, which Sau Yung heard and counted.

'What do you think the man wants?' Sau Yung asked his son while his maid went to answer the door.

'Since he knocked once first the upper trigram is 1 or ☰, metal, and the lower is 5 ☴, or wood, and both the nuclear trigrams are metal, i.e., ☰ and ☰. The hour is 10 so

---

[1] Line 3 is not necessarily bad for all situations. Each must be evaluated independently.

1 + 5 + 10 = 16. 16 ÷ 6 = 2, with a remainder of 4. Therefore, the hexagram is Hexagram 44, with a moving line in the 4th place:

'The moving line is in the trigram metal and the lower trigram is wood. Therefore, it is something metal attached to wood. I think he wants to borrow a hoe.'

'Son, your analysis is correct but at this hour of the day he does not want to borrow a hoe. Our neighbour wants an axe.'

Sau Yung was correct.

EXAMPLE 3   Plants

Early one morning Sau Yung was visiting his good friend Mr Suma and they were discussing philosophers and the *I Ching* in Mr Suma's garden.

'Can a prediction be made regarding a plant?' Mr Suma asked.

'Very definitely,' Sau Yung replied. 'Everything has a consciousness and everything has a destiny. Let's take this beautiful peony for example.'

'I'm very interested. What would you divine?' queried his friend.

It was the sixteenth day of the third month in the year of Szu (number 6) at the hour of Mao (5 a.m.–7 a.m., the fourth Horary hour).

Sau Yung used the date time method for making his prediction. He added the numbers for the year, month and day:

Year   —   6
Month   —   3
Day   —   16

and obtained a total of 25. 25 ÷ 8 = 3, with a remainder of 1, so the upper trigram is 1 or ☰, Ch'ien, metal.

To get the lower trigram he added the hour to the above total and divided by 8 again; i.e.:

25 + 4 = 29
29 ÷ 8 = 3 and a remainder of 5, the trigram for 5 being ☴ Sun, wood.

To get the moving line he divided 29 by 6 and found the result to be 4 with a remainder of 5. Therefore, the fifth line was the moving line. So he had Hexagram 44 with a moving line in the 5th position; i.e.:

Upper trigram —⦶—   Fire
——— Which change into ———
Lower trigram ———   Wood

Sau Yung then told Mr Suma, 'The flower will be trampled around noon tomorrow by a horse.'

'How did you arrive at this?' asked Mr Suma.

'The upper trigram represents metal and also horse. The lower is wood and plants. The upper conquers the lower, since metal conquers wood. The nuclear trigrams are both ☰, metal, which also indicates that wood will be conquered. The upper trigram changes into Li—Fire. This represents Wu, or the noon hour.'

The next day a group of officials came on horseback to Mr Suma's house. While there two horses shied, trampling the peonies in their fright.

EXAMPLE 4   Words

One day a guest asked Sau Yung, 'What is going to happen today?' Sau Yung decided to divine from those six words.

From the Chinese intonations he obtained ☷ for the upper trigram and ☴ for the lower (Rule 10). The numbers for these are 8 and 5. 8 + 5 = 13. Divide 13 by 6 and the result is 2 and a remainder of 1. So the bottom line is the moving line.

The hexagram is therefore Hexagram 46 ䷭

After mentally making the foregoing calculations Sau Yung told his guest, 'We are going to be invited out for a meal today. Not many guests will be present nor a great deal of food either. Just some rice and chicken.'

It happened that way that evening. (Can you analyse why? Refer to Appendix A—Table of Trigram Attributes.)

EXAMPLE 5   Man, direction and hour

While out for an early morning stroll one day Sau Yung met and spoke to a stranger, an old man travelling south-east. The man had a worried look on his face.

In the Chinese consideration of physiognomy a belief exists that an event can be foretold by the appearances of one's face. Sau Yung apparently believed this, too, so he asked the man, 'What are you worried about?'

'Nothing,' was the reply. 'I have no need to worry.'

In view of the odd expression on the man's face Sau Yung did a mental divination and told the man,

'You must be careful for the next five days or a misfortune will happen to you.'

Five days later the old man went to a banquet and died when a fishbone lodged in his throat and could not be removed.

Sau Yung's reasoning was: An old man is represented by the trigram Ch'ien ☰ which is Trigram 1. The direction south-east is Sun ☴ which is Trigram 5. The hour was Mao or 4.

To obtain the moving line add $(1 + 5 + 4)$ and divide by 6 = $10 \div 6 = 1$, with a remainder of 4. Therefore the fourth line is the moving line. The hexagram is then: ䷫

The fourth line of Hexagram 44 says, 'No fish in the tank. This leads to misfortune.' This is inauspicious. Further, the upper trigram is metal and the lower wood. Wood is conquered by metal.

In this evaluation Sau Yung considered the old man as wood since it is unlikely that an old man could conquer anything. He also took half of the total numerical value $(10 \div 2) = 5$ because the man was old and moving. Therefore the action would be fast and in this case 5 days. The nuclear trigrams are both Ch'ien, ☰, metal. Hence it is a total of three trigrams of metal against one of wood plus an inauspicious line; consequently there was no doubt in Sau Yung's mind but what something drastic was going to happen soon. He was correct.

D   *A simple method for obtaining 'Yes' or 'No' answers*

Many Westerners would like to have a definite Yes or No answer to a question. Because of the way that the *I Ching* is written, this is only possible through detailed interpretation. Also, the answer given by the *I Ching* is frequently not fully understood until after the event has occurred or the action has taken place. This does not satisfy impatient individuals who would like an immediate answer. The Western co-author of the present book also had difficulty with making interpretations, so he developed the method described below for his own use and passes it on here, with the suggestion that each prospective user place his own evaluation upon it. Some people have found it quite useful; others have not.

As is well known, the commentaries on the *I Ching* show that lines 5 and 6 represent heaven, lines 3 and 4 man, while lines 1 and 2 designate earth. Heaven, man and earth are equal partners with one another for determining the course, action or result of anything. By ascertaining whether each is positive or negative in its influence at or in any given situation, a simple Yes or No answer can be established.

The procedure is as follows:

(1) To determine whether each pair of lines representing man and earth are positive or negative apply the following:

(a) ▬▬ positive or Yes   (c) ▬ ▬ negative or No

(b) ▬ ▬ positive or Yes   (d) ▬ ▬ negative or No

The case of heaven is different, for line 5 generally is a favourable line whereas line 6 is not. So for lines 5 and 6 make (a) and (c) Yes, and (b) and (d) No.

(2) Evaluate lines 5 and 6 for heaven; lines 3 and 4 for man, and lines 1 and 2 for earth, according to Step (1) above, for the hexagram cast.

(3) If two or three of these pairs are positive, or Yes, then the answer is Yes. Three positives are stronger than just two. Similarly if two or three are negative the answer is No, with three negatives being stronger than just two. For example:

6 ▬▬ ⟩ positive		
5 ▬▬ ⟩ positive ⟩ Strong Yes		
4 ▬▬ ⟩ positive		
3 ▬▬		
2 ▬▬ ⟩ positive		
1 ▬ ▬		

6 ▬ ▬ ⟩ positive		
5 ▬▬		
4 ▬ ▬ ⟩ negative ⟩ Weak No		
3 ▬ ▬		
2 ▬ ▬ ⟩ negative		
1 ▬ ▬		

When asking a question in this manner, i.e., for a Yes or a No answer only, the text and images of the *I Ching* are not given any consideration, since all that is desired is a simple Yes or No.

3 | *Astrologies Related to the* I Ching

Introduction

Five Chinese astrologies have their basis in or are related to the *I Ching*, namely, the Astrology of the *I Ching*, Nine House Astrology, and the Astrologies of Tzu Wei, of Tzu Pin and of Tai-I. There are a number of other astrologies in use in China which, like Western astrologies, are based on the position of the sun, moon, planets and stars, but we do not consider these in this work; we merely mention them so that the reader will know that they exist. Neither can we go into full detail regarding any of the five astrologies related to the *I Ching*. However, except in the case of Tai-I astrology, we do give enough information to provide a basic understanding of the systems, although the reader must be warned that the data is necessarily incomplete, so that the predictions made should be used only as a guideline, not as sources of positive information. It is well known that Chinese scholars are profound and serious thinkers, so that it is logical to assume that these works, in their Chinese originals, are quite complete and accurate; as has already been said, anyone requiring information beyond that which is provided here is advised to research the Chinese source materials. Those wishing a preliminary understanding regarding Chinese Horary[1] Astrologies will find the present work a useful introduction. Books on Tzu Pin and Tzu Wei are available in specialist Chinese bookshops and books on Nine House Astrology are to be found in Japanese bookshops. See also the present authors' *The Astrology of I Ching* (Routledge & Kegan Paul, 1975). For further advanced study

---

[1] Horary, as used here, relates to sexagenary cycles. Do not confuse with Western mundane astrologies, in which a horoscope is cast at the time a question is asked, so as to determine the answer to the question.

the collection of ancient Chinese books *Tu Shu Chi Chun* should be consulted.

The astrologies related to the *I Ching* are based on the sexagenary (Horary) cycle system, i.e., successive sixty-year cycles based on the sun. The underlying concept is that the universe is composed of space and time, so that making predictions regarding humans and events, using intervals of time, is possible. The cycles are considered to have originated at that moment in time, thousands of years ago, when the earth, sun, moon and planets of this solar system were in a straight line. That moment marked the beginning of the first cycle.

To Chinese astrologers using time, the universe is an ordered system. Cosmic forces interact with one another, the nature of their interaction varying according to the time element. Consideration is therefore given to the influence of the planets and stars, but this is expressed indirectly, in terms of time. The earth's forces are likewise included and synthesized with the stars, but this is expressed indirectly, in terms of time. The earth's forces are likewise included and synthesized with the cosmic forces to give a single value at any given moment. This value, too, is expressed in terms of time. Life's patterns are a part of time and are predicted on the interaction of the earthly and cosmic forces as expressed in the sexagenary cycle.

The sexagenary cycles are developed from the combination of the 10 Celestial Stems and the 12 Horary (or earthly) Branches. At first glance this would seem to produce a cycle every 120 years (i.e., 10 × 12 = 120); but 60 being the lowest common multiple of 10 and 12, if one combines the 10 Celestial Stems with the 12 Horary Branches, keeping them in sequence, one obtains a 60-year cycle. (Sixty is also the lowest common denominator of ten and twelve.)

The sexagenary-cycle system is widely employed by the Chinese. In ancient times it was used as a means of telling the time, as well as for making predictions; and if the system was valid with respect to the present and the past, it was only logical to use it for the future also. To calculate time, 8 symbols were used. Four Celestial Stems out of the 10 were combined with 4 of the 12 Horary Branches to form pairs, each pair composed of 1 Celestial Stem and 1 Horary Branch symbol. One pair of symbols pinpointed the year, another the month, another the day, and the last pair the hour. Symbols, in schematized varying combinations, were used to designate all aspects of time.

Man, in Chinese thinking, is an element of time. The individual's time of birth is represented by a combination of eight symbols, the sum of the cosmic forces operating at that particular moment, synthesized with the earthly forces. This is imprinted upon him for life, making him an integral unit of time until his death, exerting his own particular influence, however great or small, wherever he is and through whatever he thinks and does. In one sense he is like a star being born which exerts a specific influence on all other stars and planets until it dies. Another analogy is that of man as a motor-generator, generating a quality and quantity of current according to the forces that impinge upon him, in conjunction with those aspects which are integral to the machine itself. The variation between persons born at the same time stems from their having different mental and physical qualities which they bring into the world with them, and upon which the cosmic and earthly forces impinge. The lives of some are therefore more auspicious than others even though the same basic forces apply.

The individual's fundamental make-up, as is well known, is fixed at the moment of birth. Some use the term energy patterns to describe the individual quality of a human being, others call it aura. Since the Celestial Stems and Horary Branches are both positive and negative, a man will experience attractions and repulsions throughout his life, depending upon the combination of influences present in his individual make-up. These attractions and repulsions can be represented by symbols of time. Being himself an element of time, man is, therefore, predictable.

Time changes as the sexagenary cycle continues but man remains the same and is, for the most part, though not unequivocably, subject to the eight symbols permanently imprinted upon him at his moment of birth. His actions and reactions are the product of those eight permanent symbols interacting with the eight symbols of time at any given moment, which can vary in force and effect from being extremely favourable to devastatingly disruptive.

Because of this thesis between heaven, man and earth, the Chinese hold man as an equal partner with heaven and earth in his life's process and development, and set a high value upon the science of astrology. Observation and analysis will verify the validity of the astrological systems described in this chapter.

THE FACTOR OF PLACE

For the reader who is not resident in China one major difficulty will be encountered in all Chinese Horary astrologies. The applicability of the astrologies so far as place is concerned is not specified. The Horary astrologies are believed to have originated in the northern part of China, along with other culture disciplines; but the exact geographical co-ordinates cannot be presented. This will mean a certain amount of possible imprecision when adjusting the predictions to other time-zones and locales. Obviously, no difficulty exists with regard to the year, month or hour, for these are handled in the standard manner (i.e., the time of day is adjusted to standard time and to the meridian of the time-zone involved). It is the day which will present problems when the location is not China or the longitude encompassed by China. This is because of that man-made obstacle the International Date Line.

According to Chinese thinking, the day in question definitely should be one day or another and nothing else is acceptable. However, no definite system has yet been devised, and, with that proviso, perhaps the best tentative solution for our purposes here is to make two horoscopes; i.e., one for the day in question and one for the ensuing day and take account of the proportional influence of each. An estimate can be made based on the ratio of the time difference between the old and the new day in China. For this purpose we will use 120° E (slightly east of Peking, but a convenient longitude) as the base from which to make and interpolate our predictions. Here is an example:[1]

[1] a Definitions:
    PST = Pacific Standard Time in the US Zone 8
    PDT = Pacific Daylight Time in the US Zone 7
    CST = Central Standard Time in the US Zone 6
    CDT = Central Daylight Time in the US Zone 5
    Standard Meridian: The longitudinal meridian on which the time zone is based, i.e., 0, 15, 30, 45, 60, 75, 90, 105, 120, 135, 150, 165 and 180 degrees.
  b Horary horoscopes are based on Standard Meridian times hence the corrections to the Standard Meridian in the examples. Further, and regrettably,

Date and place for which prediction is to be made:
        31 July 1975, 6.04 a.m. Pacific daylight time;
        Francisco, 122° 25′W, 37° 40′N.

Step 1: Convert to Standard Time: 6.04 P.D.T. = 5.04 P.S.T.

Step 2: Adjust for difference from Standard Meridian:
Standard Meridian = 120°W; difference = 2° 26′.
1° = 4 minutes of time.
2° 26′ = 9 minutes 44 seconds (use 10 minutes).
Since longitude is west of the Standard Meridian the correction must be subtracted.
Therefore: 5.04 a.m. P.D.T. − 10 minutes = 4.54 a.m. P.D.T. (meridian time).

Step 3: Develop a horoscope for 4.54 a.m. on 31 July 1975, and another for 1 August 1975 for the same time.

Step 4: San Francisco is roughly two-thirds of the way (120°W compared with 120°E) around the world from Peking, so when evaluating the influences the 1 August horoscope should be given twice as much weight as the 31 July horoscope.

In view of the differences of opinion regarding the date to be used, the reader is advised to modify the above method as he sees fit, or to use an alternative system if he wishes.

Animal symbolism in Chinese astrology

Nearly everyone has heard of the animal symbolism associated with the Chinese years, particularly at about the time of the Chinese New Year, when people speak of the forthcoming twelve-month period as being the Year of the Tiger, the Rabbit, the Dragon, etc. Very few people, however, know that the twelve representations of (a) mouse (rat); (b) ox (cattle, cow);

many zones are irregular which could produce major errors if the steps described here were not taken.

c To convert to GMT in the Western Hemisphere add the standard time zone hours to the corrected Standard Meridian time or else apply the longitudinal time difference directly to the true local time. In the Eastern Hemisphere the zone time is subtracted from the corrected Standard Meridian time.

d The book *Latitudes and Longitudes in the U.S.* published by the American Federation of Astrologers, 6 Library Court S.E., Washington, D.C. 20003 (1945) can be useful in making and understanding time corrections.

(c) tiger; (d) rabbit; (e) dragon; (f) snake; (g) horse; (h) sheep; (i) monkey; (j) chicken; (k) dog; and (l) pig, came to China from India. They reached China at about the same time as Buddhism; i.e., in the early centuries AD. In fact, some Buddhist Sutras mention these animal representations, which are associated with Indian astrology, also. Because the concept appealed to the Chinese of those days, they incorporated it into Chinese thinking and the Horary Branch system.

Essentially, however, the twelve animals have nothing to do with the original Chinese Horary Branch system, which was in existence for well over 1,000 years before animal symbolism was added to it. Few people know this, and many have tried to link the Chinese tradition with Western Mayan and Aztec cultures, in which animal symbolism also occurs.

Some scholars have gone even further and have added the Celestial Stem elements to the animal designation for the year. As has been mentioned elsewhere (see, e.g., Table 10) the Celestial Stems represent the elements earth, metal, water, wood and fire. Take 1946 as an example. This is a 'Ck' year, the Celestial Stem being 'C', which is symbolic of fire, while the Horary Branch 'k' has the same symbol as dog. So some individuals have chosen to call 1946 the 'Year of the Dog of Fire'. This is nonsense and no year was ever so named in Chinese.

There are other misrepresentations, but only one further one will be mentioned here: according to the 1970 edition of *History of Astrology* by Serge Hutin, a famous French scholar, the Tiger represents the west in Chinese astrology, whereas it is a symbol of the east for the Mayans and Aztecs. This is erroneous because Tiger (c) (see the opening paragraph above) represents the east in China also—the Horary symbols 'c' and 'd' both represent east. For the exact directions of the Horary Branches, see the Figures in the chapter on directionology.

Nine House, or Star, astrology

Nine House astrology is based on the premise that the numbers 1–9 inclusive form a complete cycle. This is true of several numerical disciplines in the East as well as in the West. The number 10 is not used, since everything in this world is considered as being in a state of constant change (one of the basic premises of the *I Ching*), and where 10 *is* referred to, it is as the number of completion.

In this form of astrology the sequence 1–9 applies not only to the year, but also to the month, day and hour of birth. To present in full all the rules and applications of this astrology would require a complete book in itself, so in this anthology we have limited ourselves to outlining the basic principles involved and showing their general application. As has been said earlier, any scholar desiring to study the subject in greater detail will find many books, in both Chinese and Japanese, dealing with it in depth. The reader of this volume will at least be able to understand the general concept and how the sequences apply, as well as being introduced to some of the basic prediction techniques. For most people this will suffice.

In Nine House astrology a man or woman is not simply born in a particular 'house', but during his or her lifetime migrates through the yearly, monthly, daily and hourly sequences many times. The belief behind this is that man can and should become as perfectly balanced as possible through facing and overcoming all the varied experiences presented to him as a result of the influences of the various 'houses'. People follow different patterns because of the influences permanently imprinted upon them at their own particular times of birth. The rules that carry them through these cycles remain constant, and it depends upon their state of wisdom as to how well they apply them. The different situations different people face are determined by their state of evolution at the time they re-enter this world. The strength and intensity of troubles or good fortune depend upon the strength and (cosmic) maturity of the individual. These considerations lend Nine House astrology a philosophical aspect as well.

That the system includes philosophical concepts is readily apparent in the fact that the sequence 1–9 for a man is reversed in the case of a woman. This makes 5 the middle number and 3 the only common number, 3 being also the minimum number required for completion of form (i.e., the triangle). Before that or beyond that human beings are either incomplete, or they are striving towards further fulfilment.

With the foregoing in mind, let us now look at the method of making predictions in Nine House astrology.

CASTING A NATAL HOROSCOPE

Step 1: Determine the number for the year of birth from Table 14.

Step 2: From Table 15 determine the number relating to the month of birth.

Table 14 *Nine House numerical designations for the year of birth*

Year	Man	Woman	Year	Man	Woman	Year	Man	Woman
1890	2	4	1916	3	3	1942	4	2
1891	1	5	1917	2	4	1943	3	3
1892	9	6	1918	1	5	1944	2	4
1893	8	7	1919	9	6	1945	1	5
1894	7	8	1920	8	7	1946	9	6
1895	6	9	1921	7	8	1947	8	7
1896	5	1	1922	6	9	1948	7	8
1897	4	2	1923	5	1	1949	6	9
1898	3	3	1924	4	2	1950	5	1
1899	2	4	1925	3	3	1951	4	2
1900	1	5	1926	2	4	1952	3	3
1901	9	6	1927	1	5	1953	2	4
1902	8	7	1928	9	6	1954	1	5
1903	7	8	1929	8	7	1955	9	6
1904	6	9	1930	7	8	1956	8	7
1905	5	1	1931	6	9	1957	7	8
1906	4	2	1932	5	1	1958	6	9
1907	3	3	1933	4	2	1959	5	1
1908	2	4	1934	3	3	1960	4	2
1909	1	5	1935	2	4	1961	3	3
1910	9	6	1936	1	5	1962	2	4
1911	8	7	1937	9	6	1963	1	5
1912	7	8	1938	8	7	1964	9	6
1913	6	9	1939	7	8	1965	8	7
1914	5	1	1940	6	9	1966	7	8
1915	4	2	1941	5	1	1967	6	9

Table 14—*continued*

Year	Man	Woman	Year	Man	Woman	Year	Man	Woman
1968	5	1	1982	9	6	1996	4	2
1969	4	2	1983	8	7	1997	3	3
1970	3	3	1984	7	8	1998	2	4
1971	2	4	1985	6	9	1999	1	5
1972	1	5	1986	5	1	2000	9	6
1973	9	6	1987	4	2	2001	8	7
1974	8	7	1988	3	3	2002	7	8
1975	7	8	1989	2	4	2003	6	9
1976	6	9	1990	1	5	2004	5	1
1977	5	1	1991	9	6	2005	4	2
1978	4	2	1992	8	7	2006	3	3
1979	3	3	1993	7	8	2007	2	4
1980	2	4	1994	6	9	2008	1	5
1981	1	5	1995	5	1	2009	9	6

Table 15   *Numerical designations for the month of birth*

Approx. date	In the year of 1, 4 & 7		In the year of 2, 5 & 8		In the year of 3, 6 & 9		24 Seasons
	Man	Woman	Man	Woman	Man	Woman	
22 Dec.–5 Jan.	1	5	4	2	7	8	Winter Solstice
6 Jan.–3 Feb.	9	6	3	3	6	9	Little Cold Severe Cold
4 Feb.–5 Mar.	8	7	2	4	5	1	Spring Begins Rain Water
6 Mar.–4 Apr.	7	8	1	5	4	2	Excited Insects Vernal Equinox

Table 15—*continued*

Approx. date	In the year of 1, 4 & 7 Man	In the year of 1, 4 & 7 Woman	In the year of 2, 5 & 8 Man	In the year of 2, 5 & 8 Woman	In the year of 3, 6 & 9 Man	In the year of 3, 6 & 9 Woman	24 Seasons
5 Apr.–5 May	6	9	9	6	3	3	Clear & Bright Grain Rains
6 May–5 June	5	1	8	7	2	4	Summer Begins Grain Fills
6 June–7 July	4	2	7	8	1	5	Grain in Ears Summer Solstice
8 July–7 Aug.	3	3	6	9	9	6	Slight Heat Great Heat
8 Aug.–7 Sept.	2	4	5	1	8	7	Autumn Begins Limit of Heat
8 Sept.–8 Oct.	1	5	4	2	7	8	White Dew Autumnal Equinox
9 Oct.–7 Nov.	9	6	3	3	6	9	Cold Dew Hoar Frost Descends
8 Nov.–7 Dec.	8	7	2	4	5	1	Winter Begins Little Snow
8 Dec.–21 Dec.	7	8	1	5	4	2	Heavy Snow

EXAMPLE:

The man who is born in the year of 9 between 8 July and 7 August will have number 9 for the month of birth. A woman who is born in the same period will have number 6 for the month of birth.

Step 3: Determine the numbers relating to the day of birth and the hour of birth. (The process for obtaining these is quite complex and will not be given in this volume. In general, the direction for the daily and hourly cycles are ascending for the early part of the year and descending for the latter half.)

Step 4: Analysis is made using year of birth, monthly, daily and hourly values and correlating the data. Year, month, day and hour each have nine segments, decreasing in significance from year of birth to hourly, the year of birth number being given the greatest weight, the hourly number receiving the least.

The authors believe that little is to be gained from the daily and hourly predictions since they are only miniaturized versions of those for the year of birth. Therefore the tendencies applicable to the numbers for month, day and hour, can be obtained by reading what is given as the year of birth prediction and then giving decreasing value to each of the others in sequence. The year of birth predictions appear at the end of this chapter.

MAKING YEARLY PREDICTIONS

The yearly predictions are made with the help of the Lo Map. (This is shown in full on page 19, Figure 7, illustrating the Magic Square of Three—a simplified version of the Lo Map—is reproduced again in this section for ease of reference.) The numbers of the Lo Map progress in an orderly sequence each year; i.e., advancing (migrating), to the place held by the next higher number the preceding year. Taking the Lo Map sequence (Figure 7) as position (a), the progression is as illustrated in Figure 12. The numbers are thought of as abstract 'stars'.

Figure 7. The Magic Square of Three (repeated)

3	8	1
2	4	6
7	9	5

(b)

2	7	9
1	3	5
6	8	4

(c)

1	6	8
9	2	4
5	7	3

(d)

9	5	7
8	1	3
4	6	2

(e)

8	4	6
7	9	2
3	5	1

(f)

7	3	5
6	8	1
2	4	9

(g)

6	2	4
5	7	9
1	3	8

(h)

5	1	3
4	6	8
9	2	7

(i)

Figure 12. Nine House yearly progressions

In the Chinese system, the number for the year is the natal number for a man for that year. A woman uses the same yearly diagram for the year in question but keeps her own natal number.

To ascertain one's yearly prediction one must superimpose the position of one's natal number on the Lo Map and find the corresponding number for that position. One begins by finding one's natal number from Table 14. One then selects the applicable diagram for the year in question from Figure 12, by matching the number for the year in question with the diagram which has that number at its centre. For example, Table 14 tells us that 1976 is a 6 year for a man and a 9 year for a woman. Since the woman uses the same yearly diagram for the year as the man, diagram (i) in Figure 12, which has 6 at its centre, applies to both men and women.

Having selected the appropriate diagram, one then superimposes it upon the Lo Map and sees which 'house' of the Lo Map corresponds to one's own number on the yearly diagram. The 'house' in which the number falls in the Lo Map is then used to determine the prediction for the 'year' (a 'year' being the period between one winter solstice and another, with the last ten days or so of each calendar year counting as part of the forthcoming year).

EXAMPLES:

(1) *Date on which prediction is made:* 27 December 1975 (the prediction being required for the coming year, of course—1976).

Person for which prediction is required: Man born 2 January 1940.

The number for 1976 is 6 (see Table 14). Man's year of birth number is also 6. 6 is in the centre position in diagram (i) for 1976. Therefore he will use the centre position of the Lo Map (Figure 7) to obtain his prediction. The centre position in the Lo Map is 5. So the yearly prediction for the House of Fire is the one which applies, and it will be valid until the winter solstice of 1976.

(2) *Date on which prediction is made:* 13 August 1976.

Person for whom prediction is required: Woman, born 13 August 1931.

The woman also uses diagram (i) of Figure 12 to obtain her prediction for 1976 (the number for the year being the number for a man for that year). Table 14 shows her year of birth number as 9. In diagram (i) in Figure 12, 9 is in the NE position. In the Lo Map the NE position is occupied by 8. Therefore, the statements for the House of Eight will give this woman her yearly prediction for 1976, which will hold good until the winter solstice of 1976.

NINE HOUSE ASTROLOGY: YEARLY PREDICTIONS

A   The house of 1: K'an ☵

This house is in the north and symbolizes winter, night, darkness, poverty, ill health, difficulties and decrease in wisdom through a number of irritating and upsetting situations. It is a period during which conforming to law and order is the best course. Research can be highly successful.

In this year one will be like the bud of a blossoming tree buried under snow which prevents it from growing. Very few things will go truly smoothly. Rather, one encounters much pressure and trouble. No matter how hard one works one's financial outlay will exceed one's income this year, as a result of increased costs and unplanned expenses. Friends and associates will be far less communicative than usual. There will be many difficulties related to any new enterprise begun this year, as well as the likelihood of being robbed, having one's confidences betrayed, or falling victim to a serious accident or illness. One must guard against hazards from water and liquids, such as floods, landslides, drowning or the consequences of drinking too much. Illicit sexual affairs are likely to be discovered and become known by many persons, with resultant difficulties.

If one remains calm, follows established routines, guards against excessive emotion and expending too much energy or spending too lavishly, the year can be turned to favourable account. Meditation, personal development and research will be very productive.

Men who are about forty-two years old and women aged about thirty-three must take particular care, for it is a very inauspicious time for them. Those whose natal stars are 2, 5, 8 or 9 have to be even more careful.

Remember, be wary of anything related to liquids; and guard against possible illness also. The kidneys, bladder, urinary canal, and sex organs are the most vulnerable areas, and menstrually related difficulties, diabetes, etc., are also indicated, as is some form of poisoning.

Emotionally, there will be many unhappy days with dark moods.

B   The house of 2: K'un ☷

Broadly speaking, this year will be quite ordinary, with nothing really unusual or outstanding happening. One's imagination and creativity will be largely inactive or not readily productive, so it is a period during which it will be better to be conservative rather than innovative.

K'un is in the south-west, the late summer period symbolically, so this is a time for reaping than planting. One's best course is to use the year to complete the necessary preliminary steps that will make it possible to take more positive action in the following year; for instance the accumulation of capital, developing acquaintances or friendships with those who may be interested in or related to a future enterprise, formulating and revising one's plans for future activity. The purchase and sale of real estate on a small scale should prove profitable, but the development of extensive areas or handling of large estates are not favoured. Many small and trying difficulties will arise.

In your relations with others don't try to lead or be boss (or to try to prove that you are), or attempt to impose your ideas and will on others this year, for such efforts are sure to backfire. Be circumspect in all you do.

Emotionally this will be a negative rather than a positive time. Self-control will minimize the negative influences if applied judiciously.

C   The house of 3: Chen ☳

This is the house of the forces of spring; i.e., generation, thunder, new life, hope, the growth of plants, arousing and revitalization. It also represents initiative for action, with resultant advancement.

In this year the stagnations of the preceding year will be brought to an end and any uncompleted ventures will come to fruition. Progress will seem rapid, but caution is still advisable, for there will be a tendency, because things seem so easy, to overlook or omit some salient or vital factor. Since advancement is rapid, great success or great failure are both possible. Great efforts will produce great results at each phase of an undertaking and in every endeavour. But one must be careful in what one desires and strives for since the results can be of considerable magnitude, both good and bad.

As for diseases and illnesses, watch out for possible accidents, liver disease, the need for psychiatric treatment, nervous problems, etc.

Those whose natal stars are 2, 5, 6, 7 or 8 must exercise exceptional caution.

D   The house of 4: Sun ☴

This is the house of meditation, concentration and penetration, as well as development, travel, intelligence, appearances and statesmanship.

In this year one's past efforts will bear fruit. Business will go smoothly, with good profits. Relations with others will be easy and generally excellent, and they will be helpful, co-operative and communicative. One will be respected and trusted. Credit rating will be high. But be exceedingly cautious, and at all costs avoid impetuosity. Rash action is unnecessary and may well negate the possible good results rather than furthering them.

This will be a good year emotionally, with much love and friendship, and one will also derive much joy and satisfaction from one's achievements.

Watch out for the after-effects of colds, and for diseases of the respiratory system and intestinal tract, as well as for paralysed nerves. Any contact with an epidemic could be disastrous. Those whose natal stars are 2, 5, 6, 7 and 8 need to be especially careful.

E   The house of 5: the middle house

This is in the centre of the fixed 'house' of nine stars and represents the zenith of accomplishment and effort, while at the same time being symbolic of the beginning of everything. It is the alpha and omega of Nine House astrology and of the philosophic concepts underlying it.

This is the house of fulfilment. Everything one has been seriously working for produces results this year. If you have been working negatively or in the wrong direction you can expect negative results and penalties. If you have been positive and working for what is right you will reap your reward sometime during this year. Since your star is in this house once every nine years it is wise to plan ahead and be certain that what you strive for and long for is right both for yourself and for anyone else effected, for the end result will come during the year in which your star occupies the centre house, if it has not materialized before then. Miscalculations or wrong desires and misguided efforts can cause needless trouble. Anything started in this year also will have greater force and durability than any initiatives undertaken during other years.

This is a year of extremes, and it will either bring you the greatest possible success, or inflict the greatest losses. This applies both professionally and personally. You can easily capture the heart of a new lover. If you already have one you may lose him or her for no apparent reason. Those already married are likely to get divorced if they are unhappy in their union. For those in business it is wisest to plan for or initiate actions which will culminate next year rather than this one.

With regard to probable illness, watch out for possible heart troubles, difficulties with any of the digestive organs, tumours, infectious diseases and the possibility of cerebral haemorrhage. Those whose natal stars are 1, 3 or 4 must be especially careful.

F   The house of 6: Ch'ien ☰

This house represents Heaven, the creative, strength, dignity, progress, upward movement, elegance and dominion. It also symbolizes late autumn, the time of fulfilment after harvest.

Ambition is the keynote of the year. It is a time when one strives diligently and perseveringly towards one's goals and purposes. This brings the individual more and more into contact with others and with the various elements of society in general. Responsibilities increase and are accepted, including possible advancements to executive, or at least supervisory, positions. It will be an active year with the possibility of much travel both locally and to more distant places.

One will have a natural tendency to make a display of abilities, and this may arouse enmity in others. One must be careful not to become arrogant, domineering or dictatorial, for one has the feeling of being right nearly all the time and therefore becomes inclined to try and impose one's will on others, who will resent this. If care is not exercised many conflicts can ensue. Any enemies made during this time are likely to remain so for an extended period.

A woman whose star is in this house will display feminist tendencies, and may try to take over some man's normal position.

As for illness, one should be wary of possible accidents while riding in anything moving, especially from sudden stoppages such as the application of brakes in a car, or a horse refusing a fence, or a bicycle running into something, etc., and being thrown to the ground. Pay special attention to headaches, brain diseases, chest diseases, excessive heat and burns, bone disease and neurasthenia.

Those whose natal stars are 3, 4 and 9 should be especially careful with respect to any of the foregoing illnesses.

G   The house of 7: Tui ☱

This house symbolizes the time of enjoyment after harvest. It is a time for laughter, gaiety and entertainment, a time to enjoy the rewards of one's past labours.

Relaxation and enjoyment are the key words. People with their natal star in this house, especially, will be inclined to take it easy, in the way that one normally does after long and strenuous exercise or work. One may receive a substantial raise, or money from an unexpected source, such as an inheritance. There will also be a tendency to spend more. Individuals will be drawn towards frequenting various places of entertainment, and to making new friends of the opposite sex, indulging more than usual in sexual and related activities and perhaps succumbing more readily to the attractions of the opposite sex. A young woman whose natal star is in this house may have her first sexual experience this year.

As for marriage, it is a year for caution and conservatism. Offers of marriage will often end up as affairs only. Partners will be secretly unfaithful either before or during marriage. The great majority of affairs will be of short duration and will prove unsatisfying.

Misunderstandings, too, are frequent this year, especially in business matters. Things may appear to go smoothly for a while and then fail at the last moment due to varying interpretations between the parties. Misrepresentations are also likely. Full details regarding monetary obligations or the availability of funds will instinctively be withheld, causing needless concern, sometimes to the point of bringing about the failure of an enterprise. Men may be susceptible to the wiles of capricious women.

As for illnesses, the most likely are those of the mouth, teeth, chest and respiratory system, as well as trouble from broken bones or as a result of accidents. Those with the natal star 3, 4 or 9 must be especially careful.

H   The house of 8: Ken ☶

Ken symbolizes the transition from winter to spring so far as the seasons are concerned, and the mountain in nature. For man it means those who are cool of feelings, stubborn and obstinate, yet developing a marked degree of honesty, nobility and sincerity. So far as activity is concerned, it is a stagnant time, a period of stillness, reform, and/or possible divergence.

In this year it is quite likely that a business venture or professional position or partnership of long-standing will come to an end, a new path being taken in another direction. Policies, modes of thinking and beliefs are likewise subject to considerable change either from an internal change of heart or as the result of external pressures of an economic or political nature, or from some government action or other matter beyond one's control. Communications and associations with others will be difficult for the most part.

Slowness in taking action is indicated. Do not rush into any situation or circumstance hastily. Be neither brash nor pushy, for any and all such actions will be resented no matter how small or well intentioned they may be. Anything of this nature will become a source of antagonism and possible even cause needless difficulties.

Caution is necessary with regard to possible injury from external sources, such as accidents caused by others, beatings, falls, etc., and one must be on guard, too, against poor circulation, broken bones, high blood pressure, arthritis and neuralgia.

Those whose natal stars are 1, 3 and 4 should be especially careful regarding all health matters and take quick action in the event of becoming ill.

I   The house of 9: Li ☲

Li is symbolic of summer, midday, the shining sun, brightness, clarity, fame and civilization.

In this year what one has done in the past will become known to the public to a greater or lesser degree. An artist or a writer, for example, may gain fame and renown. A businessman's methods and private affairs can become public knowledge, and secrets and matters that one wants to keep hidden from others can become known by many. All these aspects will work for either the benefit or detriment of the individual concerned, depending on the nature of the activity one has been indulging in. In serious wrongs, police action and lawsuits are possibilities.

In the sphere of personal relations one will make some new good friends, but, conversely, lose some long-standing ones. This is caused partly by the possibility of changing residence or professional position and partly by natural growth and development along new and different paths.

Documents will play an important role, too. There may be problems with existing documents. New documents affecting the individual may be issued. An important document involving unexpected funds may be found, or, conversely, an important document may be lost, with resultant difficulties.

Care should be exercised regarding fire, for losses from this source could be occasioned too.

As for illnesses, be careful of actual or incipient eye or heart disease, and of high fevers, neurasthenia, severe burns and epidemics. Those whose natal stars are 1, 6 and 7 need to exercise special care and caution.

NINE HOUSE ASTROLOGY: NATAL PREDICTIONS

1   The One White Water Star

1 Symbolism   The One White Water Star, ☵ (K'an), is in the north of the fixed Nine House numerical diagram. North is the beginning and end of a year, the beginning and end of a cycle, the beginning and end of a situation. The primary attributes are danger and hardship, difficulties, coolness, wintry-type situations or circumstances and matters closely associated with water, mainly in the category of those resembling a river flowing through a canyon.

2 Fortune   These people will have difficulties even in early childhood, particularly in connection with family matters, separations, finances and security. The most fortunate period will be the middle years of one's life and one should capitalize on these to gain the necessary position and stability to carry on through one's later life. Will tend to worry and fret a great deal, often needlessly.

3 Personality The One White Water Star man or woman will have an outgoing personality and will tend to please others, so attracting many acquaintances. Much of what they say and do will be of a superficial nature, while keeping their true nature hidden. They will associate with others ably and well and be flexible enough to adapt themselves to the circumstances they find themselves in. Their easy-going disposition and characteristics make them amenable even to a low position, or poverty. In general they are not sufficiently ambitious to try to change or improve their circumstances appreciably. They use flattery and false words extensively, while inwardly remaining stubborn and opinionated. However, when they have no fixed opinion themselves they will follow almost any leader or go along with the herd. This often leads to difficulties. Many born under this star tend to be loners and enjoy solitude.

They should strive to improve themselves. This relates to all aspects of their lives, professional, mental and spiritual. They should also try to be as optimistic as possible, show their appreciation of gifts and assistance and express any joyousness they feel, for this will gradually help to improve the circumstances and conditions of their lives.

4 Physical type and health prospects Definitely not robust. Will tend to be weak in nearly every physical area and to take much medicine. The man (or woman) born under this star will feel the cold more than the average person, especially in the feet, and require more warmth through extra clothing or higher surrounding temperatures than those which others need for their comfort.

The likely illnesses are those connected with the kidneys, bladder, urinary tract and sexual organs. The circulation may be poor and there is a strong probability of hardening of the arteries in later years. Men and women will be prone to sexual diseases. Women with this star will often have irregular menses.

White Water Star people cannot be classified as mentally strong, either. They will also tend to have unhappy moods resulting from too much worrying, weak nerves, emotional problems and, at sometime in their lives, may perhaps even suffer from mental instability or senility.

5 *Love and marriage* In appearance and outward actions people born under this star will seem calm and unperturbed in the presence of the opposite sex. But, in reality, love is their weakness and Achilles' Heel. Once they fall in love they become more and more deeply involved, to the point that they cannot find a way out of the biological trap. Although they are inclined to be rather unromantic and do not engage in much love play, yet they will be drawn by strong sexual desires, so strong in some cases that one might almost call them animal passions. The women will have a tendency to be 'fast', the men will tend to be las-civious. They are definitely not monogamous and will frequently want more than one lover at the same time. Nevertheless, once they become associated with someone sexually they will be re-luctant to let them go and partners will often find it difficult to break free.

6 *Financial prospects* The financial prospects for people in this category are neither favourable nor unfavourable. They will find it difficult to accumulate large incomes, or make huge profits, and will never be able to make large gains quickly. They will try to keep up with their neighbours and will frequently overspend. They never amass large savings. However, they will never suffer great or sudden losses, either. Basically, their income will come in small amounts and they will always find it difficult to balance their budgets or manage their monies. They are prone to spend excessively on medicine and alcoholic beverages or to squander money on the opposite sex. They can also be easily cheated.

If they recognize their weaknesses and do not permit them-selves to be ruled by them, they can live a comfortable yet modest existence.

7 *Choice of occupation* Since these people are somewhat phleg-matic and physically weak they will tend to do best in occupations which require thought or calmness, and are likely to do well as philosophers, reflective writers and lawyers. They also make good restaurant owners, bar-keepers, waiters, maintenance men, workers in dairies and in enterprises handling dairy or fish

products, and as fishermen, printers, oilmen, dyers or in any other activity involving liquids.

2   The Two Black Earth Star

1 *Symbolism*   This star is represented by the trigram K'un ☷, and its directional aspect is the south-west. In season it signifies the late summer and the approach of autumn. It is receptivity, bringing to completion, the masses, crowds, union organizations, followers, and so on.

2 *Fortune*   Those born in a Black Star year should not try to become leaders or be in charge of important undertakings. They are far better at being completors, assistants, or when attaining their own fulfilment through playing a supportive role to others. They are more suited to taking care of matters in conventional, old-established ways. Their attempts to be creative or innovative are, in general, foredoomed to failure. If they become bosses or supervisors they will experience many hardships and difficulties. They will be more successful in work involving the public rather than in the scientific, literary or technical vocations.

The most favourable age for these people are the years between forty-five and forty-seven. They should strive to reach their peak at this time as well as to prepare for a quieter later life.

There are two general groupings of peoples under this star. One tends to be fortunate all the time, while the other tends to be unfortunate.

Since these people are not best suited to being bosses or supervisors they should try to find a complementary working partner who is suited to taking on that role, so that they can work together as a team.

3 *Personality*   They are persevering people, with a pleasing, gentle and harmonious personality. They will enjoy helping others and once they have committed themselves their word will be their bond regardless of the difficulties involved. Otherwise, they tend to be indecisive and will have frequent doubts as to the best course to pursue. Since they are not aggressive, they do not make much money or accumulate wealth. However, being thrifty

and frugal, they never lack for modest requirements and never get into deep financial difficulties.

In their relationships with others they are inclined to be reticent, tactful and conciliatory in manner and speech.

Women of a motherly type are attracted to this type of man. Women with this natal star like and need a very strong and positive man.

Both the men and the women of the star are often obsessive about detail, sometimes to a disturbing degree.

4 *Physical type and health prospects*   Most will have corpulent bodies, only a few being slim.

With respect to eating, they will tend to fall into one of two extremes: either they eat too much, or they hardly care for food at all. Most men fall into the first group. None of them handle alcohol well. Most have a sweet tooth, and pander to that craving.

Their likely diseases are disorders of the intestinal system, those arising from overwork, skin and blood diseases and backaches.

5 *Love and marriage*   Men born under this star are not the most aggressive in character, yet are well liked by the opposite sex, for they are attentive to the needs and desires of their partner. Often, however, they carry their mania for detail into their relationships also, which can prove damaging and sometimes even disastrous.

Women of this star will have a weakness for men of tall stature, and will select as their mates men of noted athletic ability or physical prowess, or of striking good looks, good education or penetrating intelligence. When the Black Earth Star woman finds one of these qualities she is likely to surrender very easily. On the other hand, where she doesn't like a man she has no hesitation in letting him know it.

People under this star are usually deeply devoted to the partner they select. If care is not exercised their over-attention to detail can spoil what might otherwise be a very beautiful relationship. They must constantly evaluate the relationship to avoid difficulties.

Basically these people tend to use their emotions when judging the opposite sex, rather than their intelligence.

6 *Financial prospects*   Black Star persons can build up wealth only through steady saving. They will never attempt to make fortunes by speculation. Though never wealthy, they will never suffer grave financial difficulties either. Although basically frugal and thrifty, they are sometimes generous to a fault in helping friends who may have financial problems.

7 *Choice of occupation*   This star is related to the public and to the masses, so those born under it should work at occupations related to or rendering service to the public. They make good grocers, supermarket employees, shop assistants, and can also be found in farming, civil engineering, nursing, bakeries, or employments of a related nature.

3   The Three Jade Green Wood Star

1 *Symbolism*   This star is in the east and is represented by the trigram ☳, Chen. Spring, its essence, its connotations of rebirth and renewal, its blossomings and even impetuosities all are aspects of the influence of this star. In nature it is wood.

2 *Fortune*   Those born under this star will be independent in nature, or forced into independence by circumstances. They will not be helped a great deal by their parents, especially their fathers, nor receive much in the way of benefits from them. Most will leave home early and enter careers of their own choosing. Some will even leave their native land. They are ambitious and positive in thought, word and deed. Many set themselves high goals and try to attain them too rapidly and experience failure. There will be many ups and downs in their lives. Their high-spirited natures and character often lead them into difficulties, but they are quite capable of extricating themselves from these. A few will be taciturn but most will be garrulous, often 'putting their foot in their mouth'. They will show their abilities and capabilities early, some rising meteorically, the ages of thirty-four to thirty-eight being the most fortunate and propitious for them. Unless they are aware of this, benefits they might accrue during this period could be lost. This is the time during which

they can set the stage for their future. Unless this is done their old age will be difficult.

3 *Personality*   The optimism and spirit of youth will pervade their being all their lives. This produces a natural sociability and likability. On the other hand, some will tend to be so single-minded of purpose that they hurt those in their path, and many will be stubborn, obstinate and resistant to change. Their motto seems to be 'Attack is the best defence', so they will rarely retreat even in the face of great difficulties. The vast majority will achieve success through their own efforts.

4 *Physical type and health prospects*   Their physical co-ordination is generally excellent. They tend to mature early and generally are above average in physical competition. They are quick of reflex and response, talkative and not bothered by noise. They should be on guard against nervous breakdown and other mental illnesses, and may also suffer from foot troubles.

5 *Love and marriage*   Since they tend to mature earlier than average, Jade Green Wood Star people tend to have love affairs earlier and marry earlier. A few of them, though interested in the opposite sex, may delay marriage in order to achieve their other ambitions. In general they fall in love easily and won't listen to the advice of others even though they may have deliberately sought it, and they frequently act in the heat of emotion rather than with due deliberation. They will be attracted largely by the physical attributes and beauty of the other person. They are forthright in approach, both physically and mentally. Women of this star will be inclined to intense jealousy, but the men will not have the same difficulty.

6 *Financial prospects*   Jade Green Wood people love to make money and love spending it. Since they are very active they are likely to carry both activities to extremes, so, although they may make a lot of money, they will never accumulate wealth or property. They are generous to a fault. They live for pleasure and fun. Jade Green Wood people reading these lines are implored to become more frugal.

7 *Choice of occupation*   These individuals make good sportsmen, speakers, musicians, singers, teachers, writers and surgeons, and will often be found working in these or associated activities.

4   The Four Green Wood Star

1 *Symbolism*   This star is in the south-east and is represented by the trigram ☴, Sun. In terms of season, it is the time between spring and summer—the approach of summer. It is the wind blowing everywhere, dispersing all things, the time of penetration and meditation. In nature it is represented by wood.

2 *Fortune*   In general, those born under this star will be weak-willed and easily controlled by others. They are obedient to authority and seldom overstep the line. Their innate character leads to frequent changes of residence and occupation. They are indecisive and frequently change their minds, traits which dictate their likely fortune and prospects for success. Even if they work hard and steadily for a while the chances are that a change of mind or change of heart will undermine what might otherwise have been a successful undertaking. They tend to be too servile to authority and to those in authoritative positions, even to the point of harming themselves.

On the positive side, most people with this star will possess good commonsense. Their mistakes, if any, will be small ones. And when they make a mistake or encounter failure, their resilience will bring them bouncing back immediately.

The most fortunate years for these people are those of their youth and early manhood. They should try to become established before reaching the age of thirty-eight by becoming partners with or working in close co-operation with a strong and benevolent senior or superior.

3 *Personality*   As a broad generality people born under this star are indecisive and perplexed individuals. They abhor detail and are inclined to be rash and impetuous rather than practical and scientific. They are easily puzzled by complex statements and are extremely susceptible to flattery.

They are inherently good and tend to think that everyone else is good, too, so they do not adequately protect themselves against the actions and designs of others. They often become the subject of false gossip, but this does not bother them.

They should strive to achieve greater strength of character, self-confidence and the courage of their convictions, and should try also to become less sensitive in their response to others.

Generally they like to be silent but they can be talkative at times. They must be careful to avoid criticizing others thoughtlessly, and also guard against inadvertently disclosing other people's secrets, and private confidences.

4 *Physical type and health prospects* Most will have a good physique, and faces that bear a kindly expression. Don't let their early-morning nervousness and irritability fool you—this will disappear as soon as they have had some food. Their vitality is greatest after lunch.

Many have broad foreheads and they will either have a lot of hair, or else become bald relatively early in life.

As for probable illnesses they should be wary of troubles associated with their respiratory systems, organs and tracts. They are prone to haemorrhoids or intestinal difficulties, and easily succumb to epidemics. The women may have considerable difficulties in connection with their reproductive organs.

5 *Love and marriage* Persons with this star mature early mentally, physically and sexually. They have a natural sexual attractiveness and are often very attractive to members of the opposite sex.

Regrettably, they never fully understand their partners. If they did, their relationships could be wonderfully fulfilling. They do, however, tend to get deeply involved. Many of them will marry for money or status, marrying 'the boss's daughter' to gain advantage will be a commonplace. In the great majority of cases such marriages will not fulfil their intended purpose.

Green Wood Star people are not too practical when it comes to love and love's strategies and frequently experience needless hurt from teasing or words that they misinterpret.

Broadly speaking, love affairs and marriage are a source of trouble and difficulty for them. But they do not shun them.

6 *Financial prospects*   In general these people will have a fixed and steady income. Regrettably they will accumulate little, since they have a propensity to spend what they earn, as well as being seemingly vulnerable to robberies, stock market declines and other sources of sudden financial difficulty. Even if they inherit money it is soon gone.

If they learn thrift and frugality they can have a reasonably secure and satisfactory financial situation throughout their lives. But they are susceptible to others and can be easily induced to part with their money or invest it unwisely, so as well as experiencing losses, they are also unlikely to get full value from their investments.

7 *Choice of occupation*   Since dissemination is one of the symbols of this star, the more favourable occupations are in the communications field: advertising, radio, television, public relations, etc.; they also do well in transportation, and as masters of ceremonies. The manufacture and selling of wood and rope, and their associated products, are also auspicious.

5   The Five Yellow Earth Star

1 *Symbolism*   The female trigram representing the Five Yellow Earth Star is K'un, ☷, the Receptive, and the male trigram for this is Ken, ☶, Mountain.

The Five Yellow Earth Star is in the centre position of the magic square and represents the beginning and end of the cycle. It therefore symbolizes both high—mountain—and low—earth. It represents a mixture of the qualities assigned to each of these trigrams. Sometimes it is thought of as the turning point from the mundane to the spiritual.

2 *Fortune*   There are two extremes for persons with this as their natal star. Some will enjoy great success and good fortune. For others, the opposite will be true, and they will have to endure many hardships or disasters. Many of the people in this second category are likely to be imprisoned at some point in their lives.

Many unexpected things will happen to Five Yellow Star

99

people during their lives, as if they were paying off their karma at the end of a cycle and getting ready to start afresh.

As individuals, they will either be strongly positive or discouragingly negative; either ambitious or else so lackadaisical that no one will want to pay any attention to them. Their judgment is frequently unsound, since they are so materialistic that they cannot see true worth and value. They will have few real friends and at the same time more real enemies than people under any other star.

Those who are born under this star do not learn life's lessons readily. They are prone to make the same mistakes over and over again, as well as experiencing repeated failure in their efforts and enterprises. They will do best if they strive to advance in a slow and stable manner.

After the age of forty-two things should improve dramatically for them, and their surroundings and general conditions of life will be far better than they were during their earlier years.

3 *Personality* They will tend to go to extremes in whatever they do. Ethically, too, they will either be highly moral, very good people, or else totally disregard the rights and values of others and wallow in evil. Apparently there is no middle way, no golden mean, for people of this star.

They are ambitious and active individuals. They dislike being quiet. Their desire to become someone special, rise to a high position or achieve success, is stronger than average. They tend to be influential, and it is not unusual for them to be rash, or to employ unorthodox methods to attain their aims. Their goals are often over-ambitious and impractical.

Some individuals show a strong display of duality by engaging in two different occupations simultaneously. This duality also shows in sometimes being very obedient to laws and regulations while at other times flagrantly violating them. In their relationships with others they are sometimes merciful and kind, but at other times domineering and inconsiderate.

Since their self-image is high and their instinct for self-defence strong, they tend to become easily involved in arguments. On the other hand, they can endure hardship more stoically than most people, as well as overcoming their difficulties more effectively.

4 *Physical type and health prospects* Being constantly active, people with this star are for the most part healthy and strong. They have an inclination to debilitate themselves through excess. They must be careful about this.

As for sports, they are either among those who excel or those who participate in none. Those who excel have beautiful, fluid co-ordination, while the others seem to have muscles of clay.

As for likely illnesses, these people usually are strong enough to survive unusual and even bad environmental conditions, but they should nevertheless exercise care against infections such as cholera and typhoid, and also guard against diarrhoea, diseases related to blood circulation, tumours, fevers and illnesses of a similar nature. They are also prone to high blood pressure and heart disease.

5 *Love and marriage* People born under this sign have a stronger than normal need to love and to be loved. As a result they love often and passionately, although not necessarily wisely. They also like variety and change. Part of this is due to their very strong sex drive, but in part it stems from an inherent desire to dominate others. Few people would condone what Yellow Earth Star people do, nor wish to emulate them, but they themselves usually feel enriched by their experiences.

The women often have 'triangle' difficulties. They either have a second lover in reserve ready to take the first man's place, or else they get married and have one affair after another, and their carelessness in these matters inevitably leads to difficulties.

The men usually have one love which satisfies their needs so far as basic marriage relations go, but will often flirt or indulge in brief affairs just to satisfy their egos and prove to themselves that they are attractive to women, without loving the central woman in their lives any less. Five Star men frequently devote, even sacrifice, their lives to love and their success or failure in life depends to a great extent on the woman who occupies that position.

The men are much more subject to disappointment in love than the women simply because they try too hard or demand more than any woman will tolerate. So it is the women rather than the men who most often terminate the relationship. Since the males are strong and outgoing they quickly turn to a new love.

In general, neither the men nor the women can be described as good homemakers. For the most part, they unconsciously shift such responsibilities to their partners, with the result that although they appear to be in charge, in reality they are not.

6 *Financial prospects*   Money is never of grave concern to Five Star people. In general, they do not experience a serious need for money at any time during their lives. Should they lose everything, they would quickly recuperate their losses. Some will enjoy the advantage of an inheritance, but others will have to work hard for everything they get. Most will be lucky financially at some point of their lives, probably in relation to real estate or stocks and shares.

Most people born under this star tend to be parsimonious, not infrequently to the point of being downright miserly.

Chronic gambling by anyone of this category is disastrous since all will lose more than they gain. They would be well advised not to gamble at all.

7 *Choice of occupation*   People with this as their natal star are capable of success in a wide variety of professions. The best of them recognize fundamental principles for success and apply them wherever they are to whatever task they have in hand. When they undertake something they will do it to the best of their ability. The unambitious, lackadaisical ones are the exact opposite. Few Yellow Earth Star people will be found in the 'in between' category.

Those who are ambitious, with high goals—and perhaps, even, comparably high ideals—will seek positions of power and influence. They will rise to success as politicians, leaders of enterprises, military or police officers and anywhere where control and authority is exercised over others.

Those of minimal education and with no ideals will work at employment not readily sought after by others, and may be found as garbage collectors and secondhand dealers, pawnshop operators, and in all types of unskilled labour positions.

In general terms, people of this Star will be found either in the leading positions in society, or amongst its dregs, will be basically very good or very evil, outstanding as individuals or total failures. Fortunately the difference is readily discernible.

6   The Six White Metal Star

1 *Symbolism*   This is the north-west, the time between autumn and winter. It is represented by the trigram ☰, Ch'ien, the Creative.

This star represents the creative, the innovative, the actuator, the strong and the wise, the sages, and those who should be exemplary. Many will have a leaning towards spiritual growth and development and will find their psychic and intuitive powers more highly developed than in other people.

Since Ch'ien is symbolic of heaven White Metal Star people frequently strive for perfection in whatever they do.

2 *Fortune*   Those born under this star have inherent qualities of leadership. These vary in strength and quality between individuals due to differences in their days and times of births. Many will have the ability to dominate and conquer as well. All will have persistence in whatever they do. They will be constantly active, as well as moving ahead along their chosen path. In general they will determine their goals and pursue them diligently, coupling this with an effort to influence others along their path.

They are people with high ideals. They are ambitious and filled with an abundance of self-esteem, often to the point of being egotistical. They hate to lose at anything, so they study and work harder in order to know more than others, putting their increased learning to personal advantage. If they are in a low position or one that they consider undesirable, they soon find a way to rise above it. They use every means available to help themselves become at once leaders of their community, in society, in the organizations with which they are involved and in their business undertakings.

Since they are strong of will and hate to lose, they will argue at length and frequently fight others in order to get their own way. This is often trying for other people. They can sometimes be magnanimous and charitable, but this is primarily for their own reputation's sake rather than from deep sincerity. They never hesitate to use others if this will serve their purposes.

In addition to being strongly materialistic they are strongly spiritual. Their libraries will include many books on psychic, para-psychological and occult subjects. They know there is more to the mind than appears on the surface and have the courage to investigate its additional possibilities and capabilities.

Women of this star are never content to be just housewives and will be found active outside the home, engaged in society, community and business matters.

Their most productive years can vary; some reveal their talents in their teens, others after their middle years. Overall, their most fortunate period is after forty, when life truly seems to blossom for them, becoming increasingly fuller and better. The truism 'The more one demonstrates one's talents and abilities the more one achieves' truly applies to them.

Even those who for one reason or another are poorly educated tend to achieve something out of the ordinary, to the surprise of their acquaintances and society in general. Most are strong in goodness and justice. A (very) few of them, regrettably, are strong in injustice and evil.

3 *Personality*   Persons of this star like to be at the top in whatever they do and wherever they are. This takes many forms, from direct action and ambitious drive to the subtle 'modesty' of seemingly gentleness and consideration while firmly keeping one's goals in mind at all times. They seldom disclose their real purposes or aims to others. If they do, it is usually not more than showing the next step. Their self-esteem makes them recognize their own faults and drawbacks, which they do their best to conceal.

Should these persons ever lose their self-confidence they would correspondingly lose their ambition and drive. At most, though, this would be for relatively short periods only, for they are resilient, and tend to bounce back easily. When they do, they let nothing stand in their way of their efforts to regain their place at the top. This leads to their riding rough-shod over people and things along their path, often creating lasting enmities.

Being egotistic and strong-willed they cling to their opinions tenaciously. As a group they can be classed as stubborn and inflexible, although some individuals are exceptions to this rule.

Many of them are inclined to believe that others should measure up to and meet the same standards that they set for themselves.

Subordinates find them difficult, especially if they too have strong keen minds, a will towards a degree of freedom and good ideas of their own.

Six White Metal Star persons should be aware of their unusual personalities and characters and constantly try to improve themselves by being warmer and more gentle and considerate towards others.

4 *Physical type and health prospects*   There are two distinct groupings of Six White Metal Star people. One group is skinny and bony, athletically inclined and fluid in its body motions. The other group is more intellectual and spiritual with little or no ability in sporting activities. All, however, put a great deal of themselves into whatever they do.

Since they work hard at everything they should be wary of over-exertion, especially in their later years, being particularly on guard against nervous breakdown, fevers, headaches and dizziness. Other probable ailments are diseases of the lungs, heart or bones. Many are accident prone and should exercise care and caution in all they do.

5 *Love and marriage*   People born under this star like to give the appearance of nonchalance with respect to love and marriage while inwardly feeling a deep need for a strong and true relationship with a member of the opposite sex. The men and the women attain their aims in this respect in different ways.

The men are strongly egotistical and like to be approached by, flattered by, and often even controlled by females. Not infrequently this leads them into the trap of domination by strong and positive women who play a circumspect and attentive game during the courting period.

The women of this star tend towards an almost masculine aggressiveness in their relations with men. They are not averse to taking the lead in courtship and love play. When not otherwise employed they tend to devote their energies to love and lovemaking. They are wonderful homemakers, actively participating in all family affairs and even entering and taking over their husband's business if this becomes a necessity.

The men of this star try to conquer and dominate their women and demand obedience. While some women find this quality attractive, others abhor it. The men also have a tendency to blame their women rather than admit any weakness of their own.

Since they want to appear superior the men frequently cannot deny the demands which women make on them. They will assist and become involved with a supposed 'damsel in distress', who will not infrequently turn out to be merely a scheming woman.

Women of this star have similar propensities, so that both sexes often find themselves involved with more than one member of the opposite sex at a time.

Lower calibre males may even treat their women as slaves, while many of the less admirable White Metal Star women are termagants.

Separation, divorce, affairs and remarriage are common among this group of individuals.

6 *Financial prospects*   White Metal Star persons tend to think 'Big' financially. This, of course, ties in with their egotistical tendencies and longing for greatness. They are always seeking the 'great breakthrough', whether in real estate, prospecting, sky-rocketing stocks, the big winning combination if they are gamblers, or the top position within a business enterprise or other career undertaking.

In youth they tend to have heavy expenses. They will have little to spare at any given time until their middle years, when many of them will start to accumulate a fortune. In view of the duality of this star there will be some who will disdain the pursuit for money.

Most of their actions, financial or otherwise, stem from a desire to influence or impress others.

This holds true even when they are asked to lend money. Basically they are 'tight-fisted' and do not wish to lend money to anyone, but they will do so if it creates a favourable impression on others, especially if the situation is one which makes them appear generous.

The women of this star are unusually fortunate in money affairs and in handling and making money.

As for men, they fare far better when they rely on themselves rather than on others in financial matters.

7 *Choice of occupation*   Since Six White Metal Star people are egotistical and hold themselves in high esteem, they seek and strive for positions and occupations which they consider superior. Their wish is to be leaders and bosses and they actively take on as much responsibility as possible, especially if this puts them in charge of others. They deeply dislike being subordinate to others, or having to adhere to rules and policies of another's making. On the other hand, they do every task well.

They make particularly good lecturers, campaigners, evangelists, priests, ministers, psychiatrists, psychologists, counsellors, teachers, lawyers and administrators, as well as good managing directors of companies, especially those in which any form of transportation or transportation equipment is involved.

Any position or task which demands solitary or quiet action proves, in general, to be disastrous for them.

The more action and activity there is the better they seem to function, even under pressure.

7   The Seven Red Metal Star

1 *Symbolism*   Seven is in the western position on the Lo Map and is represented by the trigram ☱, Tui.

Seasonally, it is a time of joy over the reaping of the harvest. Red is the colour of the leaves in the autumn. It is also emblematic of the maturity of certain fruits and plants. The trigram ☱, Tui, represents metal, the lake and joyousness.

2 *Fortune*   This is a star of variegated aspects. Children and teenagers born under this star will be subject to many changes in their lives, and will have undergone quite a wide variety of experiences by the time they are twenty. Many of them will be spoiled or given too much freedom by their parents. This will cause some to be weaker physically than normal. Not being properly supervised, they may suffer from disorders of the stomach and intestinal tracts. After the age of twenty they become very sensitive to the moods of others and to establishing

moods in others. This, coupled with an innate ability as good speakers, makes them easily able to influence or manipulate others either for good or bad purposes.

In general, they are well known and well liked by others. They have the talent to please people through tact, grace, and saying the things that others like to hear. They are optimistic as well, so they tend to create a pleasing atmosphere wherever they are. This stems partly from a strong desire to show off, as well as a wish to be always well liked. But in part it stems from their egotism. The easiest way to make such people angry is to ignore them or (pretend) to despise them.

While pretending to like nearly everyone it is very difficult for them to give in to others or to let others take a more commanding position than they themselves hold. Their liking for others is for the most part shallow and superficial. It is deliberate and devoid of sincere feelings, yet it fools most people most of the time.

Outward appearances are very important to these persons. They like to dress well, to show off as well as to try to appear younger than they actually are.

People born under this star are very sensitive to their relations with close associates of the opposite sex. Their success or failure in any enterprise is intimately linked with their feelings, emotions and love for their 'partner', whose support and encouragement is vital in all phases of their activities.

Seven Red Metal Star people have quick and keen minds capable of grasping many details, but they hate to handle routine and matters of detail themselves. By nature they like to be free, not to be controlled or supervised by others. This frequently affects their relationships and is often an impediment to their advance into positions of responsibility and authority. However, they love to give advice to others and, when they do, for the most part it is very sound and practical. On the other hand, lone business ventures will not usually be successful.

The fortune of Seven Red Metal Star people will stabilize after they reach the age of forty and their later years will be the best years of their lives.

3 *Personality* Individuals born under this star will be seekers of happiness and enjoyment and their personalities will centre on this aim. For the most part they will participate in matters of

physical enjoyment or devise means for achieving it through games, entertainment or various forms of social activities.

They are fluent talkers and writers and tend to influence others readily and easily. They are very sensitive to the feelings of others. This enables them to gain advantage over others and to use this for personal advantage. When they associate with other sensitive people, they frequently hurt them, for they soon recognize that they are being used rather than sought as friends.

The greatest weakness of Red Metal Star people is their lack of perseverance in following anything through to completion unless goaded into doing so by others. They are also subject to moodiness, even when presenting a calm exterior. Since they are sensitive they can easily be brought out of this by others. If they operate alone they usually do not accomplish much and just end up with empty dreams.

4 *Physical type and health prospects*   People of the star are usually small in body structure and not as strong as most individuals. Their five senses are more active than in most people, so they enjoy gourmet foods, nature, good music and art.

In terms of illness, they are subject to stomach ailments, neurasthenia, chest diseases, kidney problems, venereal diseases and diseases of the mouth, teeth and tongue.

5 *Love and marriage*   These people possess a natural attraction for members of the opposite sex, as well as instinctively knowing the simplest and best means of attracting them. They can easily bring about an 'affair' or a proposal of marriage if they want to. Conversely, they are the most likely ones to terminate a relationship when it no longer satisfies them or else does not serve their purposes.

A number of people born under this star will have a series of love affairs rather than marry. This arises from their innate desire for freedom.

All of them should be cautious about choosing partners of the opposite sex as friends, as lovers, or as marriage partners, for they tend to react strongly to these persons. Great good and much happiness can come from making the right choice. So the advice is to go slowly, choose cautiously and let the head rule the heart.

6 *Financial prospects*   Money, for Seven Star people, is some-thing made to be spent. Since they like to spend a lot they are also willing to work hard to make a lot. Unfortunately they do not accumulate great amounts. On the other hand, when they run out of money they always have a fresh idea and know how to get or make more. Money, therefore, is important, but not for its own sake. Rather, it is for what one can do with it.

They should never gamble, for they are under adverse influences in this respect and will always lose in the end.

Their overall fortunes will improve in later years and they should have ample funds for a reasonably good life, even by their standards.

7 *Choice of occupation*   The Seven Red Metal Star is often called the 'Star of Dining'. Therefore, any activities associated with eating and dining are favoured, such as the management and operation of bars, restaurants, cabarets, liquor stores, deli-catessens, and food processing and food distribution systems.

Additionally, persons of this star are good talkers and speakers so they can also be lecturers, teachers, preachers, salesmen and barristers. A few will do well in banking or financial enterprises and in the entertainment field. Some may even succeed as dentists.

8   The Eight White Earth Star

1 *Symbolism*   The White Earth Star is symbolized by the tri-gram ☶, Kew, Mountain, Keeping Still. Its direction is north-west and in terms of season it is the time between winter and spring. Along with the trigram ☷ K'un, the Receptive, it is also symbolic of the earth and the earth's attributes.

2 *Fortune*   The most fortunate aspects of White Earth Star individuals is that they will benefit through inheritances. This will either be in the form of money or else of a business venture or part of one. In any event they will put the money into new use or develop the old business in a more modern way. They will be successful in these ventures.

They are people with strength of mind and strong wills, difficult to sway and often considered stubborn and anti-social by others. This stems from their enjoyment of argument and desire to impose their will on others. Part of this arises from their dislike of adapting to changes which they have not themselves originated. Many can therefore be categorized as old-fashioned conservatives, a few extremists amongst them even being isolationists.

Except when involved in an argument, Eight White Earth Star people appear to be gentle, tactful and placid. In general, they try to hide their strengths rather than display them. In a showdown, honesty conquers tact and many make themselves disliked by being too candid. The combination of hidden strength and honesty often leads them into doing things in an unusual or unexpected way.

For the most part they are solid and when they exert singleness of purpose they generally attain their goals or aims.

3 *Personality* Their personalities parallel the symbolism for this star; i.e., the mountain. They are strong of will, egotistic, uncommunicative and have a high self-esteem. They would prefer to be loners and live in a self-contained world. Their co-operation with others, when it exists, is superficial and lacks inner sincerity.

They will risk their friendships and social and professional positions for the sake of proving that they are right.

What they gain out of life is primarily achieved through singleness of purpose rather than through energy, talent or wisdom. The 'School of Hard Knocks' is their most valuable practical education. Their strong inner desires, which they do not like to make apparent, carry them through many of the rough vicissitudes of life. Those less educated or unable to disguise their inner feelings will be criticized frequently for being miserly, tight and greedy.

4 *Physical type and health prospects* In general, Eight White Earth Star people will be larger than average in size. Many of them, of both sexes, will be heavily built and well filled out. While in good condition physically, they are not sufficiently co-ordinated muscularly to be outstanding athletes.

As for physical ailments, they should exercise care regarding abnormal blood circulation, congestion of the back and shoulders, neuralgia, arterio-sclerosis and illnesses brought on by lack of exercise. They are also subject to difficulties in connection with the nose, hands and feet and to chronic constipation.

Since they have a tendency to become hypochrondiacs they should make a special effort to overcome all ailments quickly, or they will find themselves becoming ill more and more frequently.

5 *Love and marriage*   Love and marriage are important to both the men and the women of this star. Both tend to stick to their partners and both are drawn to marriage. The men, while generally slow to pick a partner, stick to the one they select and pursue her relentlessly until she capitulates. They give the impression of being reliable and trustworthy, and for the most part this is so. Furthermore, they are not easily upset by small deficiencies in matters of love, and adopt a mature approach to all situations. They respect their loved ones, protect them, give them security and do not violate their confidences. They are uncommunicative and disdainful towards women who do not interest them, often to the point of appearing anti-social.

As for the women of this star, they tend to combine love and marriage well. Quite a few will put love above all else and pick a husband who loves them honestly and sincerely rather than for other motives. They enjoy managing a home and the durability of their marriages will depend on their ability in this respect.

6 *Financial prospects*   Eight White Earth Star individuals attract money. It seems to flow towards them even from early youth. They are never short of funds for very long. Most of them will have more than ample for their needs throughout their lives.

Savings and investments are areas of active interest to these individuals. They like to have several savings accounts and it does not please them to let anyone know how much they really have. Real estate and sound stocks are also favourite forms of investment. They are practical with their money, too, and will refrain from buying needless luxuries.

A few will have a true gambling instinct and will become involved in 'get rich quick' schemes. Regrettably some of them will lose more than they gain, but it is hard to convince them of their error, and they will try and try again for that large fortune and rapid gain.

7 *Choice of occupation* Positions requiring stability, long service, honesty, reliability and service to others are favoured. Many will be found working as educators, religionists, in the police and civil service, as bank tellers and cashiers, and in certain aspects of military organization. A few will display a talent for art related to the earth, or for sculpture.

9 The Nine Purple Fire Star

1 *Symbolism* This star is represented by the trigram ☲, Li, Clarity. This is the summertime season of the south, the midday, brightness, light, fire and being a light for oneself and others. It also depicts the celestial element of fire.

Nine is the highest position of single numbers and is like the sun in the sky at midday. It indicates a goal towards which all should strive.

2 *Fortune* Basically, despite their troubles and weaknesses, Nine Purple Fire Star individuals have auspicious and satisfying lives. They are naturally attractive to others and start attracting attention to themselves early in their youth. This aids them in getting started in life. Their youth is essentially smooth and progressive. The middle years are the best years of their lives, with good fortune, health and professional situations deteriorating after the age of fifty. It is best for them to establish themselves in a career early in life and to persevere so as to get as much as possible in the way of position, salary and material wealth organized before the post-fifty decline.

External appearances are important to these people. They like a good home, expensive furniture, fashionable clothing and possessions of good quality, mainly for show. Some pursue these material aims so energetically that they tend to forget or overlook the higher values of life. Conversely, those who are interested in the higher values, or become interested in them, will tend to hold material possessions in disdain, whereas a less extreme outlook would probably be more beneficial. This hint of duality spills over into other aspects of their lives, and since other people cannot easily classify them supervisors and others in authority do not always altogether trust them.

They are very sensitive individuals, easily moved emotionally, and quick-tempered yet also quick to calm down. While reasonably well-motivated, they do not have the deep-seated singleness of purpose or the perseverance to follow matters through to great lengths.

Nine Purple Fire Star people like to have friends—up to a point. They make friends easily, and also drop them easily. They do not permit others to invade their privacy, so they rarely have any really close friends. They do have a wide acquaintanceship, however, for others like to be around these individuals because they are good conversationalists, tactful and convincing.

Their main weaknesses are that they are egotistical and hate to lose. This often results in lengthy and damaging arguments. These traits should be overcome if at all possible.

A further weakness is that they have a propensity to act impulsively, rashly and impetuously. They expect too much from others, which results in disappointment. Sometimes they will make a decision or base a course of action on too little knowledge. This, too, is a source of difficulty to them.

3 *Personality* Nine Purple Fire Star people are outgoing, materialistic, clever, devious, introspective, self-centred and have a tendency to superficiality. External appearances are very important to them. They are also artistically inclined, with a good sense of proportion and balance in the various art forms. However, they are not the most practical individuals with regard to the ordinary problems of living.

They are often hypercritical, tending to criticize extensively those things which they personally disdain, such as poverty, improper attire, weakness of character and inadequacies in general. This is primarily a reflection of what they fear in themselves.

Since these people hate to lose, they frequently will not admit their mistakes. This often offends others to the point of losing them valuable acquaintances. The same quality will tend to make them keep within their own castle and not let others enter, primarily so that they will not be hurt by them.

The women are loners, too, and try to achieve what they want singlehandedly, even if this means throwing a fit of hysterics, if they think it will serve their purpose.

4 *Physical type and health prospects* For the most part Nine Purple Fire Star people will be average in physical size, strength and abilities with only a few being tough, rugged and outstandingly athletic. Their eyes are clear, small, beautiful and penetrating. They give the impression of being observant, with a sharp and sensitive mind working away behind their eyes.

Their most likely illnesses are neurasthenia, insomnia, schizophrenia, and eye and heart diseases. Women may also have to take account of constipation, breast cancer and the possibility that they may have to have a hysterectomy.

5 *Love and marriage* Love is very important to Nine Purple Fire Star people and they are natural and attractive in this regard. They mature early and have keen feelings of love and of needing to be loved. They are sensitive to the feelings of their partners and quickly recognize their moods. Not only are they naturally sexy in voice and action but by being fluent talkers as well they can readily capture the attention of the object of their affections. They tend to let partners go rather easily since they are confident they can find someone else, so that they are rather like butterflies fluttering from flower to flower. Since they hate to lose they will be angry with any person who gives them up, while conversely expecting their partners to accept without question any termination that they themselves may originate.

As individuals they are quite possessive. They want their partner to themselves and will brook no actual or apparent infidelity. This can and does lead to many difficulties.

Both the men and the women will have fantasies about possible love affairs, even when they are married, but it rarely goes further than that.

Basically, they should try to learn to love more deeply, more sincerely and for longer periods of time.

6 *Financial prospects* Nine Purple Fire Star people are about average in matters of finances. They are neither very strong nor very weak. They will never run out of money but they will

never be truly rich either. They always want and fight to get what a peer gets for comparable service.

Expenses invariably equal income. The larger the income the greater the expenses. They love to spend what they make and their savings accounts are low to minimal.

While the desire for money is strong these persons always follow honourable means to get what they need. They abhor dishonest business practices as a means of getting money. Since they lack both perseverance and dedicated singleness of purpose, they do not amass great fortunes unless they deliberately overcome this weakness.

While not averse to gambling they never really win in matters involving chance. It is better for them to be conservative in all financial matters.

7 *Choice of occupation*   Any position which allows a degree of self-expression and freedom will suit the Nine Purple Fire Star person.

Among the more popular occupations will be those of politician, diplomat, judge, barrister, artist, author, actor, reporter, editor, advertising agent, broker, fortuneteller, beauty parlour stylist, horticulturist and any occupation in which individuality is of value.

Tzu Pin astrology

Tzu Pin is an Horary astrology with its foundations in the most advanced divination methods for applying Celestial and Horary Branch stem interactions and relationships. The usual eight symbols for the year, month, date and hour of birth are developed. The interplay of forces related to the eight symbols provides the basis for predictions affecting all the phases of life. Since the concepts and applications originate in the advanced divination methods that are associated with the *I Ching*, Tzu Pin is seen as another of the astrologies related to the *I Ching*.

In China, it is the most popular of the Horary Branch astrologies. The primary reason for this lies in the vast range of predictions which can be made—natal, ten-year, yearly, monthly, daily and even bi-hourly. The Horary symbols change for each of these segments of time and by comparing the natal elements with the elements of time involved, a forecast is available for any circumstance from a two-hour period upward. It is an interesting idea that man's fortunes are in a state of constant change as a result of the Horary symbols changing throughout each day, month and year. Carrying this one step further it gives us a basis for understanding how the relationships between people change as time progresses.

The steps required to determine the eight natal symbols are similar to those shown under the title 'The Astrology of the *I Ching*', Steps 1–6 inclusive (see pp. 164–8).

Here, however, there is one controversial aspect for Chinese astrologers, namely, the question 'When does the astrological year begin?' One has a choice between using the winter solstice or the beginning of the 'Spring Begins' period, when life seems to enter a new cycle. ('Spring Begins' is the first season of the ancient Chinese twenty-four-season system and it begins on approximately 4 February each year.) The arguments are too much involved to be discussed here. We ourselves feel that the weight of evidence indicates it is best to use the winter solstice for *I Ching* astrology, and 'Spring Begins' when making predictions by the Tzu Pin method. Thus if we assume that the astrological year 1977 would be from winter solstice December 1976 to winter solstice December 1977 it would include the dates used for the Astrology of the *I Ching*. On the other hand, the astrological year 1977 for Tzu Pin would be from approximately 4 February 1977 to 4 February 1978. Since the question of which should be used has not been solved in the last 2,000 years it is quite probable that a few years more will elapse before a final decision is made.

One other great difficulty that exists for Westerners who would like to use this astrology is that the exact time that the season 'Spring Begins' starts varies from year to year and consequently every other month of the year along with it. Tables are available in Chinese only. This makes predictions very difficult for those born at the beginning or end of a Chinese month. It also affects everyone's ten-year influence. But these points will become more clear as one works one's way through the procedure given below.

Tzu Pin astrology received its name from the famous astrologer of the Tang Dynasty, Hsu Tzu Pin (Hsu is the surname). He took the same principles as are used in advanced divination based on the *I Ching* and further expanded them into the methods and applications we now know as the Astrology of Tzu Pin. Like the other astrologies of this group it is based on eight symbols.

By carrying through the computation methods set out as Steps 1–6 in the section entitled 'Astrology of the *I Ching*' (see pp. 164–8) a birthdate can be expressed in terms of yearly, monthly, daily and hourly Celestial Stems and Horary Branches. For instance, if a person was born at 00.25 on 18 September 1934, that person's eight symbols would be:

Year	=	Ak
Month	=	Jj
Day	=	Ie
Hour	=	Ga

Note that midnight to 1 a.m. was a Ga hour while 11 p.m. to midnight of the same calendar date was an Ia hour. The first is called the early 'a' hour and the second is the night 'a' hour.

TEN-YEAR INFLUENCE SPANS

The ten-year influence span is based on the symbols for the month in which one was born, coupled with the additional consideration of whether the individual in question is Yang or Yin, male or female.

Step 1: Select the Celestial Stem and Horary Branch symbol, previously determined (as shown on p. 167), for the month in which the person was born. Enter the categories listed below and decide to which of the four the person belongs:

Yang Males: Men born in an A, C, E, G or I year
Yin Males: Men born in a B, D, F, H or J year
Yang Females: Women born in an A, C, E, G or I year
Yin Females: Women born in a B, D, F, H or J year

Step 2: Use either (a) or (b) below to determine the ten-year span symbol.

(a) For a Yang Male and Yin Female the ten-year influence symbols follow the natural order sequence of the Sexagenary cycle system (see p. 45) and proceed sequentially.

EXAMPLE:

If the natal month symbol is Ic
The first ten-year influence span symbol will be Jd
The second ten-year influence span symbol is Ae
The third ten-year influence span symbol is Bf
The fourth ten-year influence span symbol is Cg
The fifth ten-tear influence span symbol is Dh

(b) For the Yin Male and the Yang Female the ten-year influence symbols follow the reverse sequence of those shown
in (a) above:

EXAMPLE:

Suppose that the natal month symbol is Ic
The first ten-year influence span symbol is Hb
The second ten-year influence span symbol is Ga
The third ten-year influence span symbol is Fl
The fourth ten-year influence span symbol is Ek
The fifth ten-year influence span symbol is Dj

For any other ten-year influence span symbol follow either the
sequence (a) or (b) above, as appropriate.

The ten-year influence span predictions are developed from the
interaction of the symbol for the span with the eight natal symbols for that person following the interaction rules set forth in
Tables 1 and 2 and those laid down in the section entitled
'Advanced Divination' (pp. 57–67).

The degree of detail to which Tzu Pin extends itself is shown
in the calculations for determining when a ten-year cycle begins.
It is a two-step process:

(1a) For Yang males and Yin females count the days and hours
from the time of birth to the beginning of the next Chinese
month.

Or

(1b) For Yin males and Yang females count the days and
hours from the beginning of the Chinese month to the time
of birth.

Then

(2) Using the assumption that three days are equal to one year
and one hour to five days, convert the interval of days found
in (1a) or (1b) above into years and days.

EXAMPLE:

Suppose a boy and a girl were born in California at 11.45 a.m. Pacific Standard Time on 24 August 1971.[1] 1971 is an Hl year. The boy is a Yin male and the girl a Yin female. In this year, the Chinese month 'Autumn Begins' (i month) starts on 7 August at 8.40 p.m. and the White Dew (j month) begins on 8 September at 11.30 p.m. Pacific Standard Time. Therefore, they were born in 'i' month. From Table 11 or the table under Step 4 of the section on 'The Astrology of the *I Ching*', we find that the Celestial Stem of this month is C; therefore, this is a Ci month.

For the girl, the time 11.45 a.m. on 24 August to 11.30 p.m. on 8 September is 15 days, 11 hours and 45 minutes. From the assumption in (2) above this time is equivalent to:

15 days	=	5 years
11 hours	=	55 days
45 minutes	=	4 days (approximately)

Therefore, 5 years and 59 days after the time the girl was born the ten-year influence spans begin, which makes the influences:

22 October 1976 to 21 October 1986	=	Dj
22 October 1986 to 21 October 1996	=	Ek
22 October 1996 to 21 October 2006	=	Fl
22 October 2006 to 21 October 2016	=	Ga
22 October 2016 to 21 October 2026	=	Hb

For the boy, the time from 7 August, 8.40 p.m., to 24 August, 11.45 a.m., is approximately 16 days and 15 hours.

16 days is equivalent to 5 years and 122 days approximately

15 hours is equivalent to 75 days

This makes a total of 5 years and 197 days

Therefore, 5 years and 197 days after the boy was born his ten-year influences begin, which makes the influences:

9 March 1977 to 8 March 1987	=	Bh
9 March 1987 to 8 March 1997	=	Ag
9 March 1997 to 8 March 2007	=	Jf

---

[1] For time conversions see footnote p. 74.

9 March 2007 to 8 March 2017 = Ie
9 March 2017 to 8 March 2027 = Hd

Remember that these are the symbols which interact with the natal symbols to determine the predictions.

ADDITIONAL INTERACTION AMONG CELESTIAL STEMS AND HORARY BRANCHES

In addition to the interactions already shown under the chapter entitled 'Advanced Divination' the following further interactions between the Celestial Stems and Horary Branches exist.[1]

[1] Examples of these relationships for divination purposes are cited below:
a Action of the Horary Branch:

EXAMPLE:
When a and b unite they form earth.
Question: What will be the financial result of the stocks I bought today? (Time: f month, a day.)
        Hexagram cast:

money	— —	k (earth)
officer	— —	i
children	——	g
officer	——	j
parents	——	l
money	— —	b (earth)

f, the month, is fire. Fire generates earth (money). a is the day. a and b unite to form earth (money). The b in this case is the lowest line, which is also money.
Prediction: The entire situation will be very favourable.
b An example of expulsion (repulsion) has already been given on page 51.
c Triplicate Horary Unity and the Five Elements:

EXAMPLE:
Question: Will my father have a favourable recovery from his illness? (Time: b month, d day.)
        Hexagram cast:

parents	——	k (earth)
brother	——	i
officer	—⊖—	g
parents	——	e (earth)
money	—⊕—	c
children	——	a

The moving lines always have to be considered. In this case there are two: c and g.

There are two parents' lines, e and k. c, g and k combine to become fire. Fire generates earth (parents), so the prognosis is for a favourable recovery.

1   Action of the Celestial Stems

When A and F unite they form earth; i.e., when the forces of A and F meet, they combine or join together to form the force of earth. Similarly, for the other stems:

When B and G unite they form metal.
When C and H unite they form water.
When D and I unite they form wood.
When E and J unite they form fire.

2   Action of the Horary Branches

When the forces of a and b unite or combine they form the forces of earth. So we say:

When a and b unite they become earth.
When c and l unite they become wood.
When d and k unite they become fire.
When e and j unite they become metal.
When f and i unite they become water.
(When the forces of g and h unite or combine, what they become is not mentioned in the Chinese text.)

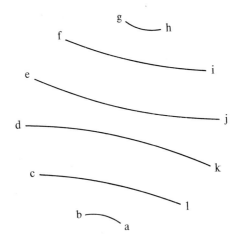

Figure 13.   Action of the Horary Branches

3   Triplicate horary unity and the five elements

When the combinations of Horary Branch forces unite or combine in the following combinations they form the elements indicated:

a, e and i form the water force.
d, h and l form the wood force.
c, g and k form the fire force.
b, f and j form the metal force.

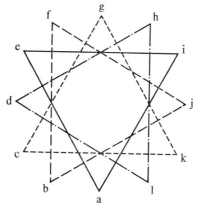

Figure 14.   Triplicate Horary unity and the five elements

4   The Expulsion (Repulsion) of Horary Branches

Opposites expel or repel each other, so we say:

a and g expel each other.
b and h expel each other.
c and i expel each other.
d and j expel each other.
e and k expel each other.
f and l expel each other.

5   The unharmonious

In Section 4 certain forces had such a strong antagonism that they expelled or repelled one another. Here the emnity is not

as intense, but nevertheless of a nature to produce discord. So
we say:

a is not in harmony with h.
b is not in harmony with g.
c is not in harmony with f.
d is not in harmony with e.
i is not in harmony with l.
j is not in harmony with k.

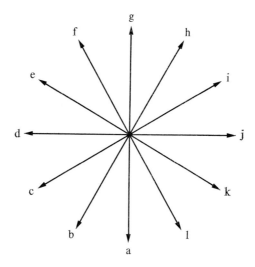

Figure 15. *The expulsion of Horary Branches*

6 Punishment

Just as in life certain people have an antipathy for each other and
constantly make things difficult for eath other, so certain Horary
forces likewise react adversely, producing hostility, malevolence,
severe criticism and ill-will. The forces which react in this
manner are spoken of as punishing each other. So we say:

a punishes d; d punishes a.
c punishes f; f punishes i; i punishes c.
b punishes k; k punishes h; h punishes b.

7   Self-punishment

Certain Horary forces when they meet a force of like nature have a very adverse effect on one another. Such forces are said to inflict self-punishment:

e punishes e.
g punishes g.
j punishes j.
l punishes l.

In addition to the rules of interactions given under the chapter 'Advanced Divination', the seven rules above should be memorized when applying Tzu Pin. They are the rules which give refinement to the predictions and consequently aid materially in their accuracy. A Western astrologer will note some similarity between these rules and the actions of Squares, Sextiles, Quincunxes, Yods, etc.

ASSOCIATIONS OF CELESTIAL STEMS IN HORARY BRANCHES

Some Chinese scholars, apparently from experience and based to some extent on propensities, have added a further refinement to the foregoing rules to reflect the carry-over of certain Celestial Stem forces into Horary Branch forces. A summary of their ascribation is:

a stores J
b stores F, H and J
c stores A, C and E
d stores B
e stores B, E and J
f stores C, E and G
g stores D and F
h stores B, D and F
i stores E, G and I
j stores H
k stores D, E and H
l stores A and I

Note that when a stores J the converse is also true; i.e., J hides in a.

In writing, the relationships of the eight symbols are shown thus:

```
        D
  Ak    E
        H

  Jj    H

        B
  Ie    E
        J

  Ga    J
```

In other words, since k stores D, E and H write $\begin{smallmatrix}D\\E\\H\end{smallmatrix}$ after k; j stores H so write H after j; e stores B, E and J so write $\begin{smallmatrix}B\\E\\J\end{smallmatrix}$ after e; and since a stores J, write J after a.

TZU PIN PREDICTIONS

A deep understanding and thorough knowledge of the intricate relationships and interactions between the forces of the eight natal symbols and the Celestial Stem and Horary Branch forces makes it possible to finely grade the Tzu Pin predictions. The eight natal symbols form the base from which interpretations and interpolations are made. Roughly speaking, the yearly Celestial Stem and Horary Branch represent one's ancestors; the monthly Celestial Stem and Horary Branch represent parents, brothers, sisters, friends and associates; the daily Celestial Stem represents oneself; the daily Horary Branch, one's spouse; the hourly Celestial Stem and Horary Branch represent one's children. From the interaction between the Celestial Stems and the Horary Branches, the approximate relationship between oneself and one's parents, brothers and sisters, friends, spouse and children can be determined. For other aspects of one's life, the rules given in this section and those relating to advanced divination, such as the material given in Tables 1, 2, 5 and 7 are incorporated. The Celestial Stem and Horary Branch interactions generate these in this astrology just as they do in the other Horary astrologies, and it is primarily through these same relationships and interactions that this astrology is also related to the *I Ching*. The full complement of rules is quite complicated and involved and requires a good memory if one is to make accurate predictions. Naturally there are variations in the quality of astrologers, and the value of their predictions in China differs in degree just as it does in the West.

Ten-yearly, yearly, monthly, daily and bi-hourly predictions can be made. The ten-year span prediction is made by noting the interaction of the eight natal symbols with the symbols for the ten-year Celestial Stem and Horary Branch forces. Similarly, the yearly prediction is made by noting the interaction of the eight natal symbols with the symbols for the yearly Celestial Stem and Horary Branch forces. The same applies to the monthly, daily and bi-hourly predictions. Bi-hourly predictions are possible, since the Horary Branch symbols change every two hours.

As for compatibility, the total interaction of the eight natal symbols involved for each person must be considered as well as their current interaction with time. Working out a few of these will give one a basis for understanding why compatibility between individuals changes frequently, often for no apparent reason. Recognizing this could make for better relations between individuals.

Obviously, the various interactions can and do cover nearly all aspects of life. This, and the fact that when predictions are made by a knowledgeable astrologer they are found to be sound and reliable, has made Tzu Pin the favourite Horary Branch astrology, and the most popular of those related to the *I Ching*.

Tzu Wei astrology

INTRODUCTION
The Astrology of Tzu Wei is said to have been created by the immortal Chen Tuan, who lived between the Five Dynasties period and the beginning of the Sung Dynasty *c*. AD 950. Who the real creator was is still debatable, for many Chinese scholars

liked to name famous ancients as the originators in order to gain acceptance for their material rather than risk producing it under their own name. For the Chinese, Tzu Wei astrology is next in popularity only to Tzu Pin.

This astrology applies sixty-three Stars to a chart consisting of the Houses of the twelve Horary Branches. The sixty-three stars, in theory, include the Plough (the Big Dipper), the stars of the middle sky and some stars from around the South Pole. Tzu Wei is the Emperor of the Stars, and it is for this reason that the astrology bears his name. Whether the horoscope chart of this astrology really indicates the position of the stars in any sense is still a question. The creator of the astrology does not mention any of the principles underlying his method. He merely sets out the procedure. Therefore the principles and basis of this astrology need to be researched further.

There is only one book on Tzu Wei astrology in Chinese and it is not an easy work to understand. Occasionally, the simplified Tzu Wei, which applies only fourteen of the sixty-three stars, is used. These fourteen stars are those considered as having the greatest influence. In fact, the complete Tzu Wei is nearly always used. The simplified Tzu Wei was probably developed in Fukien Province in China, but has never gained popularity. In this book, however, we shall set out this simplified method, so as to give the reader some idea of Tzu Wei and how it works. To try and set out the entire Tzu Wei system would be beyond the scope of this book, which deals primarily with the *I Ching*, not astrologies as such.

Tzu Wei is an astrology which involves some of the principles of the *I Ching*, together with the Ho Map, the five celestial elements, the Horary time system and the lunar calendar dates. There are approximately 125,000 basic combinations and almost limitless variations of these are possible if one takes into account all the considerations of time variation that can make some influences stronger than others in the natal pattern of individuals. In theory it can account for every type of person found in the universe as well as giving natal predictions and predictions for each year of one's life on a twelve-year cycle basis.

Essentially there are twelve Horary 'Houses' to which sixty-three 'Stars' are assigned. In this simplified version only the fourteen major stars will be considered. The term 'Stars' seems to be used figuratively, since arbitrary names are applied as a matter of convenience to represent certain influences and related considerations. The houses are symbolic of the twelve two-hour periods of the day and have special characteristics and attributes which will be discussed in greater detail below. They do, however, cover all phases of one's life. Here we will merely mention their sequence and broad representations; i.e.: (1) the Natal House; (2) the House of Brothers (sisters and friends); (3) the House of Husband and Wife; (4) the House of Children; (5) the House of Wealth; (6) the House of Sickness; (7) the House of Residence and Movement; (8) the House of Servants (subordinates); (9) the House of Position and Revenue; (10) the House of Property and Estates; (11) the House of Blessings and Virtue; and (12) the House of Mother and Father. The 'stars' are placed in the various houses according to the fixed rules from which predictions can be made.

Both the houses and the stars have the element characteristics and attributes of earth, metal, water, wood and fire. These interact favourably, unfavourably or neutrally in accordance with the concept of interaction shown originally in Tables 1 and 2 and reproduced here for the reader's convenience:

Earth generates (gives birth to) metal
Metal generates (gives birth to) water
Water generates (gives birth to) wood
Wood generates (gives birth to) fire
Fire generates (gives birth to) earth

Earth conquers water (Absorption)
Water conquers fire (Quenching)
Fire conquers metal (Melting)
Metal conquers wood (Cutting)
Wood conquers earth (Extracting)

Positive or strong negative or weak and neutral aspects of the stars are also shown. To a large extent this is predicated on the time represented by the house the star is in. For example, if the Sun Star were in the house whose time corresponded to midnight it would be weak or negative, whereas it would be positive and strong in the house of midday.

Understandably what has just been said is only a brief outline of Tzu Wei, designed to give the reader a general idea of what to expect as the material is presented.

DEVELOPING THE HOROSCOPE

Step 1: Determine the corrected date and time of birth. This is done by correcting the time to Standard Time and by applying a time correction for the difference in longitude between the place of birth and the Standard Meridian. When making the longitude correction allow four minutes for each degree of difference; add the correction if the birth place is east of the Standard Meridian, subtract it for births west of the Standard Meridian.

EXAMPLE:

Male. Born 1.21 a.m. CDT Oklahoma City, Oklahoma, 30 June 1975. Longitude 97° 31′W. Standard Meridian = 90°W. 1.21 a.m. CDT = 1.21 − 1.00 = 12.21 CST 30 June. 97° 31′ W of the Standard Meridian. Multiply 7° 31′ by 4 to obtain the correction in minutes; i.e. 7° 31′ × 4 = 28 minutes and 124 seconds or 30 minutes and 4 seconds (Note: if seconds are less than 30 drop them; if between 30–59 add 1 minute). Therefore 12.21 − 00.30 = 11.51 on 29 June. This is the sidereal time of birth for this astrology.

Next find the month applicable to 29 June 1975 from Table 11 and note this month. In this case it is g month. Only the Horary Branch of the month is used in this astrology. Ignore the Celestial Stem of the month in Table 11.

Draw a standard horoscope chart as shown in Figure 16.

Next, determine the position of the natal house in the horoscope chart using the month and hour of birth (but ignoring the year and day) and selecting the result from Table 16.

EXAMPLE:

If a person is born at 11.45 a.m. Standard Time in b month, Table 16 shows us that the position of the person's natal house is h. Write 'natal house' in square h in the horoscope chart to show its position.

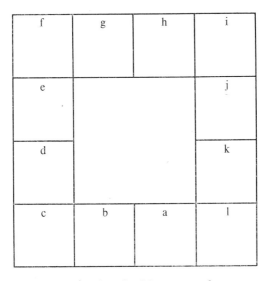

Figure 16.   *Standard horoscope chart*

Table 16   *Natal house positions*

Month	a	b	c	d	e	f	g	h	i	j	k	l
11 p.m.– 1 a.m.	a	b	c	d	e	f	g	h	i	j	k	l
1 a.m.– 3 a.m.	l	a	b	c	d	e	f	g	h	i	j	k
3 a.m.– 5 a.m.	k	l	a	b	c	d	e	f	g	h	i	j
5 a.m.– 7 a.m.	j	k	l	a	b	c	d	e	f	g	h	i
7 a.m.– 9 a.m.	i	j	k	l	a	b	c	d	e	f	g	h
9 a.m.–11 a.m.	h	i	j	k	l	a	b	c	d	e	f	g
11 a.m.– 1 p.m.	g	h	i	j	k	l	a	b	c	d	e	f
1 p.m.– 3 p.m.	f	g	h	i	j	k	l	a	b	c	d	e
3 p.m.– 5 p.m.	e	f	g	h	i	j	k	l	a	b	c	d
5 p.m.– 7 p.m.	d	e	f	g	h	i	j	k	l	a	b	c
7 p.m.– 9 p.m.	c	d	e	f	g	h	i	j	k	l	a	b
9 p.m.–11 p.m.	b	c	d	e	f	g	h	i	j	k	l	a

Step 2: Assign the remaining houses. The twelve houses move in the following sequence:

1   Natal House
2   House of Brothers
3   House of Husband and Wife
4   House of Children
5   House of Wealth
6   House of Sickness
7   House of Residence and Movement
8   House of Servants
9   House of Position and Revenue
10   House of Property and Estates
11   House of Blessings and Virtue
12   House of Father and Mother

Set them out in a counter-clockwise direction. Table 17 shows the assignments for the example we have taken.

Table 17   *Assignment of houses*

Horary Branch of Natal House	a	b	c	d	e	f	g	h	i	j	k	l
House of Brothers	l	a	b	c	d	e	f	g	h	i	j	k
House of Husband and Wife	k	l	a	b	c	d	e	f	g	h	i	j
House of Children	j	k	l	a	b	c	d	e	f	g	h	i
House of Wealth	i	j	k	l	a	b	c	d	e	f	g	h
House of Sickness	h	i	j	k	l	a	b	c	d	e	f	g
House of Residence	g	h	i	j	k	l	a	b	c	d	e	f
House of Servants	f	g	h	i	j	k	l	a	b	c	d	e
House of Position and Revenue	e	f	g	h	i	j	k	l	a	b	c	d
House of Property and Estates	d	e	f	g	h	i	j	k	l	a	b	c
House of Blessings and Virtue	c	d	e	f	g	h	i	j	k	l	a	b
House of Father and Mother	b	c	d	e	f	g	h	i	j	k	l	a

Step 3: As with Western astrologies which categorize people into fire, air, water and earth signs, Tzu Wei places them into five groupings corresponding to the five celestial elements of earth, metal, water, wood and fire. These classifications are called patterns.

The patterns themselves are important in making natal predictions. Since every star and every house has an element designation, the interaction between elements forms the basis for specific favourable and unfavourable influences. The numbers assigned to these patterns likewise play a role in determining the time at which the yearly cycles start.

For the most part the numbers assigned by the Ho Map are used for the element patterns, but this is not altogether so. The numbering is:

2 = Water pattern
3 = Wood pattern
4 = Metal pattern
5 = Earth pattern
6 = Fire pattern

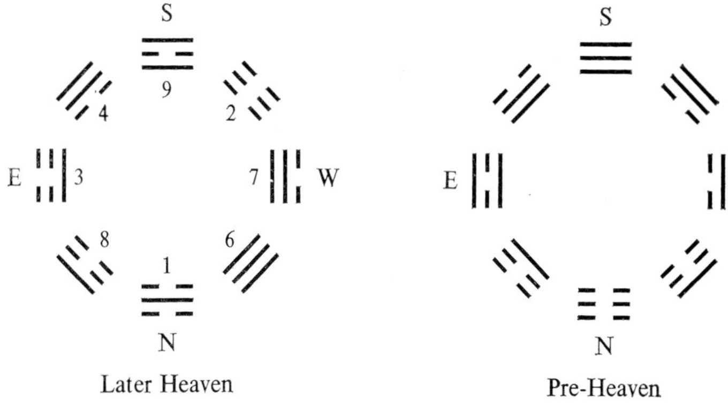

Figure 17. The Later Heaven and Pre-Heaven sequences

The Ho Map shows that wood is represented by 3 and 8; metal by 4 and 9; and earth by 5 and 10. Using these numbers 3 is assigned to the wood pattern, 4 to the metal pattern and 5 to the earth pattern. However, for water and fire the numbers are not derived from the Ho Map but by a combination of Later Heaven and Pre-Heaven trigram arrangements.

133

In the Pre-Heaven sequence shown in Figure 17 one can see that ☰ is in the south while in the Later Heaven diagram it is fire ☲ which is in the south. In the Later Heaven the number of ☰ is 6. By using the number of ☰ in the Later Heaven 6 becomes the number assigned to the fire pattern. Similarly, in the Pre-Heaven sequence, ☷ is in the north while in the Later Heaven ☵ water is in the north. The number of ☷ is 2 in the Later Heaven, so 2 is assigned to the water pattern. (Westerners may think this rather odd reasoning, but they should remember that the Chinese have found it acceptable for nearly 1,000 years.)

Ten-year cycles

When determining the ten-year influence one must first ascertain to which pattern the individual belongs and proceed from that point. For the water 2 pattern, the influence starts from age 2; for wood 3 pattern, at age 3; for metal 4 pattern, at age 4; for earth 5 pattern, at age 5 and for the fire 6 pattern, at age 6. An example is set out as Figure 18.

62-72 f	g	h	i
52-62 e	*Water 2 pattern* (Man born in positive year or woman born in negative year)		j
42-52 d		*Natal house* 2 yrs k	
32-42 c	22-32 b	12-22 a	2-12 l

f	66-76 g	56-66 h	46-56 i
e	*Fire 6 pattern* (Man born in negative year or woman born in positive year)		36-46 j
d			26-36 k
c	*Natal house* 6 yrs b	6-16 a	16-26 l

Figure 18. Establishing the ten-year cycle

Note:
(1) For a man born in a positive year and for a woman born in a negative year, the ten-year cycle goes clockwise.
(2) For a man born in a negative year and for a woman born in a positive year the ten-year cycle goes counter-clockwise.
(3) The natal house controls the years up to the pattern number.

Table 18   *Celestial Stems and their related years*

1900	G	1925	B	1950	G	1975	B
1901	H	1926	C	1951	H	1976	C
1902	I	1927	D	1952	I	1977	D
1903	J	1928	E	1953	J	1978	E
1904	A	1929	F	1954	A	1979	F
1905	B	1930	G	1955	B	1980	G
1906	C	1931	H	1956	C	1981	H
1907	D	1932	I	1957	D	1982	I
1908	E	1933	J	1958	E	1983	J
1909	F	1934	A	1959	F	1984	A
1910	G	1935	B	1960	G	1985	B
1911	H	1936	C	1961	H	1986	C
1912	I	1937	D	1962	I	1987	D
1913	J	1938	E	1963	J	1988	E
1914	A	1939	F	1964	A	1989	F
1915	B	1940	G	1965	B	1990	G
1916	C	1941	H	1966	C	1991	H
1917	D	1942	I	1967	D	1992	I
1918	E	1943	J	1968	E	1993	J
1919	F	1944	A	1969	F	1994	A
1920	G	1945	B	1970	G	1995	B
1921	H	1946	C	1971	H	1996	C
1922	I	1947	D	1972	I	1997	D
1923	J	1948	E	1973	J	1998	E
1924	A	1949	F	1974	A	1999	F

Step 4: The next step is to determine the element patterns by matching the Celestial Stem of the year of birth (see Table 18), with the Horary Branch of the natal house, as shown in Table 19.

Step 5: The position of Tzu Wei is determined by matching the element pattern with the lunar date of birth, using Table 20 to obtain the first, and the tables in Appendix B, 'The Lunar Calendar' (pp. 228–35) to establish the latter.

Table 19   *Element patterns*

Celestial Stem of year of birth	Horary Branch of natal house					
	a & b	c & d	e & f	g & h	i & j	k & l
A & F	water	fire	wood	earth	metal	fire
B & G	fire	earth	metal	wood	water	earth
C & H	earth	wood	water	metal	fire	wood
D & I	wood	metal	fire	water	earth	metal
E & J	metal	water	earth	fire	wood	water

It is no easy matter to convert solar calendar dates into lunar calendar dates, for no equivalents of the Chinese and Japanese 10,000 year calendars exist in English. It is for this reason that we have included the lunar calendar tables of Appendix B in this volume.

Table 20   *Position of Tzu Wei*

Lunar day of birth	Patterns				
	wood	fire	earth	metal	water
1	e	j	g	l	b
2	b	g	l	e	c
3	c	l	e	b	c
4	f	e	b	c	d
5	c	b	c	a	d
6	d	c	h	f	e
7	g	k	a	c	e
8	d	h	f	d	f
9	e	a	c	b	f
10	h	f	d	g	g
11	e	c	i	d	g
12	f	d	b	e	h
13	i	l	g	c	h
14	f	i	d	h	i
15	g	b	e	e	i

Table 20—*continued*

Lunar day			Patterns		
of birth	wood	fire	earth	metal	water
16	j	h	j	f	j
17	g	d	c	d	j
18	h	e	h	i	k
19	k	a	e	f	k
20	h	j	f	g	l
21	i	c	k	e	l
22	l	h	d	j	a
23	i	e	i	g	a
24	j	f	f	h	b
25	a	b	g	f	b
26	j	k	l	k	c
27	k	d	e	h	c
28	b	i	j	i	d
29	k	f	g	g	d
30	l	g	h	l	e

EXAMPLE:

Suppose that a person belongs to the earth pattern and that their lunar day of birth is 13 (i.e., the thirteenth day of the lunar month in question). Enter Table 20 and match day 13 to its corresponding pattern. You will find that in this case this is g. So write Tzu Wei in the g house of the chart.

Step 6: Ascertain the position of the other thirteen stars from Table 21. Tzu Wei is the Emperor of the Stars and all the others take their positions from his, in the order set out in that table. Insert the positions of these thirteen other stars in your horoscope chart.

Figure 19 shows a completed horoscope chart for a person born at 7.30 a.m. Standard Time on 1 November 1934, the lunar day of birth being the 25th. Prepare a chart for this person yourself and then check it against Figure 19.[1]

[1] For time conversions see footnote, p. 74.

Table 21 *Position of stars*

Star	Horary Branch occupied by *Tzu Wei*											
	a	b	c	d	e	f	g	h	i	j	k	l
Tien Chi	l	a	b	c	d	e	f	g	h	i	j	k
Sun	j	k	l	a	b	c	d	e	f	g	h	i
Wu Ch'u	i	j	k	l	a	b	c	d	e	f	g	h
Tien Tong	h	i	j	k	l	a	b	c	d	e	f	g
Dien Chung	e	f	g	h	i	j	k	l	a	b	c	d
Tien Hu	e	d	c	b	a	l	k	j	i	h	g	f
Moon	f	e	d	c	b	a	l	k	j	i	h	g
Tan Dang	g	f	e	d	c	b	a	l	k	j	i	h
Jiuh Men	h	g	f	e	d	c	b	a	l	k	j	i
Tien Siang	i	h	g	f	e	d	c	b	a	l	k	j
Tien Liang	j	i	h	g	f	e	d	c	b	a	l	k
Chi Sa	k	j	i	h	g	f	e	d	c	b	a	l
Po Chung	c	b	a	l	k	j	i	h	g	f	e	d

You will notice that in that particular chart there are no stars in the House of Parents or the House of Property. When this happens the procedure is as follows (but note that the complete Tzu Wei has sixty-three stars, so there are stars in all houses; the rules that follow therefore apply only to the simplified version of Tzu Wei):

(a) If there are no stars in the Natal House the stars of the House of Residence are assigned to the Natal House, and vice versa.

(b) If there are no stars in the House of Brothers, the stars in the House of Servants are assigned to the House of Brothers, and vice versa.

(c) If there are no stars in the House of Children the stars in the House of Property are assigned to the House of Children, and vice versa.

(d) If there are no stars in the House of Husband and Wife, the stars in the House of Position and Revenue are assigned to the House of Husband and Wife, and vice versa.

(e) If there are no stars in the House of Wealth, the stars in the House of Blessings and Virtues are assigned to this house, and vice versa.

(f) If there are no stars in the House of Sickness the stars in the House of Father and Mother are assigned to the House of Sickness, and vice versa.

So in Figure 19 one would write Tien Tong and Jiuh Men in the House of Parents, and Sun and Tien Liang in the House of Property.

Brothers	Natal	Father and Mother	Blessings and Virtues
Tien Chi	Tzu Wei		Po Chung
f	g	h	i
Husband and Wife			Property
Chi Sa			
e	7.30 a.m. Standard Time 1 November 1934 Earth pattern		j
Children			Position and Revenue
Sun Tien Liang			Tien Hu Dien Chung
d			k
Wealth	Sickness	Residence	Servants
Wu Ch'u Tien Siang	Tien Tong Jiuh Men	Tan Dang	Moon
c	b	a	l

Figure 19.   A Tzu Wei chart (simplified system)

THE MEANINGS OF THE TWELVE HOUSES
The meaning of the twelve houses is as follows:

The Natal House: One's general fortune, personality, talents, one's appearance, etc.

The House of Brothers: Determines the general fortune and tendencies of one's brothers and sisters; for instance, if a wealth star were in this house at least one of them would have wealth, etc. It also determines how many brother(s) there will be and if they will be helpful to oneself.

The House of Husband and Wife: Determines if the spouse will be a good or bad one, wise or stupid, helpful, wealthy, whether he/she have a pleasing personality, be attractive in appearance, ugly, and so on.

The House of Children: Indicates how many children there will be, their tendencies and natures, such as whether they will be good or bad, talented, whether they will give one filial love or not, etc.

The House of Wealth: Indicates how rich or poor one will be and how hard one needs to work in order to achieve material possessions.

The House of Sickness: Determines how healthy one will be, what sicknesses one will be subject to, whether or not one will be accident prone, etc.

The House of Residence: Indicates whether or not one will leave one's place of birth and establish oneself elsewhere, whether or not one will travel extensively, what one's general relations with society will be.

The House of Servants: Determines one's relationships with servants and subordinates; i.e., whether they will serve one well, be troublemakers, etc.

The House of Position and Revenue: Shows the probable occupation and level of remuneration.

The House of Property: Indicates the ownership of land, property, a home(s), buildings, etc., and whether these will be inherited, earned, lost or never attained.

The House of Blessings and Virtue: Determines how much one will enjoy or suffer in this life, one's chances of longevity, etc.

The House of Parents: Shows the relationship with parents and their general fate and their feelings towards oneself.

ASPECTS OF THE STARS

Stars exerting a good or bad influence

Each star has its own special character. They can be grouped into roughly three categories:

(1) Auspicious or good stars: Tzu Wei, Sun, Moon, Tien Tong, Tien Hu, Tien Siang and Tien Liang.

(2) Stars of middle character (i.e., those which are either mildly good, mildly bad or neutral in influence: Tien Chi and Wu Ch'u.

(3) (Generally) adverse stars: Dien Chung, Tang Dang, Jiuh Men, Chi Sa and Po Chung.

The influence of all the stars, whether good or bad, can vary according to the house in which they occur and the influence of other stars in the same house.

The stars and the Horary Branches

Whether or not a star can manifest its function fully depends on the house of the Horary Branch. If we consider the sun we know that the Horary Branches k, l, a and b represent 7 p.m.–3 a.m., the period during which the sun is normally below the horizon. Therefore, when the sun is in house k, l, a or b it is manifesting weak to zero. Table 22 shows the strength of the stars in various houses, S indicating that the influence is strong, M that the influence is mild, and W that the star's manifestation is weak.

Special considerations in relation to stars in houses

As we have already seen the stars are grouped into roughly three categories—as being auspicious, of middle character, or as adverse in influence. But there are exceptions to the general classification in the case of some stars. Those needing to know the exceptions for all stars will find the information in the Chinese sources. But, to give an example, the exceptions for Po Chung, for instance, are as follows:

(1) If Po Chung is in the House of Wealth and the Horary Branch is a, g, e or k, it becomes an auspicious star.

(2) Po Chung is a favourable star when it is in the House of Position and Revenue, regardless of the Horary Branch.

(3) If Po Chung is in the House of Servants and the Horary Branch is either a or g it is an auspicious star.

(4) If Po Chung is in the House of Property and the Horary Branch is a or g, it is a favourable star.

In all other cases Po Chung is inauspicious.

Table 22   *Influence of the stars according to house position*

| Star | Horary Branch of the house the star occupies | | | | | | | | | | | |
	a	b	c	d	e	f	g	h	i	j	k	l
Tzu Wei	M	S	S	S	M	S	M	S	S	M	M	S
Tien Chi	S	W	M	S	S	M	S	W	M	M	S	M
Sun	W	W	M	S	S	S	S	M	M	M	W	W
Wu Ch'U	S	S	M	M	M	M	M	S	M	M	S	M
Tien Tong	S	W	M	S	M	S	W	W	S	W	M	S
Dien Chung	W	M	S	M	M	W	M	M	S	M	M	W
Tien Hu	S	S	M	M	S	M	S	S	M	S	S	W
Moon	S	M	W	W	W	W	W	W	S	S	M	S
Tan Dang	S	M	M	M	S	W	S	S	W	W	S	W
Jiuh Men	S	S	M	M	M	M	S	M	S	S	M	S
Tien Siang	S	M	S	W	M	S	M	M	S	W	M	S
Tien Liang	S	S	M	M	S	W	S	S	W	M	M	W
Chi Sa	S	S	S	S	M	M	M	S	S	S	S	M
Po Chung	S	M	W	M	M	M	S	M	W	M	M	M

The influences of the stars in the different house positions

We think it will be helpful to the reader at this point if, by way of introducing him to the way in which house positions and stars interact, we show him the action of the different stars in one position. Their influence in the other eleven houses is set out on pp. 149–51.

Let us use the House of Servants and Subordinates as our example here:

Check the appropriate section of your horoscope chart. If the 'good' stars (i.e., Tzu Wei, Sun, Moon, Tien Tong, Tien Hu, Tien Siang or Tien Liang) are in the House, one will have good relationships with one's servants and subordinates; they will be co-operative and one's affairs will go smoothly. The individual knows how to command people and retain their respect.

If Tien Chi or Wu Ch'u are in this house one will not get spontaneous help from subordinates. Conversely, one will not have any great difficulty with them either.

If Dien Chung, Tang Dang, Jiuh Men or Po Chung are in this house subordinates and servants may try to harm him, take over his position, trap him, kill him or cheat him; they will co-operate reluctantly or may even deliberately slow down the pace of their work. (But note the exceptions listed for Po Chung above.)

Occupations

The occupations for which a person is likely to be most suited are determined by the star in the Natal House:

Tzu Wei	Politics, scholarship, the army (as an officer), business.
Tien Chi	Engineering and technical fields, scholarship, religion, writing.
Sun	Politics, scholarship, the arts, special enterprises.
Wu Ch'u	Engineering and technical fields, the army, the police, manufacturing enterprises.
Tien Tong	Medicine, scholarship, the arts, service.
Dien Chung	Politics, banking and financial enterprises, the army (as an officer), business.
Tien Hu	Politics, scholarship, religion, special enterprises.
Moon	The civil service, scholarship, religion, special enterprises.
Tang Dang	Engineering or technical fields, banking and financial enterprises, manufacturing, service.
Jiuh Men	Medicine, scholarship, religion, writing.
Tien Siang	Politics, scholarship, religion, service.
Tien Liang	Medicine, politics, religion, special enterprises.
Chi Sa	Engineering and technical fields, soldiering, the police, politics, general business.

Table 23 Compatibilities

Woman	TW	TC	Sun	WC	TT	DC	TH	Moon	TD	JM	TS	TL	CS	PC
Man														
TW	§§	†	†	†	*	†	*	†	=	*	*	†	*	=
TC	†	=	†	†	†	†	†	‡	‡	‡	‡	*	‡	‡
Sun	†	†	=	†	*	†	†	*	†	‡	†	‡	†	†
WC	†	†	†	=	†	†	*	†	*	†	*	†	*	=
TT	†	†	‡	‡	=	†	‡	‡	‡	=	†	‡	†	†
DC	§	§	§	†	§	=	*	§	=	§	=	†	*	=
TH	†	†	†	*	†	*	=	†	†	†	†	‡	†	†
Moon	†	‡	§	†	‡	§	‡	=	‡	†	†	§	†	†
TD	=	§	§	*	§	=	†	§	=	§	§	†	§	§
JM	§	‡	=	‡	=	‡	§	§	§	=	§	†	§	§
TS	‡	†	†	*	†	†	†	†	†	†	=	§	†	†
TL	†	‡	†	†	‡	†	†	†	†	†	†	=	†	‡
CS	‡	§	§	†	§	*	§	‡	§	§	§	§	=	§
PC	=	§	§	=	§	=	§	‡	§	§	§	§	§	=

The names of stars are abbreviated as follows in the above table:

TW — Tzu Wei	TC — Tien Chi	WC — Wu Ch'iu	TT — Tien Tong
DC — Dien Chung	TH — Tien Hu	TD — Tang Dang	JM — Jiuh Men
TS — Tien Siang	TL — Tien Liang	CS — Chi Sa	

144

Po Chung   Engineering and technical fields, manufacturing industries, business, writing.

Marriage compatibilities

Since the stars in one's Natal House express one's personality and character, a comparison of the stars in the man's and the woman's Natal Houses will indicate the degree of compatibility one may expect.

In Table 23 the following symbols are used to express the degree of compatibility:

* Greatest compatibility   † Better than average
‡ Average, i.e., sometimes good; sometimes bad.
§ Below average || Least compatibility

YEARLY CYCLES

The yearly cycles are determined by the Horary Branch of the year of birth. For those born in an i, a, or e year the k house will represent the first year of life; for those born in a c, g or k year it will be the e house; for those born in an l, d or h year it will be the b house; and for those born in an f, j, or b year it will be the h house. Once the starting point has been determined the cycles move in a clockwise direction for men and counter-clockwise for women. The yearly cycle houses are tabulated in Table 24.

EXAMPLE:

A man is born in a c year, his yearly cycle prediction for year of life 26 (i.e., the year in which he will be twenty-five to twenty-six years old) will therefore be determined by the stars in his f house.

It should be pointed out here that for the complete Tzu Wei a different set of rules apply for the first six years in the life of a child, after which the information given in Table 24 is applicable.

YEARLY PREDICTIONS

While the complete Tzu Wei takes into account the influence of the Ten-Year Cycle and the Horary Branch of the year involved, the simplified version uses only the information set out in Table

Table 24 *Yearly cycle houses*

Year of life	Horary Branch of year							
	Man				Woman			
	i	c	l	f	i	c	l	f
	a	g	d	j	a	g	d	j
	e	k	h	b	e	k	h	b
1, 13, 25, 37, 49, 61, 73	k	e	b	h	k	e	b	h
2, 14, 26, 38, 50, 62, 74	l	f	c	i	j	d	a	g
3, 15, 27, 39, 51, 63, 75	a	g	d	j	i	c	l	f
4, 16, 28, 40, 52, 64, 76	b	h	e	k	h	b	k	e
5, 17, 29, 41, 53, 65, 77	c	i	f	l	g	a	j	d
6, 18, 30, 42, 54, 66, 78	d	j	g	a	f	l	i	c
7, 19, 31, 43, 55, 67, 79	e	k	h	b	e	k	h	b
8, 20, 32, 44, 56, 68, 80	f	l	i	c	d	j	g	a
9, 21, 33, 45, 57, 69, 81	g	a	j	d	c	i	f	l
10, 22, 34, 46, 58, 70, 82	h	b	k	e	b	h	e	k
11, 23, 35, 47, 59, 71, 83	i	c	l	f	a	g	d	j
12, 24, 36, 48, 60, 72, 84	j	d	a	g	l	f	c	i

24. Keeping in mind that some aspects of the stars are good while others are malefic (see p. 141), the prediction related to each star is as follows:

Tzu Wei   Good fortune, promotion, good fortune in money and business matters.

Tien Chi   Good for taking examinations or engaging in research, the arts, literature, cultural matters and business. If the power of the star is strong it will be a joyful year; if weak, a sad year.

Sun   Auspicious for fame and money. Favourable for promotion, marriage or advancement. However, if the power of the sun is weak one may be forced to spend a considerable amount of money and also it would be best, in such a case, not to marry this year.

Wu Ch'u   Very auspicious for making or inheriting money and for material enjoyment. Should attain some degree of fame this year. If this star is weak or manifesting as a bad star, lawsuits are probable, as are losses of money, perhaps even severe debt.

Tien Tong   A very joyful event will occur within the family circle. One might marry, get a good job or make some other change for the better. It is propitious to start a new business or career this year. If the star is functioning as a bad star the family fortune will decline.

Dien Chung   Be cautious regarding any signs of disease or injuries. One's life may even be at risk. If a woman gives birth to a baby this could be difficult, even dangerous. If this star is manifesting as a good star one will have an increase in salary and perhaps even promotion.

Tien Hu   This will be an auspicious and good year. Everything will go smoothly.

Moon   One will experience romantic love. Property and estate holdings are likely to increase. If the star is functioning adversely one could be hurt by love. One should not buy real estate or lend money to others.

Tang Dang   One may be seduced by the opposite sex, losing one's virginity or money, or find oneself in a triangle situation. Women in labour will have difficult deliveries. If this star manifests as a good star, the person will make a lot of money or meet a very good lover. Do not marry this year. If a man does marry, among other hardships, his wife will wear the trousers.

Jiuh Men   Will become involved in disputes or lawsuits. If the star is manifesting as a good star, those who have not succeeded in the past will do so this year.

Tien Siang   Will have a rise in position or social status. If the star is manifesting as a bad star one might separate from one's spouse in one way or another or will experience a lowering in position or status.

Tien Liang   Will become a leader of something. If this star is

	functioning as a bad star unfortunate things will happen in the family.
Chi Sa	Everything tends to fail. Those who suffer from chronic diseases are likely to die. If this star is manifesting as a good star there will be a gain in fame or promotion.
Po Chung	One might get seriously hurt or have an operation this year. In general it is a year of bleeding. A man might conquer his wife. A woman in labour might have a hard delivery. If this star manifests auspiciously one will have unexpected good fortune.

THE FIVE ELEMENTS OF THE STARS

The elements corresponding to the stars are as follows:

1 Tzu Wei	—	earth	8 Moon	—	water
2 Tien Chi	—	wood	9 Tang Dang	—	wood
3 Sun	—	fire	10 Jiuh Men	—	earth
4 Wu Ch'u	—	metal	11 Tien Siang	—	water
5 Tien Tong	—	water	12 Tien Liang	—	earth
6 Dien Chung	—	fire	13 Chi Sa	—	metal
7 Tien Hu	—	earth	14 Po Chung	—	water

The houses have the element designations shown in Table 6 on p. 40.

There is an interaction between the stars and the houses. The rules given in Tables 1 and 2 apply here also. Thus, if a bad star is conquered by the house, it will not show the bad effect and might even end up having a good effect. Suppose that the adverse star Tang Dang (wood) is in an i or j house (both of which are metal); the star will be conquered and will not show its bad effect. If a good star is conquered by the house, it will not show its good effect; it might even show a bad effect.

There are interactions between the stars too. For example, if both the Sun (fire) and Chi Sa (metal) are in a d house (wood), the Sun will conquer Chi Sa, and the power of Chi Sa will become weak. Also, the power of the Sun becomes more powerful because the house d (wood) generates fire, which is the power of the Sun. In the interpretation of this example, the manifestations of the Sun should be given extra emphasis while those of Chi Sa may be considered as being without effect.

THE GENERAL DISPOSITION OF THE STARS
The general dispositions of the stars are characterized as follows:

Tzu Wei	The Emperor of the stars, nobleness, blessings of heaven, good fortune.
Tien Chi	The star of wisdom and cherishing goodness.
Sun	Brightness, love, generosity.
Wu Ch'u	Courage, soldierly virtue, wealth.
Tien Tong	Harmony, gentleness and modesty.
Dien Chung	Evil, depravity, vileness, cunning.
Tien Hu	Talent and mercy.
Moon	Grace, benevolence, cleverness and purity.
Tan Dang	Desire, deceitfulness.
Jiuh Men	Disputes, suspicion and dishonesty.
Tien Siang	Honesty, peacefulness and helpfulness to others.
Tien Liang	Constancy and leadership.
Chi Sa	Stubbornness and obstinacy.
Po Chung	Damage, ruin, exhaustion.

THE INFLUENCE OF THE STARS IN THE DIFFERENT HOUSE POSITIONS
This section develops the introductory passage on pp. 142–63, in which the action of the different stars in the House of Servants and Subordinates was discussed.

1   House of Husband and Wife

Tzu Wei	If a man has this star in the House of Husband and Wife he will marry a good wife who also will be a good mother to their children. If a woman has this star, she'll be a good wife and very helpful to her husband.
Tien Chi	A man will marry a woman five or more years younger than himself who will be stubborn and give him considerable trouble. A woman will marry an older husband who will be intellectual.

	If Tien Chi and Tien Liang are both in this house, a man will marry an older wife. If Tien Chi and the Moon are both in this house, the wife will be pretty and helpful.
Sun	For a man, if the power of the Sun is strong he will marry late. If a couple marry at a young age, the husband will conquer the wife. Generally auspicious for marriage.
Wu Ch'u	The spouse will be a stubborn and quick-tempered person, the couple will experience much disharmony. If marriage is deferred to a late age this can be avoided. It is best to marry a spouse of the same age. The women will have noble husbands.
Tien Tong	Both the man and the woman will have a good spouse, and they will help each other. There is a tendency to marry early but it would be better to marry a little later than normal.
Dien Chung	Will separate from spouse or spouse will die first. Will marry several times (probably three times). In general this is a bad star for marriage.
Tien Hu	Similar to Tien Tong.
Moon	Indicative of good marriage. If both sun and moon are in this house it will be a perfect marriage.
Tan Dang	Will separate from spouses and marry three times. Best marriage will occur late in life.
Jiuh Men	Will have disputes and troubles because of spouse. However, if the sun is also in this house, the couple will live harmoniously together. If Tien Chi is with Jiuh Men the man will get a pretty and helpful wife; the woman will marry a good husband.
Tien Siang	Auspicious for marriage. The man will marry a good and beautiful woman; the woman will marry a wise and noble husband.
Tien Liang	The spouse will tend to dominate the family, but it will be a good marriage otherwise. The men are likely to marry very beautiful women.
Chi Sa	Will dominate and conquer the spouse and separate. Only by marrying at a very late age can this be avoided.

Po Chung	Cannot get help from spouse. Will separate. A late marriage can probably avoid many of the troubles which will occur in an early marriage.

Note: Remember that the manner in which a star manifests itself and the effect each star produces depends on the interaction between the stars themselves and between the star and the house.

2   House of children

Tzu Wei	If the power of this star is strong, will have three boys and two girls.
Tien Chi	If the power of the star is strong will have two children. May also adopt children or acquire children as a result of a spouse's earlier marriage. Some may even have an illegitimate child.
Sun	If the power of the sun is strong will have three boys and two girls. If the power of the sun is weak will have fewer children and the children will tend to leave home early.
Wu Ch'u	Will have one or two children. Will have help from any adopted children.
Tien Tong	If the power of the star is strong will have five wise and noble children but a lesser number if the power of the star is weak.
Dien Chung	Will have one bad child. However if Tien Hu is also in this house will have three good children. If any other bad star is in the house, will not have any children.
Tien Hu	Will have five children, some of whom will be very talented.
Moon	If the power of the moon is strong will have three girls and two boys. If the power is weak will have fewer children and they will not be helpful.
Tan Dang	Will have three or four children if the power is strong but only one if the star is weak and none of the children will be helpful.
Jiuh Men	If the power of the star is strong will have two children and they will be hard to rear at first but will improve later. If the sun is also in this house

	will have one or two children and they will be easy to rear.
Tien Siang	Will have two children who will have very auspicious lives.
Tien Liang	The first child will be a girl. Will have two children if the power of this star is strong.
Chi Sa	Will probably have no children but if the couple do have one it will be a boy who will be a difficult child in many respects, perhaps even denying his parentage and foregoing his heritage.
Po Chung	If the power of this star is strong will have three stubborn children, one or more of whom will squander the family money. However, if Tzu Wei is also in this house, will have three children all of whom will be noble and good.

3   House of wealth

Tzu Wei	Will have abundant funds throughout life.
Tien Chi	It will not be easy for these individuals to make a lot of money in life; at best, hard work will result in modest accumulations.
Sun	If the power of the sun is strong will have abundant funds throughout life. If the power is weak can accumulate a small fortune only and then only by continual hard and strenuous effort.
Wu Ch'u	Will be rich in life. If the star is weak will either lose or spend all the money he can make.
Tien Tong	Will make a fortune in middle or old age. This is built up slowly by dint of hard effort. If the star is weak will lose most of what he makes.
Dien Chung	If the star is in a c or i house will make a huge fortune. If the star is weak will have difficulties in connection with money early in life, but the situation will gradually improve.
Tien Hu	One will have considerable amounts of money and perhaps even own land and houses; but one's fortunes will fluctuate.
Moon	In general will have ample amounts of money. If the moon is weak will have very few resources.

Tan Dang	If the star is strong will have a windfall. If the star is weak the person will be poor and remain poor.
Jiuh Men	Individuals here become rich by dint of hard effort; however, if they are too ambitious they may suddenly lose what they make.
Tien Siang	Will have a very comfortable income and perhaps even be or become rich.
Tien Liang	Will be rich and noble. If the star is weak will have a small fortune only and this has to be earned by hard work.
Chi Sa	Can make only a small fortune and that by being industrious and frugal.
Po Chung	If this star is in an a, g, e or k house the individual will be rich. If the star is weak one will never accumulate money; instead, one will spend any money, whether inherited or accumulated, very quickly.

4 House of sickness

Tzu Wei	Will have little sickness and few accidents in life. Any illness will be cured quickly and easily. The most likely disorders are those of the spleen, stomach, and those relating to cold, heat, the olfactory organs and vomiting.
Tien Chi	Will suffer more than normal from childhood diseases. Sicknesses at all ages will be related to the liver, gall, restlessness, convulsions from fear, chest pains, headaches and for women, irregular menses.
Sun	Will be subject to considerable heart trouble and colds, will be quick-tempered and the large intestine will tend to be too dry. If the sun is weak may suffer from eye troubles as well.
Wu Ch'u	During childhood this person's hands, feet or face may easily suffer injury. May develop TB, and suffer from vomiting or nose troubles.
Tien Tong	Will be generally healthy. Sicknesses will be related to the nervous system or the cold virus.
Dien Chung	These people's physical defences will not be

	strong. A tendency to suffer from eye diseases, a rapid pulse, colds, asthma, diseases of the sex organs, nymphomania or satyriasis, irregular menses and a general condition of low vitality. Scarring can be a further source of trouble.
Tien Hu	Will be healthy and have few illnesses in life. Might possibly suffer at some time from stomach trouble, beri-beri, dropsical swelling or numbness.
Moon	If the moon is strong will have very few illnesses. If it is weak, however, will tend to have much difficulty, mainly of a minor nature, such as neurasthenia, catarrh problems, some nervousness (in some women it may verge on hysteria) or minor respiratory ailments.
Jiuh Men	Will be subject to disorders of the spleen, stomach, skin, chest, lungs and breathing system. Will have inflammatory and blood troubles in childhood.
Tien Siang	In general will have little sickness and will be quite healthy. If this star is weak may suffer from skin diseases, jaundice, imbalances in the composition of the blood and lowered energy levels. Will have a tendency to develop bladder troubles, diabetes, gonorrhoea and similar ailments.
Tien Liang	Will have few illnesses. Such ailments as do occur are likely to relate to stomach disease, disease of the liver, poor appetite and indigestion.
Chi Sa	Is likely to have a lot of trouble in childhood. After maturity will be vulnerable to haemorrhoids and heart and lung diseases.
Po Chung	In general will have poor health. May have ulcers, inflammatory complaints, blood diseases and worm infestations in childhood. The lower part of the body will easily feel the cold, and the person with this star in the House of Health may experience frequent spermatorrhoea and be subject to ailments caused by high humidity, such as rashes, pustules, rheumatism, athlete's foot; women may be subject to irregular menses and leucorrhoea.
Tan Dang	If this star is alone in its house and its power is

strong these people will have few accidents or sickness. If the star is weak, however, they will have disorders of the feet and loins. The primary sicknesses related to this star are those associated with the lungs, stomach and the intestines, and the individual will easily feel the cold.

5 House of residence

Tzu Wei	Will travel quite a lot. Will get help from people of rank and status and have a good career.
Tien Chi	It is best to leave one's family and seek one's personal development elsewhere. If one stays at home or remains in one's native town one will have many disputes.
Sun	Will go forth into the world and develop and apply his abilities in a good career. Very ambitious. Will get much help from seniors.
Moon	If this star is strong can go out and develop a new career. If the star is weak it is better to stay with the family enterprise, for if one branches out alone, one will experience many hardships without much gain.
Wu Ch'u	Will always be busy. Dislikes being quiet. Inactivity can be ruinous to these people. Will travel much.
Tien Tong	Will travel much and will get help from others when he is away from his childhood home area.
Dien Chung	If he leaves his childhood home area he will have a good career; otherwise little or no progress.
Tien Hu	Will travel a great deal and get help from influential persons.
Tan Dang	Will leave his childhood home area. Will experience many difficulties in life.
Jiuh Men	Restless. Tends to branch out on his own. Will have an unstable life.
Tien Siang	Will travel a great deal and will be helped by influential persons.
Tien Liang	Will be successful and travel or move house with moderate frequency.

Chi Sa	Will tend to get away from the area in which he grew up and make his way alone. Whether or not it will be auspicious for him to do so will depend on other stars in this house.
Po Chung	If the star is strong he will put down roots away from his childhood home area, either with the same country or abroad. If the star is weak it is best for him to stay near his place of birth.

6   House of position and revenue

Tzu Wei	A high and honourable position can be expected.
Tien Chi	If this star is strong will have a high position; if it is weak he will have a low position.
Sun	Will attain a high position and fame. However, if the sun is weak he cannot expect a good career.
Wu Ch'u	It is auspicious to become a government administrator or military officer.
Tien Tong	If the star is strong will rise to a high position. If the star is weak will achieve only a low position.
Dien Chung	A military position is most suitable. If Tzu Wei is in this house also, a non-military position would be better.
Tien Hu	If the star is strong will attain a high position. If the star is weak will make a living by writing and will gain fame later.
Moon	If the moon is strong will have a good and fortunate career. If the moon is weak will never attain a high position and will change employment frequently.
Tan Dang	If the star is strong will attain a high position. If the star is weak probably will become a corrupt official.
Jiuh Men	If the star is strong will gain power and honour through a respected official position. If the sun is also in this house, there will be several changes of career. If the star is weak he will never rise high.
Tien Siang	If the star is strong will have a high, well remunerated position. If the star is weak he will suffer several fluctuations in his fortunes. If the

stars Wu Ch'u or Dien Chung are also in this house, he will have a good career in a country other than that of his birth.

Tien Liang	Will attain a high position and abundant income.
Chi Sa	Can have a good career in a military or government position.
Po Chung	In general will usually have to endure hard times and difficulties until middle age, when he will gain position and fame. A governmental position is more suitable than any other.

7 House of property

Tzu Wei	Will have a great deal of property.
Tien Chi	Tends to leave ancestor's estate and establish an estate of his own. He will experience some losses and gains in the process. If the star is weak he will not acquire property.
Sun	If the sun is strong he will inherit some estate and hold on to or even increase his inheritance. If the sun is weak he will not acquire property.
Wu Ch'u	Might inherit land or property. Will have some gains in property even if the star is weak.
Tien Tong	Will have few assets during the early periods of his life but will have many at a later age.
Dien Chung	Will lose all his inheritance, if any. However, if Chi Sa is also in this house he can acquire property through his own efforts.
Tien Hu	Will have several estates and considerable property and his family will flourish.
Moon	If the moon is strong will have many assets. If the moon is weak he will have neither estate nor property.
Tan Dang	If the star is strong will inherit an ancestor's estate and also acquire a new estate in his middle age. If the star is weak, no estate.
Jiuh Men	If the star is strong will have a lot of property. If the star is weak will be plagued by disputes related to property or estates (resulting even in lawsuits).

Tien Siang	Will acquire new estates.
Tien Liang	Will inherit an ancestor's estates and increase them.
Chi Sa	If another good star is also in this house he will acquire estates. If he has a bad star in the house he will probably lose all his acquisitions.
Po Chung	If this star is in an a or g house he will inherit an estate and it will flourish; otherwise no substantial acquisitions.

8 House of blessings and virtues

Tzu Wei	Will have a fortunate and enjoyable life. If the star is strong may live beyond the age of eighty.
Tien Chi	Will have many early hardships and then later an enjoyable life. If he reaches middle age he can expect to live to about sixty-two.
Sun	Will have an enjoyable and happy life and may live to be over seventy.
Wu Ch'u	For the most part, will have a hard life with few real enjoyments.
Tien Tong	Will have a long and generally happy life.
Dien Chung	Will experience mostly the hardships of life.
Tien Hu	Will have a consistent, fortunate, and stable life probably living beyond the age of eighty.
Moon	Life will be fortunate and full of honour and virtue. He will live into his seventies.
Tien Siang	Will have a fortunate and enjoyable life living into his seventies.
Tien Liang	The length of life is hard to determine. Could die young. If he has a long life, however, the later years will be rich and rewarding.
Jiuh Men	Will endure much hardship. However, if the star is strong, can have a noble life and live into his seventies.
Tan Dang	Will have an unstable and short life full of hardships.
Chi Sa	If the star is strong will have a fortunate and long life. If the star is weak will have many hardships

and only live to about the age of fifty. A woman who has this as the only star in her house will be a prostitute.

Po Chung   Will suffer many hardships and enjoy only a few pleasures in life. If the star is strong will have a long life; otherwise it will be short.

9   House of father and mother

Tzu Wei   Has rich and noble parents. No conflict with parents.

Tien Chi   If the star is strong will be born into a rich family. If the star is weak will be born into a poor family, have a concubine for a mother or may even be illegitimate.

Sun   If the sun is strong will be born into a rich and noble family. If the sun is weak will be born into an ordinary family. Will be separated early from the father, perhaps as a result of the father's death; will then dominate the mother.

Wu Ch'u   Will separate from his family early. Will derive few benefits from his parents.

Tien Tong   Will have a harmonious relationship with his parents and even receive some material benefits from them.

Dien Chung   Will separate from his parents early, perhaps even being adopted into another family or else lead a life of solitude.

Tien Hu   Will have good parents and receive benefits from them.

Moon   Will be born into a peaceful family and receive many benefits from his parents.

Tan Dang   Will have only one parent living. If the star is weak will probably have a foster-parent or step-father or step-mother.

Jiuh Men   One of his parents will leave the family or die early; otherwise this child might die before its parents. If the child is adopted, this can be avoided. If the star is weak the child will leave the family early.

Tien Siang	His parents will live long and he will receive much benefit from them.
Tien Liang	Will have good parents and receive much help from them. If the star is weak, might leave his parents early.
Po Chung	Will dominate his parents early in life. If he is reared by another family this can be avoided.
Chi Sa	Will separate from his parents and relatives early and lead a solitary life.

10   House of brothers (sisters)

Tzu Wei	Will have elder siblings from whom he receives help.
Tien Chi	Will have one or two siblings. If this star is weak he will not get on well with them.
Sun	If the sun is strong will have three siblings. If the moon is also in this house, then he will have four to five siblings. There will be harmony if the sun is strong; otherwise there will be disharmony.
Wu Ch'u	If this star is strong two siblings; otherwise one or none.
Tien Tong	If the star is strong, four to five siblings. If the star is weak two siblings.
Dien Chung	Generally two siblings. If Tan Dang is also in this house great animosity will exist between them. If Chi Sa is in this house as well, then he will have either no siblings or only one.
Tien Hu	Generally five siblings. If Chi Sa or Wu Ch'u is also in this house considerable antagonism will exist between them.
Moon	If the moon is strong, will have five siblings. If Tien Chi is also in this house then only two. If the moon is weak will not get the usual help from siblings and perhaps there will not be as many.
Tan Dang	Generally two siblings. If the star is weak will separate and go his own way early in life.
Jiuh Men	Generally will have two siblings, with whom he will not get on well.
Tien Siang	Will have two or three siblings, with whom he

will get on well unless Chi Sa is also in the house, in which case disharmony will exist.

Tien Liang	If the star is strong, will have two siblings, and the relationship between them will be harmonious. If there are more than two then disharmony will prevail. If the star is weak he will be an only child.
Chi Sa	If this is an a, g, c, or i house will have three siblings and will not get on well with them; in other cases, few or none.
Po Chung	If the star is strong there will be four siblings. If the star is weak there will be fewer, even none. The siblings will be somewhat antagonistic towards one another.

11 Natal house

Tzu Wei	Will be talented, rise rapidly and be successful. A woman with this star in the Natal house will be a good wife and mother whose husband attains a high position.
Tien Chi	Will be intellectual, yet have much common-sense; quick tempered.
Sun	Will be quick of mind, dignified and broad-minded. Will achieve wealth and fame. However, if the sun is weak, will have little dignity and a short life.
Wu Ch'u	Will have singleness of purpose and be a man of decision. Will be small in stature but have a resounding voice. Quick-tempered, easy to anger and likes to finish everything quickly. Not suited to the arts or an academic career. A military or business career is more appropriate.
Tien Tong	Will be clever, gentle and diplomatic. Will be flexible and adaptable, learning many things; but will not become a real expert in anything. Will enjoy a generally favourable and fortunate life.
Dien Chung	Will be honest, forthright and outspoken, but never see the necessity of sometimes hiding his thoughts. Can master only one field since he is

not versatile and is undiplomatic. If the star is strong he is suited to become a government administrator or military officer and will be successful in such a career. If the star is weak he will leave his family and lead a solitary life.

Tien Hu — Will be somewhat portly, round-faced, but otherwise good-looking with clear features. Will be clever, quick-minded and learn things well. Adaptable, and can make the adjustments that a situation may demand of him.

Moon — Will be gentle, handsome, merciful and attractive. If the moon is strong will have tremendous ability and be very successful. If the moon is weak will be poor for most of the time and have a short life.

Tan Dang — Will have an unstable personality and be stubborn, as well as having a quick temper. Strongly sexed and will have an insatiable propensity to gamble. If the star is in a b, e, h or k house his life could be auspicious. If the star is weak he will always be poor and will probably live a life of solitude.

Jiuh Men — If the star is strong will have a stable nature and be talented mentally and physically. Will rise high in life. If the star is weak he will be over-suspicious, find it hard to make decisions, be unable to learn well and will be difficult to get along with, and will therefore have an inauspicious life.

Tien Siang — Will be cultivated, gentle, peaceful, noble in appearance, clever and know how to deal with and command others. Will have a rich and rewarding life.

Tien Liang — Will be dignified, clever, charming, unselfish and constantly striving to help others. Will have a long, healthy and fruitful life.

Chi Sa — Will be a difficult person—rash, impatient, of unpredictable temper, selfish, loving to win and hating to lose. If the star is strong will be good at scheming and planning, and will keep his faults

in the background and have a good life. If the star
is weak he will be poor and have a short life.

Po Chung   Will be self-centred, stubborn and argumentative.
Will often indulge in speculative ventures and
takes advantage of what he thinks are good oppor-
tunities. Tends to stake all on a single throw of
the dice. Will have great fluctuations in life.

12   House of subordinates

(See pp. 142–3.)

Astrology of the I Ching

I INTRODUCTION

A variation in the interpretation of the basic *I Ching* text and
lines produces the Astrology of the I Ching. The same original
classical Chinese texts and lines are used except that the explanations are slanted towards astrological meanings rather than
philosophical, medical, religious, divination, geomancy or other
purposes. This is predicated on the concept that *I Ching* describes
the evolution of the world and encompasses everything in and of
the world. This makes an astrology derived from it not only possible but inevitable. What is different is the method of arriving
at the predictions.

As with the other astrologies related to the *I Ching* this
astrology converts the year, month, date and hour of birth into
Celestial Stem and Horary Branch symbols. As the reader will
now know from reading other sections of this work, these have
numerical values based on the Ho and Lo Maps combined with
the Earlier and Later Heaven sequences (Figures 5, 6, 8 and 9).
After obtaining and summarizing the positive and negative numbers, one enters a specific table and selects a trigram for each of
the two totals. Combining these trigrams in accordance with
specific rules establishes a basic natal hexagram from which predictions are made. Further mathematical procedures allow one to
progress to yearly and daily predictions. The astrological year is
from winter solstice to winter solstice.

II   METHOD OF CALCULATION

Step 1: Determine the sidereal time of birth. Use the method described on p. 150 for Tzu Wei Astrology.

Step 2: Select the yearly and daily cycle values from Table 25.

Table 25   *Yearly and daily cycle values*

Year	Yearly cycle	Daily cycle	Year	Yearly cycle	Daily cycle	Year	Yearly cycle	Daily cycle
1900:	37	11	1901:	38	16	1902:	39	21
1903:	40	26	1904:	41	31	1905:	42	37
1906:	43	42	1907:	44	47	1908:	45	52
1909:	46	58	1910:	47	3	1911:	48	8
1912:	49	13	1913:	50	19	1914:	51	24
1915:	52	29	1916:	53	34	1917:	54	40
1918:	55	45	1919:	56	50	1920:	57	55
1921:	58	1	1922:	59	6	1923:	60	11
1924:	1	16	1925:	2	22	1926:	3	27
1927:	4	32	1928:	5	37	1929:	6	43
1930:	7	48	1931:	8	53	1932:	9	58
1933:	10	4	1934:	11	9	1935:	12	14
1936:	13	19	1937:	14	25	1938:	15	30
1939:	16	35	1940:	17	40	1941:	18	46
1942:	19	51	1943:	20	56	1944:	21	1
1945:	22	7	1946:	23	12	1947:	24	17
1948:	25	22	1949:	26	28	1950:	27	33
1951:	28	38	1952:	29	43	1953:	30	49
1954:	31	54	1955:	32	59	1956:	33	4
1957:	34	10	1958:	35	15	1959:	36	20
1960:	37	25	1961:	38	31	1962:	39	36
1963:	40	41	1964:	41	46	1965:	42	52
1966:	43	57	1967:	44	2	1968:	45	7
1969:	46	13	1970:	47	18	1971:	48	23
1972:	49	28	1973:	50	34	1974:	51	39

Table 25—*continued*

Year	Yearly cycle	Daily cycle	Year	Yearly cycle	Daily cycle	Year	Yearly cycle	Daily cycle
1975:	52	44	1976:	53	49	1977:	54	55
1978:	55	60	1979:	56	5	1980:	57	10
1981:	58	16	1982:	59	21	1983:	60	26
1984:	1	31	1985:	2	37	1986:	3	42
1987:	4	47	1988:	5	52	1989:	6	58
1990:	7	3	1991:	8	8	1992:	9	13
1993:	10	19	1994:	11	24	1995:	12	29
1996:	13	34	1997:	14	40	1998:	15	45
1999:	16	50	2000:	17	55	2001:	18	1

Step 3: Select the symbolic combination for the yearly number by entering Table 9 on p. 45.

EXAMPLE:

Year of birth 1941

From the Table 25 (see Step 2) one finds that the yearly cycle is 18.

The symbol for 18 in Table 9 is Hf−.

Note the symbol Hf− for future reference (H is the Celestial Stem; f is the Horary Branch; − indicates that the year is a negative one).

Step 4: Select the monthly symbol by entering Table 11 on p. 46 with the Celestial Stem determined in Step 3 and the date of birth.

EXAMPLE:

5 October 1941

In Step 3 we found that the Celestial Stem symbol for 1941 was H.

Under column H in Table 11, beside the dates 8 September–7 October we find the symbol Dj.

Note Dj for later use.

Step 5: Determine the daily cycle symbol.

Since the symbols are based on the sexagenary cycles each

Table 12   *Daily cycle values (repeated)*

Day	1	2	3	4	5	6	7	8	9	10	11	12	13	14	15
Month															
Jan.	0	1	2	3	4	5	6	7	8	9	10	11	12	13	14
Feb.	31	32	33	34	35	36	37	38	39	40	41	42	43	44	45
*Mar.	59	60	1	2	3	4	5	6	7	8	9	10	11	12	13
*Apr.	30	31	32	33	34	35	36	37	38	39	40	41	42	43	44
*May	60	1	2	3	4	5	6	7	8	9	10	11	12	13	14
*June	31	32	33	34	35	36	37	38	39	40	41	42	43	44	45
*July	1	2	3	4	5	6	7	8	9	10	11	12	13	14	15
*Aug.	32	33	34	35	36	37	38	39	40	41	42	43	44	45	46
*Sept.	3	4	5	6	7	8	9	10	11	12	13	14	15	16	17
*Oct.	33	34	35	36	37	38	39	40	41	42	43	44	45	46	47
*Nov.	4	5	6	7	8	9	10	11	12	13	14	15	16	17	18
*Dec.	34	35	36	37	38	39	40	41	42	43	44	45	46	47	48

Day	16	17	18	19	20	21	22	23	24	25	26	27	28	29	30	31
Month																
Jan.	15	16	17	18	19	20	21	22	23	24	25	26	27	28	29	30
Feb.	46	47	48	49	50	51	52	53	54	55	56	57	58			
*Mar.	14	15	16	17	18	19	20	21	22	23	24	25	26	27	28	29
*Apr.	45	46	47	48	49	50	51	52	53	54	55	56	57	58	59	
*May	15	16	17	18	19	20	21	22	23	24	25	26	27	28	29	30
*June	46	47	48	49	50	51	52	53	54	55	56	57	58	59	60	
*July	16	17	18	19	20	21	22	23	24	25	26	27	28	29	30	31
*Aug.	47	48	49	50	51	52	53	54	55	56	57	58	59	60	1	2
*Sept.	18	19	20	21	22	23	24	25	26	27	28	29	30	31	32	
*Oct.	48	49	50	51	52	53	54	55	56	57	58	59	60	1	2	3
*Nov.	19	20	21	22	23	24	25	26	27	28	29	30	31	32	33	
*Dec.	49	50	51	52	53	54	55	56	57	58	59	60	1	2	3	4

* Add one day during leap years.

calendar year has a value and each day of the month has another value. By determining these and combining them we can arrive at the appropriate daily value symbol. So add the daily cycle value found in Step 2 to the daily cycle value given for the date in question in Table 12, which is repeated here for the convenience of the reader. If the total adds up to more than 60 subtract 60. Enter Table 9 with a value between 1 and 60 and select the symbol for that number. This is the daily cycle symbol.

EXAMPLE:

    5 October 1941

    Step 2 gave us 1941 daily cycle value as   46

    Table 12 shows the 5 October value as   37

                                   Total   85

Since 85 is over 60 subtract 60 and we have a remainder of 25. Table 9 shows that for 25 the symbol is Ck.

Note Ck for future use.

Step 6: Enter Table 26 with the hour of birth and the Celestial

Table 26   *Hourly Celestial Stems and Horary Branches*

Exact Time	Daily Celestial Stem				
	A & F	B & G	C & H	D & I	E & J
Midnight–1 a.m.	Aa	Ca	Ea	Ga	Ia
1 a.m.– 3 a.m.	Bb	Db	Fb	Hb	Jb
3 a.m.– 5 a.m.	Cc	Ec	Gc	Ic	Ac
5 a.m.– 7 a.m.	Dd	Fd	Hd	Jd	Bd
7 a.m.– 9 a.m.	Ee	Ge	Ie	Ae	Ce
9 a.m.–11 a.m.	Ff	Hf	Jf	Bf	Df
11 a.m.– 1 p.m.	Gg	Ig	Ag	Cg	Eg
1 p.m.– 3 p.m.	Hh	Jh	Bh	Dh	Fh
3 p.m.– 5 p.m.	Ii	Ai	Ci	Ei	Gi
5 p.m.– 7 p.m.	Jj	Bj	Dj	Fj	Hj
7 p.m.– 9 p.m.	Ak	Ck	Ek	Gk	Ik
9 p.m.–11 p.m.	Bl	Dl	Fl	Hl	Jl
11 p.m.–midnight	Ca	Ea	Ga	Ia	Aa

Stem symbol found in Step 5 and pick out the symbol for the hour of birth.

EXAMPLE:

 5 October 1941, 05.45 a.m.

 Symbol found in Step 5 is Ck.

 C is the daily Celestial Stem.

 Below C in Table 26 and across from 05.45 a.m. we find the symbol Hd.

 Note Hd for future use.

Step 7: Convert the symbols into numerical values, using Table 3 (p. 22) and the following values:

Wood		Fire		Earth		Metal		Water	
A+	B−	C+	D−	E+	F−	G+	H−	I+	J−
6	2	8	7	1	9	3	4	6	2

EXAMPLE:

 The date in question is 5 October 1941

The year 1941	= •Hf	=	4, 2, 7
The month (8 September–7 October)	= Dj	=	7, 4, 9
The day 5 October	= Ck	=	8, 5, 10
The time 05.45 a.m.	= Hd	=	4, 3, 8

 The sum of the odd numbers is 31. This is the Heavenly number.

 The sum of the even numbers is 40. This is the Earthly number.

Step 8: Enter Table 27 with the Heavenly number obtained in Step 7.

Step 8a: Enter Table 28 with the Earthly number obtained in Step 7.

Step 9: The combination of Heavenly and Earthly trigrams obtained in Step 8 will determine the natal hexagram. Which of the trigrams will be the upper trigram and which the lower one is determined on the following basis:

For Men: For positive years (even numbered) the Heavenly trigram is on top (upper). For negative years (odd numbered) the Heavenly trigram is on the bottom (lower).

For Women: For positive years (even numbered) the Heavenly trigram is on the bottom (lower). For negative years (odd numbered) the Heavenly trigram is on the top (upper).

Table 27   *Heavenly number trigrams*

1	☳	2	☷	3	☷	4	☳	5*	
6	☰	7	☶	8	☷	9	☵	10	☷
11	☳	12	☷	13	☷	14	☳	15*	
16	☰	17	☶	18	☷	19	☵	20	☷
21	☳	22	☷	23	☷	24	☳	25*	
26	☳	27	☷	28	☷	29	☵	30*	
31	☰	32	☶	33	☷	34	☳	35	☷
36	☳	37	☷	38	☷	39	☵	40*	
41	☰	42	☶	43	☷	44	☳	45	☷
46	☳	47	☷	48	☷	49	☵	50*	

* a For Upper Sexagenary Cycle years (1864–1923) use ☷ for man and ☷ for woman.
b For Middle Sexagenary Cycle years (1924–1983) use ☷ for man in even numbered years and for woman in odd numbered years.
c For Middle Sexagenary Cycle years (1924–1983) use ☷ for man in odd numbered years and for woman in even numbered years.
d For Lower Sexagenary Cycle years (1984–2043) use ☷ for man and ☷ for woman.

Table 28   *Earthly number trigrams*

2	☷	4	☰	6	☰	8	☷	10	☳	12	☷
14	☰	16	☰	18	☷	20	☷	22	☷	24	☰
26	☰	28	☷	30	☷	32	☷	34	☰	36	☰
38	☷	40	☷	42	☷	44	☰	46	☰	48	☷
50	☷	52	☷	54	☰	56	☰	58	☷	60	☷

EXAMPLE:

5 October 1941, 05.45 a.m.

1941 is a negative year.

The Heavenly number   =   31   Trigram

The Earthly number   =   40   Trigram

The natal hexagram for man is therefore Hexagram 5

The natal hexagram for woman is Hexagram 6

Step 10: In this step we have to determine the controlling line.

While the natal hexagram gives the 'broad' picture it is the controlling line of the hexagram that is important. It is from this that all subsequent patterns of hexagrams for yearly, monthly, and daily predictions are developed. And, not surprisingly, it is the time of birth which is used as the basis for determining the controlling line. There are quite a few different combinations, as will be seen, but in fact they are quite easy to obtain and simple to use.

The importance of the controlling line is that it dictates the pattern of the subsequent age subcycles and at the end of these becomes the foundation for the Later Heaven hexagram, relating to the later years of one's life. Since it influences all that follows from the time of birth onwards it is right to call it the controlling line.

The natal hexagram lines are given an alphabetical designation in a manner which will be described in the pages that follow, and it is in this way that the controlling line is found, for it corresponds to the time of birth and carries the same alphabetical desig-

Table 29   *Time of birth symbols*

Symbols:	a	b	c	d	e	f
Hours:	11 p.m. –1 a.m.	1–3 a.m.	3–5 a.m.	5–7 a.m.	7–9 a.m.	9–11 a.m.
Yang (+)	☵					

Table 29—*continued*

Symbols:	g	h	i	j	k	l
Hours:	11 a.m. −1 p.m.	1–3 p.m.	3–5 p.m.	5–7 p.m.	7–9 p.m.	9–11 p.m.
Yin (−)	䷁	䷁	䷁	䷁	䷁	䷁

nation as the latter. The different time of birth symbols are shown in Table 29.

Every hexagram, of course, has Yang or Yin lines in varying combinations. The *I Ching* system of designating these lines is shown in the examples which follow. There is one method for Yin hours and another for Yang hours. (Table 29 shows which hours are Yin and which are Yang.)

EXAMPLES:

Case 1   For the hexagram that has only one Yang line:

(a) Yang hours

```
      — —
     — f —
     — e —
  a ———— b
     — d —
     — c —
```

(b) Yin hours

```
     — k —
     — j —
     — i —
     ———— l
     — h —
     — g —
```

In other words, the Yang line is always a and b and the lowest Yin line c and the other lines are designated d, e, f in sequence from bottom to top.

Here the lowest Yin line is g and the other Yin lines above it are designated h, i, j and k. The Yang line is always l no matter where it is.

Case 2   For the hexagram with two Yang lines:

(a) Yang hours

```
      — —
      — —
  b ——— d
  a ——— c
     —f—
     —e—
```

(b) Yin hours

```
     —j—
     —i—
     ——— l
     ——— k
     —h—
     —g—
```

Note that the lowest Yang line is a and c and the upper Yang line is b and d, with the two lowest Yin lines being designated e and f respectively.

Obviously the Yin lines are designated g, h, i and k, starting with the lowest, the lower Yang line being k and the upper Yang line being l.

Case 3   For the hexagram which has three Yang lines and three Yin lines:

(a) Yang hours

```
  c ——— f
     — —
  b ——— e
     — —
  a ——— d
     — —
```

(b) Yin hours

```
     ———
  i — — l
     ———
  h — — k
     ———
  g — — j
```

The lowest Yang line is a and d, the middle one is b and e and the top one is c and f. The Yin lines are not designated.

Similar to the Yang hours except that the Yin lines are designated, with the lowest being g and j, the middle one being h and k and the top one i and l.

Case 4   For the hexagram which has four Yang lines:

(a) Yang hours

```
d ─────
c ─────
    ── ──  f
b ─────
a ─────
    ── ──  e
```

(b) Yin hours

```
    ─────
    ─────
l ─────
h ── ── j
g ── ── i
k ─────
```

The designations are in natural sequence beginning with the lowest Yang line and designating the Yang lines first, then the Yin lines.

Here the two Yin lines receive double lettering, the lowest being g and i and the upper one being h and j. The lowest Yang line is k and the next above it is l.

Case 5   For hexagrams having five Yang lines:

(a) Yang hours

```
e ─────
d ─────
    ── ──  f
c ─────
b ─────
a ─────
```

(b) Yin hours

```
g ── ── h
    ─────
l ─────
k ─────
j ─────
i ─────
```

The Yang lines are always lettered from the bottom up and the Yin line is always f.

The single Yin line receives a double designation of g and h and the Yang lines are lettered from the lowest up, with the uppermost remaining unmarked.

Case 6 For the hexagram with all Yang lines. The designations for men and women have different considerations:

Man	Woman (x and y)	
	(x) If born after winter solstice and before summer solstice:	(y) If born after summer solstice and before winter solstice:

Man		(x)		(y)	
i ——— l		a ——— d		i ——— l	
h ——— k		b ——— e		h ——— k	
g ——— j		c ——— f		g ——— j	
c ——— f		g ——— j		c ——— f	
b ——— e		h ——— k		b ——— e	
a ——— d		i ——— l		a ——— d	

Case 7 For the hexagram with all Yin lines. The designations for man and woman have different considerations:

Man (s and t)		Woman
(s) If born after winter solstice and before summer solstice:	(t) If born after summer solstice and before winter solstice:	

(s)		(t)		Woman	
i — — l		a — — d		i — — l	
h — — k		b — — e		h — — k	
g — — j		c — — f		g — — j	
c — — f		g — — j		c — — f	
b — — e		h — — k		b — — e	
a — — d		i — — l		a — — d	

It should be remembered in the development of the patterns of life the controlling line is more important than the basic hexagram since the interpretation of the meanings of the lines is always more specific than that of the hexagram as a whole. An example will show how this is obtained.

EXAMPLE:

5 October 1941, 05.45 a.m.

Table 29 shows the controlling letter as d and the hours are Yang. From Case 4 above it is seen that the Yang lines are lettered in sequence from the bottom up and then the Yin lines. The result is:

	Man		Woman
	— —		—ө—
	—ө—		————
Hexagram 5	— —	Hexagram 6	————
	————		— —
	————		————
	————		— —

The controlling line in both instances is the d line. In one case this is line 5 and in the other it is line 6. Since it is a Yang line the fact that it controls is shown by showing the Yang line as —ө—. In the event that the controlling line is a Yin line then an **x** is placed between the broken lines to show that it controls; e.g.: —x—. *Important caution: Be sure to use the right hours system (Yang or Yin), to letter the hexagram in keeping with the rules for the case involved, and to use the right letter designations for determining the controlling line.*

Step 11: Yearly, monthly and daily predictions are made by assigning nine-year spans to Yang lines and six-year spans for Yin lines, beginning with the controlling line. Then by a series of rules relating to Yin and to Yang lines for positive and negative years, a yearly hexagram can be developed for each year of one's life. These yearly hexagrams, by another series of rules and computations, are broken down into monthly and daily predictions.

An example of the yearly span phases is shown below:

10	— —	15	79	————	87
1	—ө—	9	70	————	78
43	— —	48	61	————	69
34	————	42	55	— —	60
25	————	33	49	—x—	54
16	————	24	88	— —	93

Year 1 is from birth to the next winter solstice. Also, since the astrological year begins with the winter solstice, the last seven to nine days of the preceding calendar year belong to the following astrological year; e.g., 28 December 1957 is part of astrological year 1958.

It will be seen that in the hexagrams shown above the trigrams of the natal hexagram are reversed for the years beyond forty-eight, the moving line changing both its position and its nature. This is readily understandable but to get into and explain the complex rules for determining the hexagrams for the years, months and days would require detail which would not be of value here since full predictions for natal, years, months and days cannot be presented in such drastically abbreviated form. Our recent volume *The Astrology of I Ching* (Routledge & Kegan Paul, 1976), confines itself to this single subject and treats it comprehensively.

The foregoing material, however, will in itself allow the reader to determine his natal hexagram, its controlling line and the broad influences affecting his life, information which can be helpful to him if he cares to avail himself of it. Naturally, the better one understands the *I Ching* the better the understanding one will have of its astrological implications.

Tai-I Number astrology

Tai-I Number Astrology is by far the most complicated of the astrologies related to the *I Ching*. It was invented sometime during the Ming Dynasty, AD 1400–AD 1500. Its range of computations is extraordinary, especially when one considers that Arabic numerals and mathematical systems were not used, all calculations were made from Chinese characters. The complexity of the computations was matched by the broad scope of the astrology, which was used to obtain personal horoscopes, for divination, and to obtain guidance with regard to history, wars, battles, leadership problems, the weather, and other worldly affairs. Altogether it tries to do too much in a very difficult way and hence has never gained popularity. Not a great many people even know it exists today. In the light of this we, too, will mention it only briefly.

Tai-I combines the *I Ching*, the sexagenary cycle system and Horary Branches with a series of migrating stars. For example, for a personal horoscope the stars migrate through sixteen houses consisting of *I Ching* trigrams and Horary Branch symbols. The stars bear symbolic names—King, Minister, etc.—or are given the names of famous personages or abstract qualities. The predictions vary greatly between astrologers and there are so many interactions that it is virtually impossible to get a really clear understanding of the intended meaning in any particular case.

The greatest value of Tai-I lies in its historical applications. More will be said about this aspect of it in the chapter entitled 'The *I Ching* and History' later on in this book.

4 / Tai Shuan Ching

Yang Hsiung (*c.* 40 BC–AD 18) was a great scholar in the Han dynasty. He considered himself as learned as any of the ancient sages, and therefore wrote several books which paralleled some of the treasured ancient works. *Tai Shuan Ching*, one of his well-known works, was written in imitation of the *I Ching*. In the *I Ching* there are two lines, ———— (Yang) and — — (Yin). In *Tai Shuan Ching* there are three essential lines:

———— called, One
— — called, Two
– – – called, Three

What the meanings of One, Two, and Three are is not clearly explained, so almost everyone comes up with his or her own personal interpretation. For example, one could say, 'Tao gives birth to One, One gives birth to Two, Two gives birth to Three and Three gives birth to all things' (quoted from *Tao Te Ching*). Someone else might explain One as Yang, Two as Yin and Three as the product brought of their interaction. Another supposition could be that the third element is sex. For male, Yang, and female, Yin, to be productive and produce and sustain life there must be an attraction and intercourse between them fostered by a spiritual force. This attraction, the spiritual force, or marriage itself, could each be interpreted as representing the third line.

Where the *I Ching* has hexagrams, the *Tai Shuan Ching* has tetragrams. Examples of the tetragrams are:

There are 81 (3 × 3 × 3 × 3) tetragrams in the *Tai Shuan Ching* as compared with the 64 hexagrams of the *I Ching*.

178

While the commentaries regarding the *I Ching* were written by a scholar other than the author, Yang Hsiung wrote his own commentaries on his book.

Fa Yen is another of this notable's works. It is an imitation of *The Analects of Confucius*.

Since the *I Ching* has a system of divination, Yang Hsiung introduced a system of divination into the *Tai Shuan Ching*. The composition of this again paralleled that of the *I Ching*.

Yang Hsiung did, however, alter the numerology of the *Tai Shuan Ching*, changing the values normally attributed to the Celestial Stems and Horary Branches as follows:

Celestial Stems	Number	Horary Branches	Number
A and F	9	a and g	9
B and G	8	b and h	8
C and H	7	c and i	7
D and I	6	d and j	6
E and J	5	e and k	5
		f and l	4

The *Tai Shuan Ching* never gained popularity, although scholars have known of its existence. It is said that one of the astrologies of the *I Ching*, 'Iron Plate Divine Number', adopts the numerology of the *Tai Shuan Ching*.

In the preceding chapter, 'The *I Ching* and Astrology', we make no reference to the 'Iron Plate Divine Number', for it is a concept shrouded in much mystery, and no one really knows the truth about it. The claims of those who purport to know its secret inevitably turn out to be untenable. Others believe that Sau Yung (*c.* AD 1050) invented the 'Iron Plate Divine Number'. If one cares to take the necessary trouble one can find books on the 'Iron Plate Divine Number' in almost any Chinese bookstore. But, with all the pirating that has taken place over the years, and all the misprints that have been carried forward from one version to another, the secret of this astrology will probably never be solved.

5 | *The* I Ching *and History*

The ancient Chinese tried to explain the development of Chinese history in terms of some sequences of the *I Ching* hexagrams. Only Chinese history has been researched in this manner, so whether or not these methods are applicable to the history of the world as a whole remains a subject for future study.

There are two known systems regarding the *I Ching* and history, Sau Yung's method and Tai-I Number, of which the former is somewhat better known. A detailed book on Sau Yung's method was being prepared by Professor Haui Chin Nan in Chinese at Taipei, Taiwan, in 1976. The title of the work is *Huang Chi Ching Sue*, and there is a possibility that it may be translated into English soon after publication. Anyone interested can write for further information to the EWES Society, PO Box 7–51, Taipei, Taiwan. It will be mentioned only briefly here.

Sau Yung's concept of the I Ching and history

The ancient Chinese expressed all cycles of time by one and the same system. The reader is already aware from other chapters that in Tzu Pin all the yearly, monthly, daily and hourly cycles are represented by sexagenary cycles. Similarly, in Nine House Astrology, yearly, monthly, daily and hourly cycles are all expressed in terms of nine stars.

In a sense, Sau Yung adopted a similar way of expressing the cycles of time in history. He considered that both large and small cycles of time could be represented by the same system (just as, in the West, 60 seconds = 1 minute, and 60 minutes = 1 hour). He rationalized that a year, month, day and hour could be represented by the same general system and that from these observations even much larger segments could be representatively developed, and came up with the system of equivalents set out as Table 30.

The similarity between the two systems is obvious. Taking nature as his guide, Sau Yung noted that the activities of life flourish from spring to autumn (that is, from c month to i month). He therefore posited that the activities of life and human culture start to really become manifest in the c Hui period and flourish gradually, these activities declining after time enters i Hui. Nearly all activity ceases in the l Hui, a Hui and b Hui. He further reasoned that these concepts applied not only to our present human culture, but also to an earlier culture which followed the same pattern of development and decline. He believes every human culture will be destroyed—whether by natural disaster, or as a result of self-destruction, or from some other cause. However, human beings themselves will never all die in any such major disaster; a few will always survive and go into the next Yuan to help start a new human culture. Sau even thinks that the *I Ching* may have been invented in the previous Yuan and that Fu Hsi, the Father of Chinese culture and attributed inventor of the *I Ching*, was a saint in an earlier human culture.

Table 30   *Sau Yung's system of equivalents*

Yuan (One Yuan=129,600 years)	*Segmentally equivalent to*	One year
One Yuan has 12 Hui		One year has 12 months.
The names of the Hui are a Hui, b Hui, c Hui (etc.)		The names of the months are a month,
Each Hui covers 10,800 years [Note that 129,600 $(1+2+9+6=18,$ $1+8=9).$ 10,800 $(1+8=9)]$		b month, c month, etc.
One Hui has 30 Yun		One month has 30 days
Each Yun covers 360 years		(lunar days)
One Yun has 12 Sue		One day has 12 hours
Each Sue covers 30 years		(ancient Chinese method of calculating time)

SAU YUNG'S SEQUENCE OF HEXAGRAMS

Sau's 64-hexagram circular arrangement (see Figure 4, p. 16) represents the time cycle. The 60 hexagrams (excluding Hexagrams 1, 2, 29 and 30, which represent heaven, earth, sun and moon) are assigned to one Yuan sequence. Hence each Hui gets 5 hexagrams for its share (60 ÷ 12 = 5); or, in other words, 5 hexagrams represent 1 Hui. By following certain rules each of these hexagrams subdivides into 6 hexagrams, to make up the 30 Yun. By repeating this procedure each Yun and each Sue is assigned to a hexagram for the interpretation of particular periods of time. From the hexagrams of Sue the yearly hexagrams are developed and all Chinese history is explained from the interpretation of these hexagrams.

Tai-I Number

Tai-I Number is a system of astrology which claims to be able to explain and interpret everything in the universe (see also the section on 'Tai-I Number Astrology' on pp. 176–7). It is so complicated that books explaining it are, even today, not completely understood, although it is supposed to be all-embracing. How comprehensive it really is has never been verified. In fact, the principles of Tai-I that relate to history are little known and we cannot guarantee the accuracy of this presentation. We merely set forth those aspects that in our estimation appear to have some relevance.

The astrology of Tai-I has a circular system of sixteen Houses. These are formed by dividing a circular area into sixteen equal parts. Many 'stars' migrate through the houses. Judgments are based on the position and interaction between 'stars' and the relative strength of the 'stars', since some are much stronger in influence than others. These are symbolic and abstract, having such designations as King, Minister, General, or bearing the names of famous personages, abstract qualities, and so on.

The stars represent earth, man and heaven. The stars of earth relate to earthly matters and affairs; the stars of man to individuals, leaders and families along with their characters and traits, and the stars of heaven generate special external influences. There also are specific rules for analysing the interactions between each of these, based on the hexagrams involved, the Horary Branches as correlated with the sexagenary cycles, and the stars which migrate according to formulae into given segments of a house at any specific time.

Each cycle in history is 11,520 years ($1 + 1 + 5 + 2 = 9$). Every Yang line governs 36 years. Every Yin line rules 24 years.

For instance Hexagram 44 ䷫ governs $(5 \times 36) + 24 = 204$ years. The 64 hexagrams govern 11,520 years. The sequence of the 64 hexagrams is arranged into 12 periods.

(1) THE FIRST PERIOD

At the beginning Heaven and earth were separated (quiescent). This era is depicted by Hexagram 1 ䷀ and Hexagram 2 ䷁. When Heaven and earth draw apart there is no intercourse between Heaven, Yang, and earth, Yin; this is represented by Hexagram 12 ䷋. Subsequently Heaven and earth enter into relationship again. Their coming together is shown by Hexagram 11 ䷊. These four hexagrams govern 720 years:

Hexagram 1 governs 216 years: 1197 BC to 982 BC.
Hexagram 2 governs 144 years: 981 BC to 858 BC.
Hexagram 12 governs 180 years: 857 BC to 658 BC.
Hexagram 11 governs 180 years: 657 BC to 478 BC.

(2) THE SECOND PERIOD

This is the period of intercourse between man and woman. As a result of this intercourse Ch'ien gets Yin and produces Chên ☳. Chên and Hexagram 51 ䷲ are the Eldest Son. K'un gets Yang as a result of intercourse, to beget Sun ☴. Sun and Hexagram 57 ䷸ are the Eldest Daughter. The Eldest Son and the Eldest Daughter become a couple by marriage, represented by Hexagram 32 ䷟. The intercourse between them is Hexagram 42 ䷞. Ch'ien gets Yin through a second intercourse, to raise K'an ☵. K'an and Hexagram 29 ䷜ are the Middle Son. K'un gets Yang by a second intercourse, to raise Li ☲. Li and Hexagram 30 ䷝ are the Middle Daughter. Middle Son and Middle Daughter become a couple, represented by Hexagram 63 ䷾. The intercourse between them is Hexagram 64 ䷿. By a third intercourse Ch'ien raises Ken ☶. Ken and Hexagram 52 ䷳ are the Youngest Son. K'un by the third intercourse, raises Tui ☱. Tui and Hexagram 58 ䷹ are the Youngest Daughter. The Youngest Son marries with the Youngest Daughter to become Hexagram 41 ䷨. Their intercourse is represented by Hexagram 31 ䷞.

A total of 12 hexagrams represent 2,160 years:

Hexagram 51 governs 168 years: 477 BC to 310 BC.
Hexagram 57 governs 192 years: 309 BC to 118 BC.
Hexagram 52 governs 180 years: 117 BC to AD 63.
Hexagram 42 governs 180 years: AD 64 to AD 243.
Hexagram 29 governs 168 years: AD 244 to AD 411.
Hexagram 30 governs 192 years: AD 412 to AD 603.
Hexagram 63 governs 180 years: AD 604 to AD 783.
Hexagram 64 governs 180 years: AD 784 to AD 963.
Hexagram 52 governs 168 years: AD 964 to AD 1131.
Hexagram 58 governs 192 years: AD 1132 to AD 1323.
Hexagram 41 governs 180 years: AD 1324 to AD 1503.
Hexagram 31 governs 180 years: AD 1504 to AD 1683.

(3) THE THIRD PERIOD

Man works to govern the world. The Sons follow the Father to work. Hexagram 34 ䷡ and Hexagram 25 ䷘ show the Eldest Son following the Father. Hexagram 5 ䷄ and Hexagram 6 ䷅ show the Middle Son following the Father. Hexa-

gram 26 ䷙ and Hexagram 33 ䷠ show the Youngest Son

following the Father. A total of 6 hexagrams governs 1,152 years:

Hexagram 34 governs 192 years: AD 1684 to AD 1875.
Hexagram 25 governs 192 years: AD 1876 to AD 2067.
Hexagram 5 governs 192 years: AD 2068 to AD 2259.
Hexagram 6 governs 192 years.
Hexagram 26 governs 192 years.
Hexagram 33 governs 192 years.

(4) THE FOURTH PERIOD

The woman rules the family and helps the man. The Daughters

follow their Mother. Hexagram 20 ䷓ and Hexagram 46 ䷭

show the Eldest Daughter following the Mother. Hexagram 35

䷢ and Hexagram 36 ䷣ show the Middle Daughter follow-

ing the Mother. Hexagram 45 ䷬ and Hexagram 19 ䷒ show

the Youngest Daughter following the Mother. A total of 6 hexagrams govern 1,008 years:

Hexagram 20 governs 168 years.
Hexagram 46 governs 168 years.
Hexagram 35 governs 168 years.
Hexagram 36 governs 168 years.
Hexagram 45 governs 168 years.
Hexagram 19 governs 168 years.

(5) THE FIFTH PERIOD

The Mother raises and instructs the Sons. Hexagram 16 ䷏

and Hexagram 24 ䷗ show the Eldest Son following the

Mother. Hexagram 8 ䷇ and Hexagram 7 ䷆ show the

Middle Son following the Mother. Hexagram 23 ☷☶ and Hexagram 15 ☷☶ show the Youngest Son following the Mother. A
total of 6 hexagrams governing 936 years:

Hexagram 16 governs 156 years.
Hexagram 24 governs 156 years.
Hexagram 8 governs 156 years.
Hexagram 7 governs 156 years.
Hexagram 23 governs 156 years.
Hexagram 15 governs 156 years.

(6) THE SIXTH PERIOD

The Daughters follow their Father. Hexagram 9 ☴☰ and
Hexagram 44 ☰☴ show the Eldest Daughter following the
Father. Hexagram 14 ☲☰ and Hexagram 13 ☰☲ show the
Middle Daughter following the Father. Hexagram 43 ☱☰ and
Hexagram 10 ☰☱ show the Youngest Daughter following the
Father. A total of 6 hexagrams lasting 1,224 years:

Hexagram 9 governs 204 years.
Hexagram 44 governs 204 years.
Hexagram 14 governs 204 years.
Hexagram 13 governs 204 years.
Hexagram 43 governs 204 years.
Hexagram 10 governs 204 years.

(7) THE SEVENTH PERIOD

After the Father and Mother are gone, the Eldest Son will take
over the Father's place. The Middle Son and the Youngest Son
follow the Eldest Son. Hexagram 40 ☳☵ and Hexagram 3 ☵☳ show the Middle Son following the Eldest Son. Hexagram
62 ☳☶ and Hexagram 27 ☶☳ show the Youngest Son follow-
ing the Eldest Son. A total of 4 hexagrams governing 672 years:

Hexagram 40 governs 168 years.
Hexagram 3 governs 168 years.
Hexagram 62 governs 168 years.
Hexagram 27 governs 168 years.

(8) THE EIGHTH PERIOD

The Eldest Daughter takes over the Mother's place. The Middle Daughter and the Youngest Daughter follow the Eldest Daughter. Hexagram 37 ䷤ and Hexagram 50 ䷱ show the Middle Daughter following the Eldest Daughter. Hexagram 61 ䷼ and Hexagram 28 ䷛ show the Youngest Daughter following the Eldest Daughter. A total of 4 hexagrams governing 768 years:

Hexagram 37 governs 192 years.
Hexagram 50 governs 192 years.
Hexagram 61 governs 192 years.
Hexagram 28 governs 192 years.

(9) THE NINTH PERIOD

The Middle Daughter follows the Eldest Son. The Youngest Daughter follows the Eldest Son and the Middle Son. Hexagram 55 ䷶ and Hexagram 21 ䷔ show the Middle Daughter following the Eldest Son. Hexagram 54 ䷵ and Hexagram 17 ䷐ show the Youngest Daughter following the Eldest Son. Hexagram 60 ䷻ and Hexagram 47 ䷮ show the Youngest Daughter following the Middle Son. A total of 6 hexagrams governing 1,080 years:

Hexagram 55 governs 180 years.
Hexagram 21 governs 180 years.
Hexagram 54 governs 180 years.
Hexagram 17 governs 180 years.
Hexagram 60 governs 180 years.
Hexagram 47 governs 180 years.

(10) THE TENTH PERIOD

The Middle Son follows the Eldest Daughter (Hexagram 59 ䷺ and Hexagram 48 ䷯). The Youngest Son follows the Eldest Daughter (Hexagram 53 ䷴ and Hexagram 18 ䷑) and the Middle Daughter (Hexagram 56 ䷶ and Hexagram 22 ䷕). A total of 6 hexagrams governing 1,080 years:

Hexagram 59 governs 180 years.
Hexagram 48 governs 180 years.
Hexagram 53 governs 180 years.
Hexagram 18 governs 180 years.
Hexagram 56 governs 180 years.
Hexagram 22 governs 180 years.

(11) THE ELEVENTH PERIOD

The Eldest Son and the Eldest Daughter are gone, the Middle Son and the Youngest Son rule the world. A total of 2 hexagrams governing 336 years:

Hexagram 39 ䷦ governs 168 years.

Hexagram 4 ䷃ governs 168 years.

(12) THE TWELFTH PERIOD

The Middle Daughter and the Youngest Daughter rule the world. This is a bad period, one of many disasters. A total of 2 hexagrams governing 384 years:

Hexagram 38 ䷥ governs 192 years.

Hexagram 49 ䷰ governs 192 years.

It is a time of revolution and of change; a new saint will be born at this time, to prepare men for the next cycle of history.

6 | *The* I Ching *and Meditation*

Meditation, basically, is the process of quieting the mind to, usually, the low alpha and theta levels of brain-wave activity and then either concentrating on some material object, thought or idea or keeping the mind positively (never negatively) as quiescent as possible for the purposes of gaining knowledge or as a way to spiritual development.

It is not our intention to present a concept of meditation, for there are quite enough in existence already. Furthermore, each person will find the form of meditation that is most appropriate for him at any given time. 'Seek and ye shall find' that which is right for you. Once you start meditating, though, you should be aware that certain physiological and mental changes can and, in the ardent meditator, do take place. The physiological ones are based on the normal changes that occur in an individual's life as represented by the first six hexagrams of the House of Ch'ien and the House of K'un in the book of the *I Ching*. Some people consider that the House of Chen ☲☲ and the House of Sun ☰☰ reflect spiritual progress and development through meditation. Here we are not discussing spiritual development *per se*. That in itself is subject matter for a book. One need only say here that the entire *I Ching* provides guidelines for spiritual development and progress for anyone who cares to study and apply them. The physiological changes need to be understood. They reflect the physical aspects of meditation related to the *I Ching*, and, while the average meditator of today need not be concerned with any of these physical changes, anyone who takes meditation exercises seriously should have an understanding of at least the basic physiological considerations.

In the Chin dynasty, AD 265–420 a famous immortal, Po

Yang Wei, wrote a book called *Chang Tong Ch'u* in which he applied the *I Ching*, the five elements and the thoughts of Lao Tze to a discussion of advanced meditation. So far as is known he was the first person to apply the *I Ching* to advanced meditation, and his theory of progressive cycles of meditation is an interesting one.

Progressive cycles of meditation

In the course of advanced meditation one will repeat cycles similar to those of the moon many times. Each is at a higher level than the preceding one. Each is a step in achieving clarity and understanding of a phase of spiritual development when singleness of mind in respect to a specific goal is applied. The actual process of meditation is in an advanced stage when one has learned to concentrate, can maintain a single thought or idea to the exclusion of all others for long periods of time, and can quickly and fully enter the meditative state at any time anywhere. The level of development of an individual is the sum total of the cycles he has experienced.

The actual moon cycles are shown in Figure 20. Note, however, that the periods between the phases shown vary in length. This indicates that the gaining of clarity and understanding regarding any problem or matter is not an even progression, as anyone will agree. By the '15th' one has attained full clarity. Thereafter it is a process of assimilation and of making the

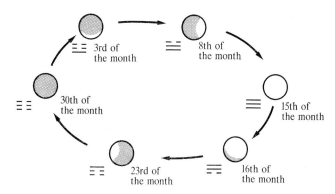

Figure 20.   The cycles of the moon

matter meditated upon a permanent part of one's subconscious self.

The moon cycle of thirty days (approximately) is used as an analogy for the internal process which is taking place, but in actual practice many meditative cycles will be much shorter than thirty days, while others may take a year or more. The sequence, however, will follow the moon cycle shown in the Figure.

Physiology and meditation

There are some Taoist concepts related to the *I Ching*, which were developed in the Tang and Sung Dynasties. Taoism ascribes certain hexagrams as being representative of the physical state of an individual's vitality with respect to age. These form the basis of the concept of the relationship of advanced meditation to physiology. For a boy, the hexagrams are:

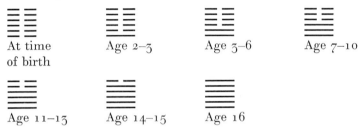

At time of birth	Age 2–3	Age 3–6	Age 7–10

Age 11–13	Age 14–15	Age 16

The sixteen-year-old boy or the fourteen-year-old girl are represented by Hexagram 1 of the *I Ching*, which shows the highest level of vitality. The best time for a person to learn and practise advanced meditation is at this age, before one has experienced sex or started to menstruate; i.e., when one is at the peak of vitality. Young people can attain results rapidly and easily if they start at this age. However, being young and not knowing what Tao is, nor what its benefits and blessings are, instead of wanting to practise advanced meditation teenagers are more likely to follow the natural instinct that leads them to love and sex. Once they menstruate, or have nocturnal emissions or sexual experiences, they start to lose their vitality.[1]

[1] The Chinese theory of the representation of *I Ching* to age is presented above. Recognizably there are variations in practical life, but these are not discussed in the Chinese text *Huang Ti Nei Ching*, an ancient and famous book on Chinese medicine.

The sequence of hexagrams for a man continue as follows, showing how his vitality declines with age.

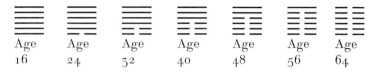

Age	Age	Age	Age	Age	Age	Age
16	24	32	40	48	56	64

The corresponding ages for women allow approximately six to seven years for each progressive hexagram, instead of the eight years shown for men. At the age of forty-nine approximately, women reach the stage of Hexagram 2, when their menses stop. Obviously, the younger a person is, the more inherent vitality he or she will have and the easier and faster it is for them to make progress in advanced meditation, so as to regain their vitality and attain longevity.

The increase in vitality of an older person is expressed by the following sequence of hexagrams. This same sequence, in fractional variation, can apply if one reverses one's vitality before reaching Hexagram 2.

The above sequence also symbolizes rejuvenation. The woman whose menses have stopped will resume her menses. Later, after making more progress, her menses will terminate again but this time she will have returned to her youth, before her menses first began.

The progress and the change in spiritual development of an individual, like the vitality of the body, are also expressed by the same sequence of hexagrams. Hexagram 1 again represents the point of highest achievement. (One famous sage in the Tang Dynasty picked the name 'Pure Yang' for himself, which is Hexagram 1.)

Hexagram 24—Return (earth's thunder returning) is used to express the explosion of (awakening) the Chi[1] routes and Chakras. At this stage one can hear the sound of explosion (sounds produced by the vibrations of the Chi moving through the Chi

---

[1] Chi is man's vital energy which flows through, sustains and gives life to his body. Acupuncture is based largely on tapping and correcting the flow of this energy through the invisible veins.

veins). These sounds are even audible to others if they are close or put their ear to the body.

In Taoism, achievement is classified into two major states of interaction between Yin and Yang, through the intercourse between K'an ☵ and Li ☲. When uniting together in one way, ䷾, they symbolize completion. When put together the opposite way, ䷿, they symbolize beginning. They represent the beginning and ending of various stages of subdevelopment, and like the moon cycles can be repeated at ever higher levels.

The intercourse between Ch'ien and K'un represents the ultimate stage, when one can relate and fully integrate oneself with the whole universe.

Chen Tuan, the sage who invented Tzu Wei, used the terms Wu Chi (Wu means nothingness) and Tai Chi to explain advanced meditation. In Taoist books the concepts of the *I Ching* are often mentioned in relation to meditation.[1]

Physiology and the I Ching

Man is represented by ☵, woman by ☲. The final object is to become ☰. This is attained when the male and the female blend fully. It is easier for a woman to achieve this than a man, since the woman has only one Yin line to change, whereas man has two. In practice women are not usually as persistent as men, and their wisdom often seems to be gained at a slower rate.

In terms of the human body, for man the back is Yang and the left is Yang. For women, the front is Yang and the right is Yang. These factors also affect the spiritual progress of men and women.

In view of the physiological changes that take place in advanced meditation only a great Master can guide both men and women. It often happens that a male instructor misguides a female student, not from intent but from lack of knowledge and experience regarding the physiology and psychological make-up of women. Therefore, advanced meditation should be undertaken carefully and under competent supervision.

[1] One should check with the *Tao Chun* which is a compilation of about 1,300 Taoist Sutras and books.

Chi Mai and Yin Yang

Chi Mai is the route of Chi through the body or the invisible veins through which it flows (Mai meaning roughly 'vein'). There are both Yin and Yang veins. For man, Tu Mai is Yang and Zun Mai is Yin. For woman, Tu Mai is Yin whereas Zun Mai is Yang. Therefore, man should endeavour to open the Tu Mai first while the woman should obtain a breakthrough of the Zun Mai first. According to Taoism there are eight major Chi Mai. Besides the Tu Mai and Zun Mai there are Tai Mai (very important for women), Chong Mai (also called Middle Mai), Yang Wei, Yin Wei, Yang Chiao and Yin Chiao. These carry life, vitality and energy to the various parts of the body, especially to the Chakras.

Once the Chi Mai have been opened through advanced meditation the individual cannot be treated in the usual manner by medical doctors, for they do not have any understanding of the attained physical states and many of the medications they would be likely to prescribe would be harmful to the individual and set him back. Thus advanced meditators should select their doctors with great care and preferably choose those who are knowledgeable regarding advanced meditation, or else find a Master of meditation who is also a fully trained physician. Regrettably in this day and age such people are virtually non-existent.

7 | *The* I Ching *and Geomancy*

Geomancy, the process of selecting the most auspicious areas for action or inaction, such as the place of work, sleep, interment, direction in which to move, etc., is an art. As an art there are many schools of thought regarding the most successful methods to use and each school derides all the others, claiming its own as the sole correct method. None of the methods is sufficiently clear in itself to be understood or employed by the mass of people. The books on geomancy are either incomplete, or else the material is presented in an ambiguous style, open to several different interpretations. Chinese 'Masters' of geomancy do not teach it in a way that makes it readily understandable either. What we shall be giving here is a brief description of a form of geomancy related to the *I Ching*, and some aspects of its purported benefits.

There are two major systems of geomancy. One applies principles similar to those of Tzu Pin (see pp. 116–27), which uses Celestial Stems and Horary Branches and stars for the determination of locations, positions and directions for specific purposes. This system will not be discussed here, for it is too complex to be of benefit to the general reader. The second system relates to the Lo Map and Sau Yung's circular arrangement of the sixty-four *I Ching* hexagrams. It is thought to have been developed in the Sung Dynasty (AD 960–AD 1279), when the Lo Map also first appeared.

It classifies aspects as either positive or negative. The Negative House relates to interment, while the Positive House concerns the activities of life. Both are important to the Chinese, but they seem to give more consideration to the negative aspects, for they see these as being of a more permanent nature, many aspects of the Positive House being beyond the individual's control. (It is interesting to note in passing that some high officials of China are said to have employed 'masters' of geomancy for the selection of their own interment sites and even supervised their construction.)

The Negative House

It is assumed that the bones (not the flesh) of a dead body will, when interred, absorb some form of Chi[1] and will reflect this Chi on members of the family and descendants—an idea that seems to have its basis in scientific fact, since the atomic structure of the bones of children is similar to that of their parents and a form of resonance or empathic vibration can and does exist between children and deceased parents. This can be auspicious or not depending on the favourableness of location of the burial site and the direction in which the body is laid in rest. Some people consider it best if a site can be chosen in which no subsequent influence can be exerted, but others believe that the site should be as auspicious as possible, since the influences can help the children and descendants achieve rank, wealth, position, fame, a happy life, etc. (This largely accounts for all the burial sites one sees dispersed across the whole Chinese countryside, rather than being concentrated in cemeteries as in Western countries—although some cemeteries have come into existence in modern times.) Of course, like any other radiological influence, it diminishes with time.

The factors influencing the choice of burial site include the relation of the site to water—since rivers and lakes will determine the degree of wealth and property the children can attain; its proximity to mountains—which will establish the children's prospects of achieving fame and how many children of their own they will have; and so on. Naturally, if one believes in applied Negative House geomancy, one will want to obtain the best possible results and will go to great lengths to try and achieve them.

The Positive House

As stated above the Positive House relates to the activities of life, such as where one should work, live, sleep and the best direction

[1] See footnote, p. 192.

in which to travel to attain the greatest happiness, wealth and longevity.

There are at least two other systems of geomancy which use the theories of the *I Ching* as their basis. The most popular in China is the one related to the *I Ching* and Nine House Astrology.

In this, the natal stars of individuals are the basis from which computations and considerations are made. Everyone has his own natal star (see Table 14, p. 78). The trigrams corresponding to these are:

1 ☵ water	4 ☴ wood		6 ☰ metal		
2 ☷ earth	5 ☶ earth (man)		7 ☱ metal		
3 ☳ wood	5 ☷ earth (woman)		8 ☶ earth		
	9 ☲ fire				

From the foregoing people are divided into either an East group or a West group, according to their trigrams:

The East group trigrams are: ☳, ☴, ☵, ☲ or, those having 1, 3, 4 or 9 as their natal star.

The West group trigrams are: ☶, ☷, ☱, ☰ or, those having 2, 5, 6, 7 or 8 as their natal star.

These are further categorized as positive or negative, as indicated in Figure 21, which parallels the Later Heaven sequence, and are then applied to the appropriate subject categories.

1   SLEEPING

East group people should sleep on the positive side of West group individuals; i.e., to the north-west, north, north-east or east. Which means that West group people must sleep on the negative side of the East group, or to the south-east, south, south-west, or west. This applies to brothers, sisters, friends and associates. It is also desirable to employ these directions when two people are working on a common project. For two individuals in the same group the sleeping position does not matter.

EXAMPLE:

Suppose I am sick. I belong to the East group. My brother, who is in the West group, comes over to take care of me. If he sleeps on my positive side it will tend to prolong my sickness. If he sleeps on my negative side it will hasten my recovery.

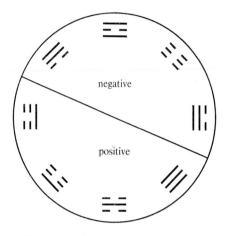

negative

positive

Figure 21.   Positive and negative trigrams in geomancy

2   MOVING

East group individuals should always move in a positive direction (north-west, north, north-east or east) for the results to be auspicious, whereas West group should move towards the negative (south-east, south, south-west, or west) directions to avoid inauspicious results.

Obviously, there are times in life when moves must be made in directions which are inauspicious. In such cases, according to the principles of geomancy, the move must be made in two parts, one temporary and the other permanent. The temporary move is made in an adverse direction for a period of forty-nine days. At the end of that time the individual can move to his permanent location and have full and beneficial results from the move.

EXAMPLE:

Suppose I am an East type living in Memphis, Tennessee, and am required by my employer to move to Los Angeles, California, which is west of Memphis. In such a case it would be desirable for me to move to somewhere like Long Beach (also west of Memphis but south of Los Angeles) for forty-nine days and then move to Los Angeles (to the north or positive direction) at the end of that time.

3 USAGE OF ROOMS

Certain rooms are considered more propitious and beneficial than others in every house, building or structure. This is based on the interaction of the trigrams representing the direction of the gate or main entrance to the establishment, with the trigrams representing the direction of the rooms, using the Later Heaven sequence directions and applying the interactions given in Tables 1 and 2 (p. 21). It is also dependent on the direction in which the building faces.

The rooms themselves are assigned names depending on their degree of auspiciousness and the nature of their influence. The names are as follows, their disposition being as indicated in Figures 22 and 23:

Heavenly Doctor
Vitality
Longevity
Five Ghosts
Six Devils
Disaster
Termination of Life (e.g., when Yin conquers Yang it becomes the Termination of Life).

The designations for East group and West group individuals shown in Figures 22 and 23, are for one-storied buildings. Multistoried and split-level buildings have complex rules which are not appropriate here. Furthermore, not every structure has rooms of equal size, so when analysing a building the direction of a room in relation to the main entrance becomes more important than its size. Inauspicious rooms should be used for storage, or as baths, kitchens, utility rooms, etc.

Another consideration lies in the fact that this form of geomancy is based in part on natal stars. As the reader already knows, the natal stars migrate yearly (see Figure 12, p. 82). The effects of this can best be illustrated by an example:

EXAMPLE:

A man, who has cancer, has the natal star 9 ☲, fire, and is an East group individual.

By 1976 star 6 is in the centre position (see Figure 12 or refer to Figure 24 in this chapter).

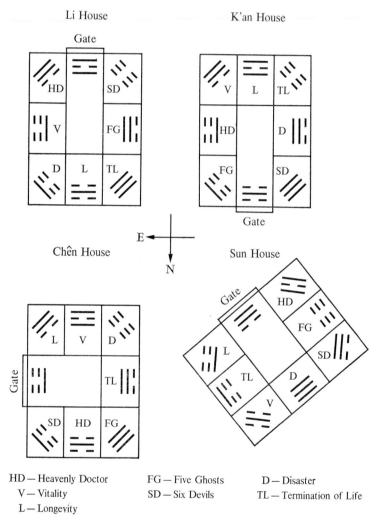

HD — Heavenly Doctor   FG — Five Ghosts   D — Disaster

V — Vitality   SD — Six Devils   TL — Termination of Life

L — Longevity

Figure 22. The four East houses

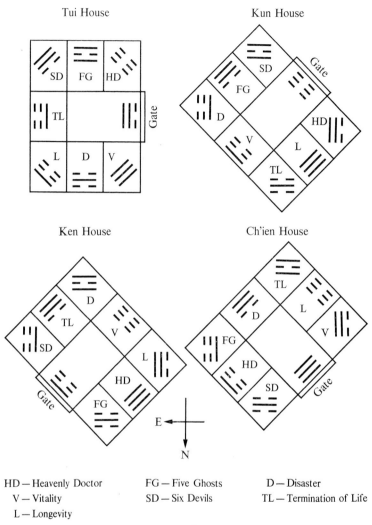

Tui House   Kun House

Ken House   Ch'ien House

HD — Heavenly Doctor   FG — Five Ghosts   D — Disaster
V — Vitality   SD — Six Devils   TL — Termination of Life
L — Longevity

Figure 23. *The four West houses*

Remember it is the stars which migrate (numbers 1–9) while the trigrams remain fixed (Later Heaven sequence). The fixed trigrams are called Houses, K'an ☵ for instance, being a house in the north while Li ☲ is a House in the south.

Whether or not a room is auspicious to an individual is

judged from three interactions: the individual with the house; the individual with the star; and the interaction between the star and the house. When the house or the star 'generate' the individual it is very auspicious; but not when the opposite is the case. Also, the interaction between the star and house has only a weak effect on the individual. It is inauspicious for the individual to be 'conquered' by the star, or the house.

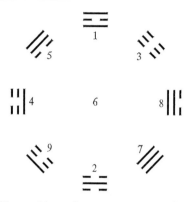

Figure 24. The position of natal stars in the Lo Map in 1976

To continue the analysis of our example, since the individual is 9, fire, if he sleeps in the north room it will be inauspicious. The north room is K'an ☵, water, which conquers fire. In the case we are citing it is a double inauspicious room, since fire generates earth and the star of position 2 is earth. Thus the individual would be giving forth rather than receiving. To be auspicious the person should receive benefits. By checking further, we find that both the east and the south-east rooms are wood. Since wood generates fire these rooms would be favourable. By the same system of interactions, the south-west room —which is earth and generated by fire—would be unfavourable. If he sleeps in the north-west room the individual will conquer both the star, 7, metal, and the House Ch'ien ☰, metal, and this will result in a little or no inauspiciousness. Obviously, in this example, rooms which generate fire are the most favourable and a room which is itself fire will be next most favourable, whereas those which conquer fire will be most inauspicious and those which are generated by fire will be unfavourable but to a lesser degree. Lastly, those conquered by fire are a little inauspicious, or even neutral, but definitely not of help.

Thus, in 1976, the individual in our example should live in an East group house and sleep (work) in an east room. The east room is wood and the migrating star there is number 4 in 1976, which is also wood. Both generate fire. Of the East group houses the K'an Houses in which the east room is the Heavenly Doctor would be the best one, with the Sun House, where east is longevity, next best and Li House, where east is vitality, third in auspiciousness. Naturally, the east room of the K'an House, which is the Heavenly Doctor would be best for the recovery of our patient, if he were ill.

In 1977 for the East group there are two rooms in the diagram which will be wood, i.e., 3 and 4, in the east and south-east (see Figure 25). Both of these generate fire, so would be favourable.

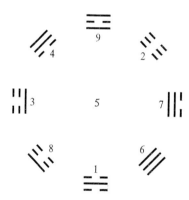

Figure 25.   The migration of stars in 1977

In this particular case the east room, Yang, is better than the south-east, which is Yin. Number 9 star is Yin. Yin and Yin are helpful but not as powerful as Yang helping Yin.

The foregoing presentation gives a simplified summary of a geomancy related to the *I Ching*. In fact, though, as has already been said, this geomancy has many complex ramifications if one is to attempt it seriously. Many additional factors need to be considered, such as the relationship to the nearby town, other buildings in the locality, the presence of roads, streams, lakes, railways, etc. Each such factor can be ascribed an appropriate trigram (see Appendix A) and as such has an interaction with everything else, either for good or for bad.

Geomancy can have many uses if one believes in the efficacy of the principles involved. It is an art to evaluate properly all the factors which need to be considered. The influence generated can effect the relationships of individuals, of families, relate to business or office assignments, affect the areas of most effective productivity, or the rotation of products and crops, and so on. It can be the basis for analysing why one year is good but another is not, even though the same principles have been employed—though without making the necessary changes to one's work, living areas, etc. Here, as in all other matters, the individual must decide for himself what he will believe and how much he can accept.

8 | Directionology

Directionology is the art of selecting the best direction to take in order to achieve successful results in a venture or undertaking. Those who use it believe that everything in life is subject to higher influences and that when one works with these influences one can expect the final result to be more propitious than if one had not. They also believe that if one acts in a way that is contrary to these outside influences, the results could even be negative. A number of systems of directionology have been invented for use by these believers. Since variations in systems and in interpretations are possible, its successful practice is considered an art.

Directionology is especially popular in Japan, where it is even used by many on a daily basis, but not nearly so popular in China. This is somewhat surprising, since geomancy, a sister belief of directionology, is used quite extensively in that country. Both Chinese and Japanese systems exist. The one we shall be discussing is the one in popular use in Japan. It is an extension of Nine House (Star) Astrology, and is based to some extent on the principles of the *I Ching* (the most popular Chinese system of directionology is based on Tzu Pin Astrology; it, too, applies some of the principles of the *I Ching*).

There are two major and one minor difference between Chinese and Japanese Nine House astrology and directionology, even though the Japanese version had its origin in China.

(1) On the basis that men and women are different, the Chinese assign different yearly and monthly stars to them (see Table 14 for yearly stars and Table 15 for monthly stars), whereas in the Japanese system the women use the same yearly, monthly and daily stars as the men. To the Chinese the

Japanese system sounds incorrect; no doubt, the converse is
true for the Japanese.

(2) The other difference in the application of directionology
lies in the areas of influence allocated to each trigram, as
Figure 26 shows. The Chinese, following the Lo Map, allo-
cate 45° to each trigram; the Japanese, 30 to 60 degrees;
again, the Chinese and Japanese each feel that their system
is more correct. (But note that the Japanese system was
originally the same as the Chinese.)

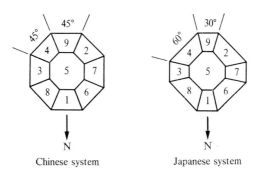

Chinese system   Japanese system

Figure 26.   Areas of trigram influence in Chinese and Japanese
directionology

(3) A third difference, as regards usage, exists between the
Japanese and Chinese systems. The Chinese use Nine
House Astrology in the development of their geomancy but
it plays no part in personal horoscopes, while in Japan it is
quite popular for both personal horoscopes and directionology.

Establishing the directions

The primary principles involved in directionology are the assignment of the appropriate trigrams to self, or to goals, aims or purposes, noting the interaction (Tables 1 and 2 on p. 21) with the
directional trigrams for the year, month or day in question. For
selecting one's star use Tables 14 and 15 (pp. 78–80) for the
yearly and monthly stars. Disregard the numbers assigned to
women in these figures, for, as has been stated above, in the

Japanese system the women use the same yearly, monthly and daily star as the men. For the daily stars, the daily numbers assigned for 1977 and 1978 are presented in Tables 31 and 32 in

Table 31 *The daily nine stars in 1977*

Day	1	2	3	4	5	6	7	8	9	10	11	12	13	14	15
Month															
Jan.	1	2	3	4	5	6	7	8	9	1	2	3	4	5	6
Feb.	5	6	7	8	9	1	2	3	4	5	6	7	8	9	1
Mar.	6	7	8	9	1	2	3	4	5	6	7	8	9	1	2
Apr.	1	2	3	4	5	6	7	8	9	1	2	3	4	5	6
May	4	5	6	7	8	9	9	8	7	6	5	4	3	2	1
June	2	1	9	8	7	6	5	4	3	2	1	9	8	7	6
July	8	7	6	5	4	3	2	1	9	8	7	6	5	4	3
Aug.	4	3	2	1	9	8	7	6	5	4	3	2	1	9	8
Sept.	9	8	7	6	5	4	3	2	1	9	8	7	6	5	4
Oct.	6	5	4	3	2	1	9	8	7	6	5	4	3	2	1
Nov.	2	1	1	2	3	4	5	6	7	8	9	1	2	3	4
Dec.	2	3	4	5	6	7	8	9	1	2	3	4	5	6	7

Day	16	17	18	19	20	21	22	23	24	25	26	27	28	29	30	31
Month																
Jan.	7	8	9	1	2	3	4	5	6	7	8	9	1	2	3	4
Feb.	2	3	4	5	6	7	8	9	1	2	3	4	5			
Mar.	3	4	5	6	7	8	9	1	2	3	4	5	6	7	8	9
Apr.	7	8	9	1	2	3	4	5	6	7	8	9	1	2	3	
May	9	8	7	6	5	4	3	2	1	9	8	7	6	5	4	3
June	5	4	3	2	1	9	8	7	6	5	4	3	2	1	9	
July	2	1	9	8	7	6	5	4	3	2	1	9	8	7	6	5
Aug.	7	6	5	4	3	2	1	9	8	7	6	5	4	3	2	1
Sept.	3	2	1	9	8	7	6	5	4	3	2	1	9	8	7	
Oct.	9	8	7	6	5	4	3	2	1	9	8	7	6	5	4	3
Nov.	5	6	7	8	9	1	2	3	4	5	6	7	8	9	1	
Dec.	8	9	1	2	3	4	5	6	7	8	9	1	2	3	4	5

this section. For purposes other than self use the Table of Trigram Attributes (Appendix A) on pp. 218–27. To select the appropriate yearly Nine House diagram see Figure 27. By calculating back-

Table 32   *The daily nine stars in 1978*

Day	1	2	3	4	5	6	7	8	9	10	11	12	13	14	15
Month															
Jan.	6	7	8	9	1	2	3	4	5	6	7	8	9	1	2
Feb.	1	2	3	4	5	6	7	8	9	1	2	3	4	5	6
Mar.	2	3	4	5	6	7	8	9	1	2	3	4	5	6	7
Apr.	6	7	8	9	1	2	3	4	5	6	7	8	9	1	2
May	9	9	8	7	6	5	4	3	2	1	9	8	7	6	5
June	6	5	4	3	2	1	9	8	7	6	5	4	3	2	1
July	3	2	1	9	8	7	6	5	4	3	2	1	9	8	7
Aug.	8	7	6	5	4	3	2	1	9	8	7	6	5	4	3
Sept.	4	3	2	1	9	8	7	6	5	4	3	2	1	9	8
Oct.	1	9	8	7	6	5	4	3	2	1	9	8	7	6	5
Nov.	4	5	6	7	8	9	1	2	3	4	5	6	7	8	9
Dec.	7	8	9	1	2	3	4	5	6	7	8	9	1	2	3

Day	16	17	18	19	20	21	22	23	24	25	26	27	28	29	30	31
Month																
Jan.	3	4	5	6	7	8	9	1	2	3	4	5	6	7	8	9
Feb.	7	8	9	1	2	3	4	5	6	7	8	9	1			
Mar.	8	9	1	2	3	4	5	6	7	8	9	1	2	3	4	5
Apr.	3	4	5	6	7	8	9	1	2	3	4	5	6	7	8	
May	4	3	2	1	9	8	7	6	5	4	3	2	1	9	8	7
June	9	8	7	6	5	4	3	2	1	9	8	7	6	5	4	
July	6	5	4	3	2	1	9	8	7	6	5	4	3	2	1	9
Aug.	2	1	9	8	7	6	5	4	3	2	1	9	8	7	6	5
Sept.	7	6	5	4	3	2	1	9	8	7	6	5	4	3	2	
Oct.	4	3	2	1	9	8	7	6	5	4	3	2	1	1	2	3
Nov.	1	2	3	4	5	6	7	8	9	1	2	3	4	5	6	
Dec.	4	5	6	7	8	9	1	2	3	4	5	6	7	8	9	1

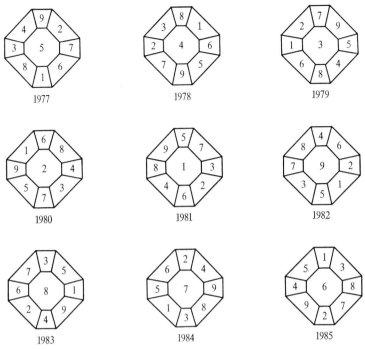

Figure 27. *Areas of trigram influence 1977–85*

wards or forwards the proper diagram for any year can be determined. They repeat every nine years.

For the reader's convenience the value of the yearly and monthly stars along with their auspicious directions have been set out in tabulated form as Table 33. The adverse directions for natal stars are also summarized, as Table 34. There are other more general adverse directions, which we shall discuss below.

The numerical value, the corresponding trigram, the designation and the colour name are for the stars as follows:

1 ☵
water, white

4 ☴
earth, black

3 ☳
wood, jade green

2 ☷
wood, green

5 earth, yellow

6 ☰
metal, white

7 ☱
metal, red

8 ☶
white

9 ☲
fire, purple

The most important step in directionology is choosing the right star for the length of time involved in the activity, purpose or aim. This should be based on when the effect will begin to show and the duration of the effect. For example:

(a) If the daily star is used the effect will begin to show on the 4th, 7th or 10th day and last for not longer than 60 days.
(b) If the monthly star is used the effect will start to show in the 4th, 7th or 10th month and last not longer than 60 months.
(c) If the yearly star is used the effect will start to show in the 4th, 7th or 10th year and last not longer than 60 years.

Table 33 *Summary of auspicious directions*

Natal star	Star of natal month	Auspicious directions
1	1	3, 4, 6, 7
1	2	6, 7
1	3	4
1	4	3
1	5	6, 7
1	6	7
1	7	6
1	8	6, 7
1	9	3, 4
2	1	6, 7
2	2	6, 7, 8, 9
2	3	9
2	4	9
2	5	6, 7, 8, 9
2	6	7, 8
2	7	6, 8
2	8	6, 7, 9
2	9	8
3	1	4
3	2	9
3	3	1, 4, 9

Table 33—*continued*

Natal star	Star of natal month	Auspicious directions
3	4	1, 9
3	5	9
3	6	1
3	7	1
3	8	9
3	9	4
4	1	3
4	2	9
4	3	1, 9
4	4	1, 3, 9
4	5	9
4	6	1
4	7	1
4	8	9
4	9	3
5	1	6, 7
5	2	6, 7, 8, 9
5	3	9
5	4	9
5	5	2, 6, 7, 8, 9
5	6	2, 7, 8
5	7	2, 6, 8
5	8	2, 6, 7, 9
5	9	2, 8
6	1	7
6	2	7, 8
6	3	1
6	4	1
6	5	2, 7, 8
6	6	1, 2, 7, 8
6	7	1, 2, 8

Table 33—*continued*

Natal star	Star of natal month	Auspicious directions
6	8	2, 7
6	9	2, 8
7	1	6
7	2	6, 8
7	3	1
7	4	1
7	5	2, 6, 8
7	6	1, 2, 8
7	7	1, 2, 6, 8
7	8	2, 6
7	9	2, 8
8	1	6, 7
8	2	6, 7, 9
8	3	9
8	4	9
8	5	2, 6, 7
8	6	2, 7
8	7	2, 6
8	8	2, 6, 7, 9
8	9	2
9	1	3, 4
9	2	8
9	3	4
9	4	3
9	5	2, 8
9	6	2, 8
9	7	2, 8
9	8	2
9	9	2, 3, 4, 8

Table 34   *Summary of inauspicious directions for natal stars*

Natal star	Adverse directions
1	1, 2, 8, 9
2	1, 2, 3, 4
3	2, 3, 6, 7, 8
4	2, 4, 6, 7, 8
5	1, 3, 4
6	3, 4, 6, 9
7	3, 4, 7, 9
8	1, 3, 4
9	1, 6, 7, 9

ADVERSE DIRECTIONS

In addition to the inauspicious directions for natal stars which we have summarized as Table 34, there are further generally adverse directions. Namely:

(a) 5 yellow is always the worst possible direction.
(b) The opposite direction of 5 yellow is also bad.
(c) The opposite direction of the Horary Branch of the year (see Figure 28 and its note).
(d) The opposite direction of the Horary Branch of the month (see Table 11, p. 46).
(e) The direction of one's own yearly star.
(f) The opposite direction of (e) above.
(g) The direction of one's own monthly star.
(h) The opposite direction of (g) above.

The examples that follow will show the application of the foregoing rules and the material summarized in Tables 33 and 34 and Figure 28.

1   SHORT TRIP

For a short trip which can be finished in 1–60 days use the 9 daily stars.

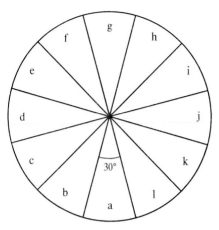

Figure 28. The yearly Horary Branches

Note:

1972 is an a year	1973 is a b year	1974 is a c year
1975 is a d year	1976 is an e year	1977 is an f year
1978 is a g year	1979 is an h year	1980 is an i year
1981 is a j year	1982 is a k year	1983 is an l year
1984 is an a year, etc.		

Since, for example, 1978 is a g year, therefore north would be unfavourable.

EXAMPLE:

Suppose a person was born in the year of 9 and the month of 9. By checking Table 33, which shows the most auspicious directions, one finds that this person's most favourable directions are 2, 3, 4 and 8.

If the person wants to take a business trip to the east, say from London to Berlin, he should start the trip on those days when the stars 2, 3, 4 or 8 are in the east. His best choice of days will be those whose diagrams are as follows:

	3 8 1	4 9 2	5 1 3	9 5 7
east ⟵	2 4 6	3 5 7	4 6 8	8 1 3
	7 9 5	8 1 6	9 2 7	4 6 2
	Daily star	Daily star	Daily star	Daily star
	4	5	6	1

During October 1975 these diagrams occur
when the daily star is 4—on 5, 14, 23 October (and 1 November)

when the daily star is 5—on 4, 13, 22 and 31 October
when the daily star is 6—on 3, 12, 21 and 30 October
when the daily star is 1—on 8, 17, 26 October (and 4 November)

The foregoing would therefore be the most propitious dates during October 1975. The same principles can be employed for any time-span.

As a matter of further refinement one can select the appropriate trigram and trigram number relating to the purpose of the trip from the Table of Trigram Attributes (see Appendix A). Suppose that the above trip was in connection with wheat sales (farm products) then star 2 would be applicable when it was in the east, which in the foregoing case would be on 5, 14 and 23 October. If it had been in connection with communications star 3 would apply and the best dates would have been 4, 13 and 22 October.

2 HOLIDAYS

If a person wants to take a vacation (1–60 days) he will have the best results when his auspicious stars are in the direction in which he wants to go.

EXAMPLE:

Suppose the 9–9 person (in 1 above) wants to go from London to Scotland for his holiday. He should start when his lucky stars 2, 3, 4 and 8 are in the north. His best days will be those when the diagrams are as follows:

	5	1	3	6	2	4	7	3	5	2	7	9
north	4	6	8	5	7	9	6	8	1	1	3	5
↓	9	2	7	1	3	8	2	4	9	6	8	4
	Daily			Daily			Daily			Daily		
	star			star			star			star		
	6			7			8			3		

(Remember that in the use of directions related to the *I Ching*, north is towards the bottom of the page and south is towards the top.)

3 LONG TRIP

If a person wants to take a long trip or to make a change of residence of an estimated duration of 1–5 years, the monthly stars should be used.

EXAMPLE:

Suppose the 9–9 person in 1 above wants to go from San Francisco to Japan to stay about two years; the auspicious stars, 2, 3, 4 and 8 would apply and he would use the following diagrams:

8	4	6		9	5	7		1	6	8		5	1	3	
7	9	2		8	1	3		9	2	4		4	6	8	⟶ west
3	5	1		4	6	2		5	7	3		9	2	7	
Monthly				Monthly				Monthly				Monthly			
star				star				star				star			
9				1				2				6			

(For the seasons corresponding to the monthly stars see Table 15 on pp. 79–80.)

If one should wish the venture to be as perfect as possible it should be started on an auspicious day, using the method described in 1 or 2 above, as well as considering the favourableness of the year. For the individual in the example we have just given, the year 1976 would be an auspicious one for moving to the west.

Other applications

The numerous other possible applications of directionology include the following:

(a) *Persuasion—influence:* If, for example, a man wants to persuade a woman to marry him, or wants to take an important examination (or other matters of a similar nature) the direction of star 4 will bring best results. This is because that star symbolizes marriage, winning fame, statesmanship, etc. Of course other directions will also be suitable so long as they are favourable to oneself. However, the direction of 4 star will prove the most auspicious.

(b) *Asking favours:* If one wants to ask a favour of another person, especially if that person is an important one, then the direction of star 6 is the most auspicious.

(c) *Hospital direction:* If one needs to go to hospital because one has, say, a liver ailment, it is best to go in the direction of star 3, for this star is associated with the liver. For other ailments consult the Table of Trigram Attributes (Appendix A) and determine the applicable star.

(d) *Special case:* Unfortunately some stars are always bad for some people. One can gain the benefits of these stars if one waits until one's own favourable stars are in the house of the otherwise unfavourable star.

EXAMPLE:

Suppose an individual has a natal star of 2 and a monthly star of 3. His favourable direction is 9 (see Table 33). He can gain the benefits of star 1 (assuming star 1 to be unfavourable to him) by waiting until star 9 is in the north, the house of star 1, ☵, and take whatever action he has in mind at that time. Similarly, if he wanted to get the advantage that star 3, ☳, might have to offer he could wait until star 9 was in the east and then use that direction.

Summary

The foregoing material can be summarized as follows. The principles of the interactions of the *I Ching* trigrams are employed in directionology to determine the auspicious or unfavourable directions for doing anything. These interactions are between both the trigrams representing the individual involved, and the trigrams representing the direction, goal, aim or purpose of the intended activity. If one believes in the interactions set out in Tables 1 and 2 and agrees with the fundamental principle of assignment of the numbers 1–9 to years, months, and days, then one will find that the directionology we have outlined has a valid basis. However, before using it for an important decision, we would suggest that the reader experiments first to obtain answers to less important questions, so that he can decide for himself whether the results are valid or not. If they are, then he can add this procedure as another tool for making his life more meaningful and more successful. This same principle applies in general to all the material presented in this anthology.

Appendix A | Table of Trigram Attributes

Trigram	Ch'ien ☰	K'un ☷	Chên ☳	K'an ☵
Family member	Father	Mother	Eldest Son	Middle Son
Primary attribute	Creative	Receptive	Arousing	Danger Hardship
Symbolized by	Tiger Horse Lion	Cow Mare Ant	Eagle Dragon Swallow Cicadas	Pig Rat Fox Bat
Later Heaven direction	NW	SW	E	N
Season	Approach of winter	Approach of autumn	Spring	Winter
Persons (see also *Occupations*)	Sages Elderly men Husbands Presidents Chairmen of boards Dictators Military commanders Kings Prime ministers	Elderly ladies Wise women The masses Multitudes Groups Congregations Unions	Men aged 23–40 (approx.) Princes Famous personages Innovators Constructors Inventors	Men aged 16–22 (approx.) Troublemakers Evil doers Sick persons Troubled individuals Strongly sexed persons Promiscuous persons The dead

Trigram	Ch'ien ☰	K'un ☷	Chên ☳	K'an ☵
Occupations	Government service Industrial machinery Sports equipment Lawyers Jeweller Salesman Priest Teacher	General services Obstetrician Hospital doctor Antique and curio dealer Nurse Gardener	Television industry Munitions industry Technician Engineer Musician Sportsman	Printing and dyeing Fishing industry Chemist Masseur or Masseuse Fisherman Prostitutes Philosopher Writer
Physiognomy	Skull, head	Abdomen	Vocal system	Ear
Internal representation	Mind (pineal gland)	Stomach Spleen Lower region	Feet Liver	Sex organs Kidneys and urinary systems
Sites	Temples Shrines Churches Convention halls Stadiums Arenas Encampments Fortifications Racetracks Schools Universities Congress Parliament Offices Mountain retreats	Doctors' surgeries Fields Farms Empty land Uncultivated areas Ghettoes Bottom of the sea Mobs Large gatherings	Communication areas TV stations Radio stations Lecture halls Auditoriums Power stations Forests Buildings and houses being built or remodelled	Rivers Wells Convalescent homes Waterworks Hospitals Funeral parlours Brothels Waterfalls Hot springs Bars Liquor stores

Trigram	Ch'ien ☰	K'un ☷	Chên ☳	K'an ☵
Weather	Clear Crisp and cold High-pressure areas	Cloudy in low-pressure areas	Clear and mild Thunder-storms Hurricanes Typhoons	Heavy rains Floods Cold Darkness
Illnesses	Broken bones Heart attacks Migraines Lung ail-ments Swellings	Skin diseases Blood diseases Goitres Tongue and throat ailments Digestive tract ail-ments Congestion	Disorders of the nervous system Ulcers Tumours Hysteria Phobias Liver diseases Foot ail-ments	Kidney ailments Earache Venereal diseases Haemor-rhoids Abnormal menses Melan-cholia Neuras-thenia
Food products	Fresh fruits Soya Natural teas Uncooked vegetables (other than green) Rye Oats	Yams Taro Sweet potatoes Natural cereals Wheat Rice Desserts Sugar Snacks Powdered and ground foods Hors d'oeuvres	Green vegetables Citrus fruits Bamboo shoots Plums Grapefruits Prunes Peaches	Liquors Beers Salt Soya sauce Soft drinks Seaweed Raw fish Dairy products Saltwater fish

Trigram	Ch'ien ☰	K'un ☷	Chên ☳	K'an ☵
Plants	Chrysanthemums Fruit trees Herbs Fruit-tree blossoms	Peanuts Potatoes Taro Bulb flowers	Evergreens Bamboos Fresh-sprouting plants Blossoming trees and plants	Reeds Lotuses Lilies Swamp plants Algae
Material possessions	Cars Aeroplanes Precious gems and jewellery Bicycles Watches Clocks Stamps Insignia Protective devices Round items	Square items Clothing (general) Cotton and cotton products Mattresses Cushions Pillows Sheets Suitcases	Noise-making objects Rockets Guns Fireworks Gunpowder Organs Pianos Trumpets Flutes Clarinets Records Telephones Bells Gongs	Paints Varnishes Coal tar and its products Petrol Oils Inks Waistbands Generic medicine
Rooms	Study	Kitchen	Living room	Bathroom
Man's progress	Eventual oneness with universal brotherhood	Philanthropy Receptiveness True and impartial rendering of service	External and internal growth	Baptism Cleansing

Trigram	Ch'ien ☰	K'un ☷	Chên ☳	K'an ☵
Additional attributes of trigram	Action Creativity Sagacity Wealth and nobility High status Courage Bravery Boldness Daring Happiness Content- ment Charity Leadership Fulness Forgiving Roundness Day Heaven Golden white	Receptivity Earth Masses Reverence Perse- verance Caution Thrift Modesty Humility Tran- quillity Obedience Respect Yellow Sweet Night Stinginess	Freshness Greenness Newness Uplifting lectures Determina- tion Renewal Birth Sunrise (dawn) Flight Surprise Business Industry Manufac- turing Engineering	Dangers Confined activity Narrow limits Hidden crimes Robberies Close inter- personal activities Worries Perse- verance Cunning Midnight Canyons Gorges Dish- washers Washing machines Azure Inland water activities Refrigera- tors Roads
Approximate correspond- ence with calendar	7 Nov.– winter solstice	7 Aug.– autumn equinox	Vernal equinox– 5 May	Winter solstice –4 Feb.

Trigram	Ken ☶	Sun ☴	Li ☲	Tui ☱
Family member	Youngest son	Eldest daughter	Middle daughter	Youngest daughter

Trigram	Ken ☶	Sun ☴	Li ☲	Tui ☱
Primary attribute	Keeping still	Penetration	Clarity	Joyousness
Symbolized by	Dog Bull Ox Leopard Mouse	Cock Chicken Crane Snake Earthworm Unicorn	Pheasant Goldfish Crab Shrimp Oyster Turtle	Sheep Birds Simians Deer Elk
Later Heaven direction	NE	SE	S	W
Season	Approach of spring	Approach of summer	Summer	Autumn
Persons (see also Occupations)	Men under 16 Hunch-backs Sincere people Lazy people Prisoners Convicts Faithful people	Women 21–40 (approx.) Business-men Travellers Thinkers Meditators	Women 15–20 (approx.) Beauties Wise and intelligent people Beneficent people Public servants Funda-mental-ists	Women under 16 Daughters Immature people Incompe-tent people Prostitutes
Occupations	Monk Taoist practi-tioner Priest Minister Clergyman	Removals industry Shipping Building and furniture construc-tion Advertising	Writer Artist Artisan Optome-trist War cor-respond-ent Armourer	Public re-lations Entertain-ment industry Savings and loans Taverns

Trigram	Ken ☶	Sun ☴	Li ☲	Tui ☱
		Communications industry Travel agent Guide Teacher	Book dealers Beautician Publisher Diplomat	Lecturer Banker Dentist
Physiognomy	Hand	Leg	Eyes	Mouth
Internal representation	Back	Nervous system Breathing system	Blood system and heart	Speech organs
Sites	Hotels Motels Apartment buildings Walls Graves Gates Paths Castles Palaces	Forest glades Libraries Studies Research centres	Lighthouses Airway beacons Schools Theatres Court houses Scenes of fire Department stores City streets at night	Lakes Valleys Marshes Bars Liquor stores Drinking houses Low-lying land
Weather	Cloudiness that is clearing	Wind Windstorms usually with clouds Tornadoes	Clear, warm and dry	Rain Fog Smog
Illnesses	Nasal difficulties Arthritis Fatigue	Colds Hyperactivity Intestinal upsets	Mental illnesses Brain tumours	Chest and breast difficulties

Trigrams	Ken ☶	Sun ☴	Li ☲	Tui ☱
	Muscular difficulties Leg disorders Constipation	Spine trouble	Heart ailments Blood disorders High fevers Eye diseases	Pelvic disorders Hip joint disorders Skull injuries
Food products	Preserved foods Avocadoes Mushrooms Cooked cereals	Pasta Onions Leeks Garlic Cauliflowers	Dried foods Shellfish Colourfully prepared foods Peanuts	Coffee Tea (other than natural) Wine Mutton Fish Honey
Plants	Nut trees Mangoes Avocadoes	Grass Poppies Lilies	Maples Watermelons Red peppers Tomatoes	Magnolias Gardenias Lake plants Mangrove trees Ginger and other hot spice plants
Material possessions	Non-moving items (such as items stored together, piled together, or assembled together in fixed positions)	Blowers Fans Vacuum cleaners Ropes Wire String Thread Lumber Cabinets Drawers Posted items Railways Pencils	Books Paintings Calligraphy Ornaments and decorations Lights Pots Kettles Cheques Stocks Bonds Silent weapons	Non-wind musical instruments Articles that give pleasure

Trigrams	Ken ☶	Sun ☴	Li ☲	Tui ☱
	Tables Warehouses Screens Storage bins Beds	Air-conditioners	Arrows Protective devices	
Rooms	Bedroom	Hallway	Patio Porch	Playroom (area)
Man's progress	Inner perception and introspection	Reflexion Concentration Penetration	Being a light for self and others	Recognition of spirituality and the joy of giving
Additional attributes of trigram	Mountains Late winter Tardiness Stubbornness Candour Savings Frugality Caution Independence	Credit Late spring —early summer Intellectual activities Neatness Statesmanship Mid-morning Care Faraway places Esoteric subjects Relaxation Hypnotism Aviation Psychology Psychiatry Supermarkets	Intelligence Sound judgment Midday Brightness Impulses Acridity Electricity Medical practice Newspapers Magazines Bookstores	Red Sea-going activities Musical arts Gentleness Joy and joyfulness Lawsuits Litigation Expressed sexual desire Laughter Arguments Setbacks or failures Damage Hardware stores

Trigrams	Ken ☶	Sun ☴	Li ☲	Tui ☱
Approximate correspondence with calendar	5 Feb.– vernal equinox	5 May– summer solstice	Summer solstice– 7 Aug.	Autumn equinox– 7 Nov.

Appendix B / The Lunar Calendar

The lunar month is either thirty or twenty-nine days long. There are seven leap months every nineteen years, the term 'leap month' meaning that the same month is repeated. In the tables which follow, the first day of each month in the solar calendar from 1910 to 1990 is designated with its corresponding date in the lunar calendar. L means that the month is a long month, with thirty days: S means that it is a short month, with twenty-nine days. For example, 1 January 1910 is 11S–20. This means that it is the 20th day of the 11th short month (i.e., a month of twenty-nine days) of the lunar calendar.

When a month is not shown, the length of that month should be calculated. For instance, when we compare 1 December 1910 and 1 January 1911, we notice that the 11th month that separates them is not shown. This is because neither 1 December 1910, nor 1 January 1911 fell in the 11th month, although of course there was an 11th month. As to whether that month was a thirty-day or twenty-nine-day month, the reader can ascertain this by subtracting the earlier date designation from the later one.

Note the use of the prefix L to designate a leap month. For example, 1 August 1911 is L6S–7; this means that it is the 7th day of the 6th leap (i.e., repeated) month, and that the 6th month is a short month.

	1910	*1911*	*1912*	*1913*	*1914*	*1915*
1 Jan.	11S–20	12S–1	11L–13	11S–24	12L–6	11S–16
1 Feb.	12L–22	1L–3	12L–14	12L–26	1L–7	12L–18
1 Mar.	1S–20	2S–1	1L–13	1L–24	2L–5	1L–16
1 Apr.	2L–22	3L–3	2S–14	2L–25	3S–6	2S–17
1 May	3S–22	4S–3	3L–15	3S–25	4L–7	3L–18
1 June	4S–24	5S–5	4S–16	4L–27	5S–8	4L–19
1 July	5L–25	6L–6	5S–17	5S–27	L5L–9	5S–19
1 Aug.	6S–26	L6S–7	6L–19	6S–29	6S–10	6L–21
1 Sept.	7L–28	7S–9	7S–20	8S–1	7L–12	7S–22
1 Oct.	8S–28	8L–10	8S–21	9S–2	8S–12	8L–23
1 Nov.	9L–30	9L–11	9L–23	10L–4	9S–14	9S–24
1 Dec.	10L–30	10S–11	10L–23	11S–4	10L–15	10L–25

	1916	*1917*	*1918*	*1919*	*1920*	*1921*
1 Jan.	11S–26	12S–8	11L–19	11L–30	11L–11	11L–23
1 Feb.	12S–28	1L–10	12S–20	1S–1	12L–12	12L–24
1 Mar.	1L–28	2S–8	1L–19	1S–29	1S–11	1L–22
1 Apr.	2L–29	L2S–10	2S–20	3S–1	2L–13	2S–23
1 May	3S–29	3L–11	3S–21	4S–2	3S–13	3L–24
1 June	5S–1	4S–12	4L–23	5L–4	4S–15	4S–25
1 July	6L–2	5L–13	5S–23	6S–4	5L–16	5S–26
1 Aug.	7L–3	6L–14	6L–24	7S–6	6S–17	6L–28
1 Sept.	8S–4	7S–15	7S–26	L7L–8	7S–19	7S–29
1 Oct.	9L–5	8L–16	8L–27	8L–8	8L–20	9L–1
1 Nov.	10S–6	9L–17	9L–28	9S–9	9S–21	10S–2
1 Dec.	11L–7	10S–17	10S–28	10L–10	10L–23	11L–3

	1922	*1923*	*1924*	*1925*	*1926*	*1927*
1 Jan.	12L–4	11L–15	11S–25	12S–7	11S–17	11L–28
1 Feb.	1L–5	12L–16	12L–27	1L–9	12L–19	12S–29
1 Mar.	2S–3	1S–14	1S–26	2S–7	1S–17	1L–28
1 Apr.	3L–5	2L–16	2L–28	3L–9	2S–19	2S–29
1 May	4L–5	3L–16	3L–28	4S–9	3L–20	4L–1
1 June	5S–6	4S–17	4S–29	L4L–11	4S–21	5S–2
1 July	L5S–7	5L–18	5L–30	5L–11	5L–22	6L–3
1 Aug.	6L–9	6S–19	7S–1	6S–12	6S–23	7S–4
1 Sept.	7S–10	7L–21	8L–3	7L–14	7L–25	8L–6
1 Oct.	8S–11	8S–21	9S–3	8L–14	8L–25	9S–6
1 Nov.	9L–13	9S–23	10L–5	9S–15	9S–26	10L–8
1 Dec.	10S–13	10L–24	11S–5	10L–16	10L–27	11L–8

	1928	*1929*	*1930*	*1931*	*1932*	*1933*
1 Jan.	12L–9	11L–21	12L–2	11L–13	11L–24	12L–6
1 Feb.	1S–10	12L–22	1S–3	12S–14	12S–25	1S–7
1 Mar.	2L–10	1S–20	2L–2	1L–13	1L–25	2L–6
1 Apr.	L2S–11	2L–22	3L–3	2L–14	2L–26	3L–7
1 May	3S–12	3S–22	4S–3	3S–14	3L–26	4S–7
1 June	4L–14	4S–24	5S–5	4L–16	4S–27	5L–9
1 July	5S–14	5L–25	6L–6	5S–16	5L–28	L5L–9
1 Aug.	6S–16	6S–26	L6S–7	6L–18	6S–29	6S–10
1 Sept.	7L–18	7S–28	7S–9	7S–19	8S–1	7L–12
1 Oct.	8S–18	8L–29	8L–10	8S–20	9S–2	8S–12
1 Nov.	9L–20	10L–1	9S–11	9L–22	10L–4	9L–14
1 Dec.	10L–20	11L–1	10L–12	10S–22	11S–4	10S–14

	1934	*1935*	*1936*	*1937*	*1938*	*1939*
1 Jan.	11S–16	11S–26	12S–7	11L–19	11L–30	11S–11
1 Feb.	12L–18	12L–28	1L–9	12S–20	1L–2	12L–13
1 Mar.	1S–16	1S–26	2S–8	1L–19	1L–30	1L–11
1 Apr.	2L–18	2S–28	3S–10	2S–20	3S–1	2L–12
1 May	3S–18	3L–29	L3L–11	3S–21	4S–2	3S–12
1 June	4L–20	5L–1	4S–12	4L–23	5L–4	4S–14
1 July	5L–20	6S–1	5S–13	5S–23	6S–4	5L–15
1 Aug.	6S–21	7L–3	6L–15	6S–25	7S–6	6S–16
1 Sept.	7L–23	8L–4	7L–16	7L–27	L7L–8	7S–18
1 Oct.	8S–23	9S–4	8S–16	8S–27	8S–8	8L–19
1 Nov.	9L–25	10L–6	9L–18	9L–29	9L–10	9S–20
1 Dec.	10L–25	11L–6	10L–18	10L–29	10L–10	10L–21

	1940	*1941*	*1942*	*1943*	*1944*	*1945*
1 Jan.	11S–22	12S–4	11L–15	11S–25	12S–6	11L–18
1 Feb.	12L–24	1L–6	12S–16	12L–27	1L–8	12L–19
1 Mar.	1L–23	2L–4	1L–15	1S–25	2S–7	1S–17
1 Apr.	2L–24	3S–5	2S–16	2L–27	3L–9	2S–19
1 May	3S–24	4L–6	3L–17	3S–27	4S–9	3L–30
1 June	4L–26	5L–7	4L–18	4L–29	L4L–11	4S–21
1 July	5S–26	6S–7	5S–18	5S–29	5S–11	5S–22
1 Aug.	6L–28	L6L–9	6L–20	7L–1	6L–13	6L–24
1 Sept.	7S–29	7S–10	7S–21	8S–2	7S–14	7S–25
1 Oct.	9L–1	8S–11	8L–22	9L–3	8L–15	8L–26
1 Nov.	10S–2	9L–13	9S–23	10S–4	9L–16	9L–27
1 Dec.	11L–3	10S–13	10L–24	11L–5	10S–16	10L–27

	1946	*1947*	*1948*	*1949*	*1950*	*1951*
1 Jan.	11S–28	12L–10	11L–21	12L–3	11S–13	11L–24
1 Feb.	12L–30	1L–11	12L–22	1L–4	12L–15	12S–25
1 Mar.	1L–28	2L–9	1L–21	2S–2	1S–13	1L–24
1 Apr.	2S–29	L2S–10	2S–22	3L–4	2L–15	2S–25
1 May	4L–1	3S–11	3L–23	4L–4	3L–15	3L–26
1 June	5S–2	4L–13	4S–24	5S–5	4S–16	4L–27
1 July	6S–3	5S–13	5L–25	6L–6	5L–17	5S–27
1 Aug.	7L–5	6S–15	6S–26	7S–7	6L–18	6L–29
1 Sept.	8S–6	7L–17	7S–28	L7S–9	7S–19	8L–1
1 Oct.	9L–7	8S–17	8L–29	8L–10	8S–20	9S–1
1 Nov.	10L–8	9L–19	10L–1	9S–11	9L–22	10L–3
1 Dec.	11S–8	10S–19	11S–1	10L–12	10S–22	11S–3

	1952	*1953*	*1954*	*1955*	*1956*	*1957*
1 Jan.	12L–5	11S–16	11L–27	12L–8	11L–19	12L–1
1 Feb.	1S–6	12L–18	12S–28	1S–9	12L–20	1L–2
1 Mar.	2L–6	1S–16	1L–27	2L–8	1S–19	1L–30
1 Apr.	3S–7	2L–18	2S–28	3S–9	2L–21	3L–2
1 May	4L–8	3S–18	3L–29	L3L–10	3S–21	4S–2
1 June	5S–9	4S–20	5S–1	4S–11	4L–23	5L–4
1 July	L5L–10	5L–21	6L–2	5S–12	5S–23	6S–4
1 Aug.	6S–11	6L–22	7S–3	6L–14	6S–25	S7–6
1 Sept.	7L–13	7S–23	8L–5	7S–15	7L–27	8L–8
1 Oct.	8L–13	8L–24	9L–5	8L–16	8S–27	L8S–8
1 Nov.	9S–14	9L–25	10S–6	9S–17	9L–29	9L–10
1 Dec.	10L–15	10S–25	11L–7	10L–18	10S–29	10S–10

	1958	*1959*	*1960*	*1961*	*1962*	*1963*
1 Jan.	11L–12	11S–22	12S–3	11L–15	11S–25	12S–6
1 Feb.	12S–13	12L–24	1L–5	12S–16	12L–27	1L–8
1 Mar.	1L–12	1S–22	2S–4	1L–15	1S–25	2S–6
1 Apr.	2L–13	2L–24	3L–6	2S–16	2L–27	3L–8
1 May	3L–13	3L–24	4S–6	3L–17	3S–27	4S–8
1 June	4S–14	4S–25	5L–8	4S–18	4S–29	L4S–10
1 July	5L–15	5L–26	6L–8	5L–19	5L–30	5L–11
1 Aug.	6S–16	6S–27	L6S–9	6S–20	7L–2	6S–12
1 Sept.	7S–18	7L–29	7L–11	7L–22	8L–3	7L–14
1 Oct.	8L–19	8S–29	8S–11	8L–22	9S–3	8S–14
1 Nov.	9S–20	10S–1	9L–13	9S–23	10L–5	9L–16
1 Dec.	10L–21	11L–2	10S–13	10L–24	11L–5	10L–16

	1964	*1965*	*1966*	*1967*	*1968*	*1969*
1 Jan.	11L–17	11L–29	12S–10	11L–21	12L–2	11S–13
1 Feb.	12S–18	12L–30	1L–12	12S–22	1S–3	12L–15
1 Mar.	1L–18	1S–28	2L–10	1L–21	2L–3	1S–13
1 Apr.	2S–19	2L–30	3L–11	2L–22	3S–4	2L–15
1 May	3L–20	4L–1	L3S–11	3S–22	4L–5	3S–15
1 June	4S–21	5S–2	4L–13	4L–24	5L–6	4L–17
1 July	5S–22	6S–3	5S–13	5L–24	6S–6	5S–17
1 Aug.	6L–24	7L–5	6S–15	6S–25	7L–8	6L–19
1 Sept.	7S–25	8S–6	7L–17	7S–27	L7S–9	7L–20
1 Oct.	8L–26	9S–7	8S–17	8L–28	8L–10	8S–20
1 Nov.	9S–27	10L–9	9S–19	9S–29	9S–11	9L–22
1 Dec.	10L–28	11L–9	10L–20	10L–30	10L–12	10S–22

	1970	*1971*	*1972*	*1973*	*1974*	*1975*
1 Jan.	11L–24	12L–5	11S–15	11S–27	12L–9	11S–19
1 Feb.	12S–25	1S–6	12L–17	12L–29	1L–10	12L–21
1 Mar.	1L–24	2L–5	1S–16	1L–27	2L–8	1L–19
1 Apr.	2S–25	3S–6	2L–18	2S–28	3S–9	2L–20
1 May	3S–26	4S–7	3S–18	3L–29	4L–10	3S–20
1 June	4L–28	5L–9	4S–20	5S–1	L4S–11	4L–22
1 July	5S–28	L5S–9	5L–21	6L–2	5S–12	5S–22
1 Aug.	6L–30	6L–11	6S–22	7S–3	6L–14	6S–24
1 Sept.	8S–1	7S–12	7L–24	8S–5	7S–15	7L–26
1 Oct.	9L–2	8L–13	8S–24	9L–6	8S–16	8S–26
1 Nov.	10L–3	9L–14	9L–26	10L–7	9L–18	9S–28
1 Dec.	11S–3	10L–14	10L–26	11S–7	10L–18	10L–29

	1976	*1977*	*1978*	*1979*	*1980*	*1981*
1 Jan.	12L–1	11S–12	11S–22	12S–3	11L–14	11L–26
1 Feb.	1L–2	12L–14	12S–24	1L–5	12S–15	12L–27
1 Mar.	2L–1	1L–12	1L–23	2S–3	1L–15	1S–25
1 Apr.	3S–2	2S–13	2S–24	3S–5	2S–16	2L–27
1 May	4L–3	3L–14	3L–25	4L–6	3S–17	3S–27
1 June	5S–4	4L–15	4L–26	5S–7	4L–19	4S–29
1 July	6L–5	5S–15	5S–26	6L–8	5S–19	5L–30
1 Aug.	7S–6	6L–17	6L–28	L6L–9	6L–21	7S–2
1 Sept.	8L–8	7S–18	7S–29	7S–10	7S–22	8L–4
1 Oct.	L8S–8	8L–19	8L–30	8L–11	8L–23	9L–4
1 Nov.	9S–10	9S–20	10S–1	9L–12	9L–24	10S–5
1 Dec.	10L–11	10L–21	11L–2	10S–12	10S–24	11L–6

	1982	*1983*	*1984*	*1985*	*1986*	*1987*
1 Jan.	12L–7	11L–18	11L–29	11L–11	11S–21	12S–2
1 Feb.	1L–8	12L–19	12L–30	12L–12	12L–23	1L–4
1 Mar.	2S–6	1L–17	1L–29	1S–10	1S–21	2S–2
1 Apr.	3L–8	2S–18	3L–1	2L–12	2L–23	3L–4
1 May	4S–8	3L–19	4L–1	3L–12	3L–23	4S–4
1 June	L4S–10	4S–20	5S–2	4S–13	4S–24	5L–6
1 July	5L–11	5S–21	6S–3	5L–14	5L–25	6L–6
1 Aug.	6S–12	6L–23	7L–5	6S–15	6L–26	L6S–7
1 Sept.	7S–14	7S–24	8S–6	7L–17	7S–27	7L–9
1 Oct.	8L–15	8S–25	9S–7	8S–17	8L–28	8L–9
1 Nov.	9S–16	9L–27	10L–9	9S–19	9S–29	9S–10
1 Dec.	10L–17	10S–27	L10S–9	10L–20	10L–30	10L–11

	1988	*1989*	*1990*
1 Jan.	11S–12	11L–24	12L–5
1 Feb.	12S–14	12S–25	1S–6
1 Mar.	1L–14	1L–24	2L–5
1 Apr.	2S–15	2S–25	3S–6
1 May	3L–16	3S–26	4S–7
1 June	4S–17	4L–28	5L–9
1 July	5L–18	5S–28	L5S–9
1 Aug.	6S–19	7L–1	6S–11
1 Sept.	7L–21	8L–2	7L–13
1 Oct.	8L–21	9S–2	8S–13
1 Nov.	9S–22	10L–4	9L–15
1 Dec.	10L–23	11L–4	10L–15

Appendix C | Applicability of Advanced Divination, Tzu Pin and Astrology of the I Ching in the Southern Hemisphere

Certain aspects of advanced divination, Tzu Pin and the Astrology of *I Ching* are based on the Celestial Stems, Horary Branches and Sexagenary Cycles for the time and location under consideration. Intensive research by Dr Chu into the applicability of values and methods of calculation failed to reveal any consideration being given to the Southern Hemisphere in the ancient Chinese texts. It is believed that this stems largely from the fact that the word *China* in Chinese is *Jung Gwo* and means 'Central Country'. This meaning apparently was taken quite literally, leaving it up to those outside China to adjust as best they could to the central source.

As a result of his research Dr Chu has developed the following system of applicability for those in the Southern Hemisphere.

Everyone knows that the Southern Hemisphere is the counterpart of the Northern Hemisphere, i.e., when it is summer in the north it is winter in the south, the circulation of the ocean and wind-storm currents are reversed, etc., indicating different influences acting on each area. While the applicable sidereal hours remain the same for the same longitude, the point of reference for calculations in the Southern Hemisphere must be a point diametrically opposed to the point used in the Northern Hemisphere. One of the first things this does is to offset the astrological year by six months from that in the Northern Hemisphere, i.e., from what we call summer solstice to summer solstice in the Northern Hemisphere to what is known as winter solstice to winter solstice in the Southern Hemisphere, roughly 22 June to 21 June.

EXAMPLE:

1929 astrologically is from 22 June 1929 to 21 June 1930 approx. in the Southern Hemisphere. Similarly, 1978 is from 22 June 1978 to 21 June 1979 approx.

It will be noted that the Sexagenary sub-cycles shown in the subsequent Table C1 commence 'five' years later than those in the Northern Hemisphere. In actuality it is five and a half years, as the astrological years start six months apart.

Since the Southern Hemisphere is the counterpart of the Northern we must use opposites when considering the time and location in the Southern Hemisphere. Now the astrological year in the north is from 22 December to 21 December approx. whereas in the south it is 22 June to 21 June approx. with the year in the south commencing six months later than the corresponding year in the north (astrologically). In actuality then, for an 'A' year in the north the first half will be an 'E' half-year in the south and the last half-year an 'F' half-year in the south. By progression we see that the next 'A' year for the south will be the astrological year 1989 or from 22 June 1989 to 21 June 1990. Further, the opposite of the Horary Branch symbol 'a' is 'g' so an 'a' day in the Northern Hemisphere is a 'g' day in the Southern. These differences form the basis of the values in the subsequent tables being different from those shown in the main section of this book for the Northern Hemisphere. The months are calculated the same way in both hemispheres, but as will be noted when working with the tables, their effects are opposite. The sidereal times are the same in both hemispheres for the same longitude but the horary symbols may vary according to the Celestial Stem used.

The method of calculation and the steps are the same as those described under the section Astrology of *I Ching* pp. 163–75 except that the following tables are substituted for the corresponding tables in or mentioned in the referenced section.

Table C1   *Monthly Celestial Stems and Horary Branches*

Month	Season		Applicable years				
			A and F	B and G	C and H	D and I	E and J
January	−	Slight Heat / Great Heat	Hh	Jh	Bh	Dh	Fh
February	+	Autumn Begins / Limit of Heat	Ii	Ai	Ci	Ei	Gi
March	−	White Dew / Autumnal Equinox	Jj	Bj	Dj	Fj	Hj
April	+	Cold Dew / Hoar Frost Descends	Ak	Ck	Ek	Gk	Ik
May	−	Winter Begins / Little Snow	Bl	Dl	Fl	Hl	Jl
June	+	Heavy Snow / Winter Solstice	Ca	Ea	Ga	Ia	Aa
July	−	Little Cold / Severe Cold	Bb	Db	Fb	Hb	Jb
August	+	Spring Begins / Rain Water	Cc	Ec	Gc	Ic	Ac
September	−	Excited Insects / Vernal Equinox	Dd	Fd	Hd	Jd	Bd
October	+	Clear and Bright / Grain Rains	Ee	Ge	Ie	Ae	Ce
November	−	Summer Begins / Grain Fills	Ff	Hf	Jf	Bf	Df
December	+	Grain in Ears / Summer Solstice	Gg	Ig	Ag	Cg	Eg

Table C2 *The twenty-four seasons in the Southern Hemisphere*

Name	Month	Hexa-gram	Date (1975)	Time (GMT)*	CLS**
Slight Heat	(−)6th	䷤	1–05–75	23·18	285
Great Heat			1–20–75	16·37	300
Autumn Begins	(+)7th	䷋	2–04–75	10·59	315
Limit of Heat			2–19–75	6·50	330
White Dew	(−)8th	䷓	3–06–75	5·06	345
Autumnal Equinox			3–21–75	5·57	360
Cold Dew	(+)9th	䷖	4–05–75	10·02	15
Hoar Frost Descends			4–20–75	17·07	30
Winter Begins	(−)10th	䷎	5–06–75	3·27	45
Little Snow			5–21–75	16·24	60
Heavy Snow	(+)11th	䷳	6–06–75	7·42	75
Winter Solstice			6–22–75	0·26	90
Little Cold	(−)12th	䷞	7–07–75	17·59	105
Severe Cold			7–23–75	11·20	120
Spring Begins	(+)1st	䷦	8–08–75	3·45	135
Rain Water			8–23–75	18·24	150
Excited Insects	(−)2nd	䷴	9–08–75	6·33	165
Vernal Equinox			9–23–75	15·55	180
Clear and Bright	(+)3rd	䷜	10–08–75	22·02	195
Grain Rains			10–24–75	1·06	210
Summer Begins	(−)4th	䷻	11–08–75	1·03	225
Grain Fills			11–22–75	22·31	240
Grain in Ear	(+)5th	䷾	12–07–75	17·47	255
Summer Solstice			12–22–75	11·46	270

Note:
* GMT: Greenwich Mean Time.
** CLS: Celestial longitude of the sun.

Table C3 *Upper cycle (1989–2048)*

Year	Yearly cycle	Daily cycle	Year	Yearly cycle	Daily cycle	Year	Yearly cycle	Daily cycle
1989	1	52	1990	2	57	1991	3	2
1992	4	7	1993	5	13	1994	6	18
1995	7	23	1996	8	28	1997	9	34
1998	10	39	1999	11	44	2000	12	49
2001	13	55	2002	14	60	2003	15	5
2004	16	10	2005	17	16	2006	18	21
2007	19	26	2008	20	31	2009	21	37
2010	22	42	2011	23	47	2012	24	52
2013	25	58	2014	26	3	2015	27	8
2016	28	13	2017	29	19	2018	30	24
2019	31	29	2020	32	34	2021	33	40
2022	34	45	2023	35	50	2024	36	55
2025	37	1	2026	38	6	2027	39	11
2028	40	16	2029	41	22	2030	42	27
2031	43	32	2032	44	37	2033	45	43
2034	46	48	2035	47	53	2036	48	58
2037	49	4	2038	50	9	2039	51	14
2040	52	19	2041	53	25	2042	54	30
2043	55	35	2044	56	40	2045	57	46
2046	58	51	2047	59	56	2048	60	1

Table C4 *Lower cycle (1929–88)*

Year	Yearly cycle	Daily cycle	Year	Yearly cycle	Daily cycle	Year	Yearly cycle	Daily cycle
1929	1	37	1930	2	42	1931	3	47
1932	4	52	1933	5	58	1934	6	3
1935	7	8	1936	8	13	1937	9	19
1938	10	24	1939	11	29	1940	12	34
1941	13	40	1942	14	45	1943	15	50
1944	16	55	1945	17	1	1946	18	6
1947	19	11	1948	20	16	1949	21	22
1950	22	27	1951	23	32	1952	24	37
1953	25	43	1954	26	48	1955	27	53
1956	28	58	1957	29	4	1958	30	9
1959	31	14	1960	32	19	1961	33	25
1962	34	30	1963	35	35	1964	36	40
1965	37	46	1966	38	51	1967	39	56
1968	40	1	1969	41	7	1970	42	12
1971	43	17	1972	44	22	1973	45	28
1974	46	33	1975	47	38	1976	48	43
1977	49	49	1978	50	54	1979	51	59
1980	52	4	1981	53	10	1982	54	15
1983	55	20	1984	56	25	1985	57	31
1986	58	36	1987	59	41	1988	60	46

Index

Index